Monograph 44

THE AMERICAN ETHNOLOGICAL SOCIETY

June Helm, *Editor*

VOYAGERS
OF THE
VITIAZ STRAIT

A Study of a New Guinea Trade System

by *Thomas G. Harding*

UNIVERSITY OF WASHINGTON PRESS

Seattle and London

Preface

THIS MONOGRAPH describes a native trading system of New Guinea. The aims are empirical or ethnographic; no major theoretical hypotheses or methodological refinements are put forth. Nevertheless, any ethnographic study must employ some assumptions, and these must be made explicit.

The investigation itself was prompted by a perspective recently espoused by several students of cultural evolution, among them Goldschmidt (1959), Lesser (1961), and Service (1962). This view holds that a significant portion of the environment of a culture consists of surrounding or neighboring cultures, and that essential attributes of a culture are consequently the product of adaptation to its cultural or superorganic environment. In Lesser's phrasing, ethnographic reality consists of "social fields" or networks of communities. Cultures are molded by their particular engagements within a wider field of relations. The present essay, of course, is concerned with a specific social field, a trading network, and with the manner and consequences of the participation of a number of societies in this network.

Anthropologists studying the economic institutions of simple societies have tended increasingly to become polarized into two groups. One group considers primitive economic systems to be radically different—different in kind—from modern market economies, and therefore not amenable to analysis by formal economics. The second group treats the difference as merely one of degree, thus bringing all societies within the competence of formal analysis and theory. Logical argument (e.g., Dalton, 1961; Burling, 1962; LeClair, 1962) has illuminated the important issues without resolving them, and it appears at this point that applications of either the "substantive" or the "formal" perspective will be more useful than further argument.

It seems unnecessary for the present purpose, then, to enter into the theoretical ramifications of the controversy outlined above. It is essential to make clear, however, that I have been guided by the substantive perspective in both the analysis underlying this study and in the field investigation preceding it. If my understanding of substantive economics as espoused by Polanyi and his associates (see Polanyi, Arensberg, and Pearson, 1957) is correct, the approach does not entail a set of specific methods for analyzing economic phenomena. Rather, it invokes a general methodological orientation. Among the main elements of this orientation are the following: In the study of economic life (1) the central task of the investigator is to *discover* the institutions, motives, and processes by which various societies are sustained and provisioned in a material sense; and (2) this is best accomplished by not assuming beforehand the presence of any specific types of institutions or patterns of motive in the societies investigated. In more practical terms, this means that folk evaluations of economic practices should be given their due, without, however, completely sacrificing the comparative interests that the investigator brings to his study; and secondly, rather than selecting data to fit established categories or models derived from Western economic systems, the choice and use of technical concepts should be shaped primarily by the nature of the objects of study. If this sounds like little more than a call for intelligent application of the conventional anthropological axiom of cultural relativism to the study of economy, then so be it.

Predictably, I had to adopt methods in addition to and different from those normally employed by ethnographers engaged in studying single communities. The trade system that I report on here consists of people and goods in constant motion. If more than a parochial viewpoint were to be achieved, I had to move too. In particular, I worked among the communities along a trade route that runs south from Sio, on the north coast of the Huon Peninsula, to the base of the Sarawaged Range, a distance of about twenty miles (see Map 3). I visited most of the principal trading communities at one time or another, and gathered further data from informants from localities that I did not visit. I did not embark on any long overseas voyages in sailing canoes. Economics and not navigation was my primary concern, but aside from this consideration, sailing the waters of the Vitiaz Strait during the season of the Southeast Trade winds requires courage and daring beyond the normal call of duty.

Eleven months—from September of 1963 to August, 1964 —were devoted to the field investigation of the trade system. I stayed about six months at three different times in Sio, over two months in the Komba-Selepet region. I paid brief visits to Gitua and to the Rai Coast villages as far west as Roinji. Marshall D. Sahlins, who joined me in the field in June, 1964, and I spent one month working in the Siassi-Umboi area. Concluding the field trip, we stopped briefly at the Arawe Islands in New Britain and at Malisega, a mainland community of Tami Islanders southwest of Finschhafen (see Map 1).

The data were collected largely in the form of census materials, maps, genealogies, biographies of overseas and local traders, records of transactions, observations of trade in progress, and informants' discussions and opinions on all aspects of native trading.

All inquiries were conducted in Neo-Melanesian (Pidgin English). The lingua franca of modern New Guinea, Neo-

Melanesian has served as the language of overseas and local native trading for a half-century. I endeavored to learn relevant specialized vocabularies in the local vernaculars. (Six Melanesian and three non-Melanesian languages are represented in the communities studied.[1])

As I anticipated, the problems of rapport encountered in working in this many communities (two dozen) were considerable. These problems were mitigated by the fact that I moved through existing social channels of the trade system. I owe my good fortune in this respect to my Sio informants and traveling companions. Their friendship and assistance, and their trust in me and my objectives, which they communicated to their non-Sio friends, greatly expedited the investigation at all stages.

In its original form, this essay was submitted as a doctoral dissertation in the Department of Anthropology, University of Michigan. Dr. Marshall D. Sahlins, who rendered valuable advice as chairman of my doctoral committee, conceived the field project on which the study is based. In addition, he provided encouragement and advice while I was in the field, and he joined me in New Guinea for the last phase of the field trip. I am indebted also to the other members of the committee, Professors Elman R. Service, Leslie A. White, and Eric R. Wolf, and Dr. L. A. Peter Gosling of the Department of Geography, University of Michigan.

Field work was made possible by a grant from the National Science Foundation, Washington, D.C., and a Research Training Fellowship (predoctoral) awarded by the Social Science Research Council, New York. A fellowship awarded by the Horace H. Rackham School of Graduate Studies, University of Michigan, enabled me to devote full time to writing the original version.

A number of scholars read the research proposal pre-

[1] On the New Guinea mainland, Sio, Gituan, and Tami are Mn, Komba and Selepet are non-Mn. In the archipelago, Siassi, Kaimanga, and Barim-Arop are Mn, Kovai is probably non-Mn.

sented by Sahlins and myself, and their appraisal proved helpful in selecting the field site. For their criticisms and suggestions we are grateful to Doctors Ann Chowning, Anthony Forge, Ward Goodenough, Murray Groves, Ian Hogbin, Peter Lawrence, Mervyn Meggitt, Douglas Oliver, Richard Salisbury, Peter Vayda, and James Watson.

During a two-month stay in Sydney, my mentor and advisor was Dr. Peter Lawrence of the University of Sydney, who gave generously of his time and knowledge. Dr. Ian Hogbin offered helpful advice based on his knowledge of native trading in the Huon Gulf. Charles Rowley, then Principal of the Australian School of Pacific Administration in Mosman, put the resources of the Hallstrom Library at my disposal. The advice of Joe Hicks and Jim Hunter, Patrol Officers, aided me in outfitting myself for the field.

I am grateful to W. C. Groves, former Director of Education in Papua–New Guinea, and his wife for their warm hospitality in Melbourne, and to Mr. Groves for allowing me to go through his field notes on Sio.

In New Guinea, officers of the Department of Native Affairs rendered practical advice and material assistance on numerous occasions. I wish to thank R. I. Barclay and G. A. Heriot, Patrol Officers, Kabwum; Roger Lee, P.O., Siassi; Peter Worsley, P.O., Kalalo; Gordon Smith, Assistant District Officer, Finschhafen; and Len Aisbett, A.D.O., Aitape, and his wife Margaret. L. A. Tilley, Agricultural Officer, Kabwum, supplied recent agricultural and economic statistics for the Komba and Selepet Census Divisions.

For their hospitality and assistance I am indebted to Basil Kidd, Co-operative Officer, Finschhafen; Rev. Fred Wagner, Ulap Mission; Father Wilhelm Sasse at Mandok; Jeff Hall, skipper of the M.V. *Morobe;* Geoff Griffiths of Madang; Allan Gilbert, skipper of the M.V. *Sirius;* the Rev. and Mrs. James Klein, Awelkon Mission, and the clerical and lay workers of the Australian Lutheran Mission, Siassi. Dr. John Kuder, President of the Lutheran Mission, New Guinea, provided helpful information before and since the field trip.

Ted Foad of Finschhafen made possible my trip to the Rai
Coast.

Of my numerous New Guinea informants, I wish to mention in particular Babwa and his son Setepana, Koli, and
Advent Tarosi, all of Sio.

I am grateful to Richard Luplow, University of Michigan,
for his fine translations from the Russian of extracts from the
diaries, ethnographic notes, and articles contained in Baron
Maclay's *Collected Works* (1951–54). George Aspbury of
the Department of Geography, University of Michigan, prepared the maps, and Richard V. Humphrey, University of
California, Santa Barbara, drew the figures.

Contents

Illustrations

VOYAGERS OF THE VITIAZ STRAIT
A Study of a New Guinea Trade System

I

Introduction

FROM THE TIME of such accounts of native trade as
Malinowski's pioneer studies of Mailu (1915) and the
Massim region (1922) and Seligman's study, *The Melanesians of British New Guinea* (1910), it has been generally
thought that Melanesia as a whole could be divided into a
number of economic provinces or trading systems.[1] This
essay describes a system of intertribal trade in northeastern
New Guinea. It is based on an investigation concerned
generally with intercultural relations. During the course of
this investigation into the networks linking the societies
chosen for study, trade emerged as the most significant
aspect of intercommunity relations.

The trade system links several hundred communities located on opposite sides of the Vitiaz Strait,[2] a stormy pas-

[1] See, for example, Tueting's (1935) scheme in which Melanesia is
divided into eleven major provinces. Northeast New Guinea is one of the
trading provinces.

[2] The Strait is named after the Russian corvette, *Vitiaz*, which brought
the famous naturalist Miklucho-Maclay (Baron Maclay) to the Rai Coast
in 1871. Maclay was the first European to record information on native
trading in the Vitiaz Strait. He lived on the Rai or Maclay Coast for
over two years, between 1871–72 and 1876–77. (See Maclay, 1951–54,
and the biography by Greenop, 1944.)

In 1700 the English navigator William Dampier discovered that New

sage two hundred miles long and thirty to forty miles wide, which divides the northeastern mainland of New Guinea from the Bismarck Archipelago. Unlike the trading "rings" of Papua, the trade system of the Vitiaz Strait is organized around a few centers. From these centers a small number of traders, in great two-masted canoes, range over an extensive land and sea area. Their voyages connect the islands forming the northern side of the Strait with the mainland to the south. Traffic moves over open water, along the coasts, and over mountains, crossing some of the world's most rugged terrain. Exchange takes place in markets—traditional meeting places for trade purposes—on the platforms of sailing canoes, in conjunction with festivals, and during the inter-village visiting of trade-friends. The types of articles exchanged number only about three dozen; the social links or trade-friendships through which they are exchanged number in the thousands.

While it is difficult to fix the outer limits of the trade system, it is safe to estimate that about 150,000 people live within its bounds. Most of these people are horticulturists subsisting chiefly on the cultivation of taro or yams, and residing in communities that range in size from about 80 to 1,500 persons. A few of these communities, such as the Siassi Islanders, are highly specialized as traders. Others are specialist producers of pots, wooden bowls, bows and arrows, and drums, while still others supply raw materials and food. Specialization of production is also delimited on a broader areal basis—coasts and mountain interior, savanna and rain forest, mainland and archipelago.

The island and coastal peoples fringing the Vitiaz Strait speak related Melanesian languages, which as a group have been named "Graged-Siassi," for two languages at opposite

---

Guinea and New Britain were divided by the Vitiaz Strait. Approaching from the east along New Britain's south coast, he did not sail into the Strait, but veered north through the passage between the western tip of New Britain and Umboi Island (Dampier, in Masefield, ed., 1906, II).

ends of the Strait.[3] This grouping includes about three dozen languages or dialects (see Schmitz, 1960, pp. 28–45). The interior peoples and a few coastal villagers speak non-Melanesian languages.

Although there is considerable variation in some features of culture, the Vitiaz Strait constitutes an artistic province.[4] In addition to similarities in styles of decorative art, most societies of the Strait are patrilineal. Communities generally consist of a number of patrilineal lineages—named, exogamous, and corporate groups.

Paralleling the lineage organization are men's ceremonial houses, which are the most important political and ritual groups. The requirements of local political and ceremonial systems, of which the men's houses are the functioning units, include specific kinds of imported goods. Among the Siassi overseas traders, the men's house provides the framework for organizing trading expeditions and for allocating the profits

[3] The linguistic picture for the Melanesian languages of the area is evidently more complex than it appears in Schmitz's summary. Dyen's recent study suggests New Britain—because it presents the area of greatest concentration of diverse languages—as a probable homeland of the Austronesian languages (Grace, 1964, p. 367). Grace would enlarge the homeland to include "a more general area consisting of northeastern New Guinea and the neighboring islands." Much of this larger area, of course, is enclosed within the boundaries of the Vitiaz Strait trading system.

While the relationships of Melanesian languages within the Strait are still to be worked out, Murdock's recent summary (1964, pp. 119–22) of Dyen's classification points to some interesting relationships to languages in other parts of the Austronesian world. The language of Tami, one of the main groups of overseas traders, shares 18.7 per cent cognates with Palauan. The Arawe Islanders of southwestern New Britain are another group of traders. Their language (Pilelo) is "isolated," i.e., its "shared cognates with other Austronesian languages are few, or random . . ." (*ibid.*, p. 118) —and it shares 10.6 per cent with Polynesian. Kalingi of northwestern New Britain, still another language of the trade system, is also an isolated language, and it shares 18 per cent with Fijian. Sufficient linguistic data are not at hand, but comparison might well show a percentage of shared cognates between the language of the Siassi traders and Fijian to be similar to the figure for Kalingi and Fijian.

[4] Bodrogi (1959) distinguishes Astrolabe Bay and Tami-Huon–style provinces, with a possible transitional zone along the western Rai Coast.

of trade. In these ways the men's ceremonial house has a substantial impact on the conduct of trade.

The trading system of the Vitiaz Strait influences the cultural landscape, and the cultural life, speech, and even physical characteristics of the peoples within its scope. Foot-worn grooves in the earth and stone mark trade routes, and at their termini bits of volcanic glass, stone tools, and pottery fragments will remain in the ground to attest to trade for millennia to come. The trade system depends on but also helps to determine the constitution of local biotic communities—the prevalence or absence of such plant species as coconut, sago, cedars, black palm, and other economic and food plants.

The cultures of the Vitiaz Strait are shaped not only by their physical habitats, but by their particular cultural environments, which are structured largely by external exchange relations. Some cultures, in particular, are molded by their functional role in trade, so that while there are "mountain people" and "beach people," there are also complementary ways of life founded on trade: trading cultures and importing cultures.

The welter of languages characterizing New Guinea as a whole is evident on a smaller scale in the Vitiaz Strait region. There are several dozen distinct languages, but multilingualism is characteristic of the area, and any attempt to establish the relationships of the many languages should take into account the historic lines of communication that emerge from a study of the trade system. There is evidence, also, that the use of a lingua franca—specifically, a pidgin form of the Siassi language—predates the modern spread of Neo-Melanesian.

In some cases the tasks imposed by local economic specialization underlying trade are reflected in human physique, in bodily specialization. Yet the channels of trade, through which there is a flow of people as well as of goods, cause the spread and recombination of human characters.

Chapter II sets forth the boundaries of the trade system

and the kind of subregions it comprises. The people of the Vitiaz Strait classify themselves either as "bushmen" or "sea people," and Chapter III treats the variations in maritime capabilities exhibited by the "sea people." Chapter IV provides a detailed list of the articles of exchange. Chapter V describes Sio and its hinterland, one of a number of local trading spheres that compose the larger system. In Chapter VI attention shifts from the New Guinea mainland to the archipelago and the Siassi traders, the main group of overseas traders. In the following chapter, "The Economics of Status and Group Relations in Siassi and Kovai Society," consumption is viewed in its institutional context. The sociological aspects of trade-friendship are the subject of Chapter VIII, "The Social Basis of Trade." Chapter IX is devoted to a discussion of the major changes that have occurred in native trading during the last eighty years. The final chapter probes the functions of overseas trade from the larger perspectives of Melanesian economy and cultural adaptation.

For the most part, native trading clings to traditional patterns, values, and motives. In the chapters that follow, I describe the trade system as I found it, so that it is proper to speak in the present tense. In appropriate contexts, however, the "ethnographic present," referring to aboriginal times or some "slice of time" from 1884 (when Germany assumed control of New Guinea) to 1964, is employed. Where they are pertinent to the subject at hand, historical changes are described. I hope that the resulting shifts in verb tense do not produce confusion and that, in any case, the full discussion of change in Chapter IX will answer questions that seem unresolved along the way.

To avoid the repetition of cumbersome geographical references I have adopted the following terms: "Outer islands" will refer to Arop (Long), Tolokiwa, and Umboi (Rooke, Rook) Islands. "Archipelago" designates the "outer islands" plus western New Britain. "Mainland" means the mainland of New Guinea between modern Finschhafen and Astrolabe Bay. "Western Strait," the domain of the Bilibili traders, includes the mainland coast from Cape Rigney at the eastern edge of Astrolabe Bay to Cape Croisilles in the north, together with Karkar (Dampier) and Bagabag (Rich) Islands, and the extensive archipelago of small islands along the Madang Coast (Bilibili, Jabob, Siar, Graged, and others).

The eastern boundary of the Maclay or Rai Coast has not been firmly fixed by past usage.[5] I choose to place the boundary at the Kwama River just west of Sio. This boundary indicates the eastern extent of Maclay's explorations, and, more important, it is an ecological boundary. To the east of this point, *kunai* grass (*Imperata* sp.) is the prevailing vegetation, while rain forest predominates along the coast to the west.

[5] Baron Maclay himself was inconsistent. He wrote: "I am naming here 'Maclay Coast' the part of the northeastern shore of New Guinea between the capes Erempi and Teliat [Sio] or, in conformance with maps, approximately from Cape Kruazil to Cape King William" (1951–54, II, p. 398, n.). From Sio, Maclay wanted to go to Cape King William, twenty-five miles further east, but the Bilibili canoemen with whom he was traveling refused to venture beyond this point, which was the eastern terminus of their trading sphere.

II

Boundaries and Spheres of Trade

THE TRADE SYSTEM of the Vitiaz Strait is a "system" by virtue of the annual voyages of the Siassi Islanders. Linking numerous communities of the New Guinea mainland and of the Bismarck Archipelago, these overseas voyages sustain a significant development of interregional specialization and create thereby a regional economy.

The outermost limits of Siassi sailing help to define the area of the Vitiaz Strait system, but they underestimate the actual territorial scope of the trade. For Siassi contacts are limited to coastal and island communities which, if they are not themselves prominent manufacturing-trading groups, at least function as points for the collection and forwarding of goods from beyond the Siassi orbit. Each of this series of communities has its hinterland, composed of a dozen or more villages, often one or more ethnic or "tribal" blocs. These immediate hinterlands, with which the Siassi traders have no direct contact, may be said to form the boundary of the system. Viewed schematically, the territorial plan is radial: overseas routes, radiating like the spokes of a wheel, connect the center at Siassi with a large number of coastal villages. These port villages, either directly or via hinterland middlemen, are linked with an even larger number of inland communities. The area thus defined within northeastern New Guinea includes the Tami Islands; the coast of the Huon Peninsula as far south as Finschhafen, the Rai Coast to its western end at Astrolabe Bay, together with the hinterlands of these coasts, which are bounded on the south by the Sarawaged and Finisterre ranges; Arop, Tolokiwa, and Umboi Islands; the Siassi Group; the northwestern tip of New Britain (Cape Gloucester [Kalingi]) and the south coast of New Britain as far as and including the Arawe Islands.

The trade system is not a closed system. In the first place, the hinterland communities have relations of their own which face away from the Vitiaz Strait, and some of these were critical in the past for the movement of such goods as stone axes (e.g., the north-south routes across the Sarawaged-Finisterre ranges linking the north Huon and Rai Coast regions with the southern Huon Peninsula and the Markham Valley). Because of these "external" relations, there is an outward flow of local goods and an inward flow of "alien" manufactures which at many points cross the territorial boundaries defined above. Thus, Huon Gulf pots enter the area via the Tami Islands; obsidian from New Britain was brought to the Huon Gulf by the Siassi and then Tami traders.

A second consideration, before the question of boundaries can be decided, is the former role of the Tami and Bilibili Islanders, trading-manufacturing communities located at the southeastern and western extremities, respectively, of the Vitiaz Strait. The Tami Islands, about ten miles southeast of modern Finschhafen, face in two directions: toward the Huon Gulf to the south and toward the Vitiaz Strait to the north. Within the Huon Gulf the Tamis acted as the chief carriers in a trade system (Hogbin, 1947) which, though smaller, was comparable in major respects to that of the Vitiaz Strait. Sailing north to Siassi and to New Britain, Tami traders carried pots from the Huon Gulf and the finely carved hardwood bowls for which they are famous. They had and still have direct and cordial relations with the Siassi Islanders.

Bilibili Island, located in Astrolabe Bay just off the Madang Coast, allowed its traders, like the Tamis, to make the best of two economic spheres. The Bilibili people were also adventurous sailors, traders, and canoe builders and, in addition, they manufactured earthenware pots, their chief stock-in-trade. Within their own bailiwick at the western end of the Strait, the Bilibili sailors ranged over an extensive area: along one hundred miles of coast to the north, to Karkar Island, to the nearby villages of Astrolabe Bay, and along the entire Rai Coast (see Chap. IX, n. 9; also see Finsch, 1914, p. 273). It appears that they may also have sailed directly to Umboi Island and the Siassi Group.[1]

The often casual observations of the early travelers and explorers in northeastern New Guinea, though suggestive, are not sufficient to settle the question of the trading contacts of the Bilibili and Tami sailors within the Vitiaz Strait in precise detail (see Chap. IX). Nevertheless, it seems clear that the Tami and Bilibili traders were not regarded as interlopers in a Siassi preserve. Relations between the Siassis and Tamis were intimate and critical for their respective trading interests (see Chap. VI). The trading contacts of the Siassis and Bilibilis overlapped along an approximately one-hundred-mile stretch of the Rai Coast, west from Sio.

Conditions of wind and weather, combined with the frequency of sailing, indicate that these three trading peoples probably came into contact with each other's provinces. For example, a Tami canoe sailing north to Siassi in the season of the Southeast Trades risks being blown westward by any gale that might arise. Similarly, a Bilibili canoe crossing to Karkar Island during the Northwest Monsoon might be blown to the Siassi Group. These sailors wait for favorable conditions to sail, of course, but I do not want to imply that they cannot cope with adverse conditions should they arise.

[1] One must speak of Tami and Bilibili trading voyages in the past tense. See Chapter IX.

Although the canoes are unable to tack, and are too heavy and unwieldy to paddle for any distance, they are handled with great skill. With regard to Aramot canoes, a wartime intelligence report advised: "In the hands of an expert skipper and crew they will sail through almost anything, if the reason be sufficiently important" (AGS, 1943, p. 62).

Nevertheless, in the four to ten hours that crossings may require, the weather can and often does change profoundly.[2] Running in front of a strong wind, with the crew in full control of the vessel, a trip extending the length of the Strait (about two hundred miles) either to the east or west might take only one to two days. The small cargo vessels currently plying the waters of the Vitiaz Strait make the trip from Finschhafen to Madang in about thirty hours; in a good wind the large double-masted canoes of the Siassis and Tamis achieve equal or greater speed, up to eight or nine knots (AGS, 1943, p. 62). In view of the strong currents encountered in the Vitiaz Strait, a drift voyage by a disabled canoe might not take much longer.[3]

---

[2] A wartime intelligence report makes the following observations on off-shore conditions in Siassi: "Prevailing winds are from the southeast during May to November and from the northwest during January and February. March, April and December are uncertain months, where winds may be expected from almost any quarter, often springing up and dying down very suddenly. . . .

"The southeast winds usually reach rather high velocities and continue so for long periods of time.

"The northwest winds rarely last more than 5–6 days, after which a period of 2 or 3 days of almost complete calm may be expected. They usually rise very suddenly and fade out as suddenly as they come. This may happen 2 or 3 times in 24 hours" (AGS, 1943, pp. 55, 61).

[3] "A strong current flowing from the southeast, both through Dampier and Vitiaz Straits, is in evidence almost the whole year round, subsiding only during periods of strong winds from the northwest, when it sometimes turns in an opposite direction. . . .

"The strongest current is usually experienced just west of the long reef extending westward from Malai Island, where currents of 3½ to 4 knots are not uncommon during the southeast winds" (*ibid.*, pp. 55, 61).

In the 1930's a Malai canoe was disabled by high seas after leaving Finschhafen, and, proceeding past Arop Island, it went ashore on the Madang Coast after being adrift for six days. A trailing canoe, in trouble

Primarily because of the known two-way role played by the Tami Islanders, connecting as they did the Huon Gulf system with that of the Vitiaz Strait, and the possibility that Bilibili Island played a similar role in the west, it is unwise to attempt to specify rigid boundaries. Indeed, it may be best to consider the Huon Gulf on the one hand, and the Astrolabe Bay–Karkar Island trading area on the other, as components of a larger system centered in and embracing the Vitiaz Strait. This larger area, incidentally, coincides with the distribution of a type of two-masted canoe distinguished not only by its great size (often sixty feet in length), but by a two-tiered central platform, edge-to-edge fastening

---

itself in the high seas, refused to jettison its cargo, but did take aboard one man and one child, and reached Malai. The remaining eight men, two women, and children drifted ashore near Madang and lived there for eight months on government provisions. Returning home by a mission vessel, they found that they had long been mourned as dead.

Expectably, accounts of forced and drift voyages occur frequently in legend throughout the region. Some examples: The Mandoks relate that their original trading contacts with the Arawe Islands in southern New Britain were established by the survivors of a fleet which was blown to the eastward during a crossing from Sio, on the New Guinea mainland, to Siassi.

The Gituans trace their origins to tiny Pore Island (near Mandok) in the Siassi Group. Two canoes carrying migrants left Pore for the New Guinea mainland, one arriving at Gitua. The other, disabled by a broken outrigger, drifted far to the west to Malalomai. According to the Gituans, their dialect and that of Malalomai are mutually intelligible, a fact which they discovered to their great surprise in post-European times.

The Sios and Gituans explain their warlike relations in the recent past as the result of the massacre of two Sio crews which were blown back to Gitua during a crossing to Siassi. In retaliation, so the account runs, the Sios mounted a massive predawn attack in which all but one family (or lineage) of Gituans were killed.

The Komba and Selepet, neighboring mountain tribes of the Huon Peninsula, claim descent from drift voyagers from Siassi who landed and sojourned on the Sio-Gitua Coast before becoming the pioneer colonists of their mountain area.

Parkinson reported drift voyagers or their descendants from the Massim area of Papua in New Britain. He found natives from the D'Entrecasteaux Group at South Cape and, he writes, "on Cape Gloucester I met with people from the Trobriand Islands, who had resided there so long, that they spoke the language of the local inhabitants . . ." (1907, p. 241).

of wash strakes or planks, and particularly, as noted by Finsch, who observed their distribution in 1894, the elaborately carved prow-boards (1914, p. 477).

By narrow definition the trade system of the Vitiaz Strait is impressive for its size. The physical scope of the wider system outlined above may be gauged by the following statistics: it includes several hundred coastal communities dotted along one thousand miles of coastline (in New Guinea and New Britain), a total population (1964), including the populous interior sections, of nearly a quarter of a million—all this knit together by three groups of seafaring traders who collectively could not have numbered more than about twelve hundred[4] in aboriginal times.

LOCAL SPHERES OF TRADE

Long-distance trade linking the two sides of the Vitiaz Strait—mainland and archipelago—is in the hands of the Siassi Islanders. In the past the Tami sailors regularly penetrated the eastern Strait, while the Bilibili traders seem to have been largely confined to the west where, from Astrolabe Bay, the New Guinea coastline turns northward forming the boundary of the Strait itself.

Within the super-trade sphere defined by the trading contacts of the overseas traders lie numerous local trading spheres, relatively self-contained constellations of inland and coastal communities which are linked at one or more points

[4] Early estimates of the population of the trading groups are as follows:

Islands	Population	Date	Sources
Bilibili	200–250	1884–85	Finsch, 1888, p. 81
Tami	180	*ca.* 1900	Neuhauss, 1911, I, 133
	(225	*ca.* 1910)	Neuhauss, 1911, I, 133
Siassi			
Aramot	156	1926	Chinnery, n.d., p. 46
Mandok	120	*ca.* 1910	Neuhauss, 1911, I, 135
Malai	300	*ca.* 1910	Neuhauss, 1911, I, 135
Tuam	250	*ca.* 1910	Neuhauss, 1911, I, 135
	1,206		

In 1963 the four Siassi Island villages alone had a population of 1,685. Aramot—398; Mandok—343; Malai—448; Tuam—496 (Village Registers).

to the larger system. Siassi and Umboi Island, Sio and its hinterland, Tami and the Yabim and Bukaua villages of the opposite mainland, are examples of such local spheres of trade. The latter, in turn, are composed of productively specialized communities.

The local spheres—of which there are dozens—differ with regard to the products exchanged and the frequency, urgency, and organization of exchange. In later chapters two of the most important local trading areas, Siassi-Umboi in the archipelago and the Sio-Komba region on the mainland (Maps 3 and 4) will be described in detail. Here I am concerned with general characteristics.

The largest number of local trade provinces are to be found on the New Guinea mainland, the coast and its mountainous hinterland extending from the region of Finschhafen to Astrolabe Bay. Geography has conditioned the formation of these spheres, which are generally similar in form throughout the area.

The coast is narrow, consisting of a series of wide level capes rather than a continuous plain. Human settlement here is thin and widely dispersed; often neighboring villages are separated by as much as fifteen miles. Rising abruptly behind the coastal plain is a mountain range varying between three thousand and six thousand feet in altitude. Further south and running parallel to the coastal range are the towering Sarawaged and Finisterre ranges (up to thirteen thousand feet). The bulk of the population is settled in the rugged plateau country between the front and main ranges (altitudes range from about twenty-five hundred to seven thousand feet). At regular intervals swift streams, with their headwaters in the main range, flow through deep gorges on their northerly courses to the coast. These river gorges, together with mountain spurs running outward from the main range, divide the country into a series of parallel blocks, ten to fifteen miles wide and fifteen to twenty miles deep. Each of these territorial blocks is further segmented from north to south into several topographic zones: coastal plain, front range, interior plateau, and the high main range (Fig. 1).

Figure 1. Schematic Representation of Local Trade Spheres (I, II, III)

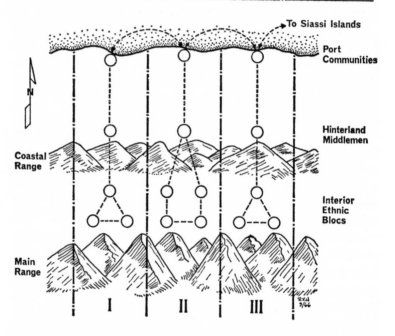

The major trade routes transect these zones, connecting the coastal villages with settlements in the mountains and plateaus. Typically, one or more coastal communities are linked with one or two ethnic units of the interior. It is this kind of topographic unit that forms, then, a local trading sphere. Trade routes connecting the various communities of the highland sections converge on a beach village, which in turn is the point of articulation with the larger system—i.e., a port-of-call for overseas traders.

Within each sphere the main movements are north-south. Highland products flow to the coast, coastal products and overseas imports move inland. Typically there is a two-step movement; the settlements of the front range, which have direct relations with the beach, forward goods to the more remote interior (see Fig. 1).

Description of the inland-coast trading regions in western New Britain must await publication of results of field work recently undertaken.[5] The terrain is neither as rugged nor as regularly patterned as that just described for mainland New Guinea, but it is likely that local trading provinces can be delineated. In New Britain, also, a number of ethnic-linguistic groups have, as archaeologists say, coastal and inland facies. This occurs on the mainland as well, for example, among the Bukaua of the southern Huon Peninsula, who are divided into inland taro producing villages and coastal fishermen. In these cases the "tribal" group forms a local trade sphere of its own.

The geographic patterning of local trading into coast-inland spheres does not preclude exchange relations between these spheres. On the mainland similarities of language and culture cut across the boundaries of the coast-inland spheres along an east-west line, uniting the non-Melanesian speaking societies of the highlands on the one hand, and the Melanesian speaking societies of the littoral on the other. There is, in particular, a great deal of coastwise traffic. For example, the inland trading of the Rai Coast villages depends in part on the exchange of pottery—which they do not manufacture —for highland products such as tobacco and bows. The pots, which may pass through many hands before reaching their final destinations, move eastward along the coast from Astrolabe Bay and westward from Sio. Travel and communications in an east-west direction in the interior are complicated by the deep gorges and steep ridges that must be crossed—one is moving against the grain of the country. Skirting the headwaters of the rivers near the base of the

[5] Ann Chowning and Jane Goodale recently completed ethnographic field work in the interior of southwestern New Britain, and in August, 1964, Philip J. C. Dark and Joel Maring completed a survey of the Kalingi, Barriai, and Kombe areas of the northwestern coast preparatory to a lengthier study. It is hoped that the results of this work will help to clarify patterns of trade in New Britain.

main range, however, affords relatively easy passage from one major sector to another.

OVERSEAS TRADING SPHERES

The three groups of island traders and the domains in which they concentrated their efforts have already been described: the Bilibili Islanders in the western Strait, the Siassis in the central and eastern portions, and the Tamis in the Huon Gulf. The question remains, however, whether some division of the area into separate trading spheres did not occur among the Siassis—the largest and now the only active group of traders. We must rely here on two kinds of information: (1) statements by modern informants regarding past and current voyaging, and (2) records of actual voyages. A large number of "sailing biographies" collected by Marshall D. Sahlins at Mandok Island indicate the pattern of voyaging, but similar data for Aramot, Tuam, and Malai are unfortunately not available (see Table 5, Chap. VI).

Originally, there were five groups of overseas traders: Paramot, located on the western coast of Umboi Island, the two tiny islets of Mandok and Aramot just off the southern tip of Umboi, and the two largest islands of the Siassi Archipelago, Tuam and Malai, located seven to ten miles out in the Strait (Map 4). Paramot ceased manufacture of ocean going canoes and abandoned overseas voyaging a long time ago, so that the supply of canoes for the four island groups now comes exclusively from Mandok and Aramot. These two groups sail less than they used to. Because all of the large canoes are sold to Tuam and Malai, the people from Mandok and Aramot must hire canoes from the other two groups when they wish to make overseas expeditions. The chief sailors, then, are Tuam and Malai, and of these, the Malais seem to be the more far-ranging.

All five groups sailed to Arop Island, crossed the Dampier Strait to New Britain and the Vitiaz Strait to New Guinea, but according to informants there was division of territory.

Tuam, Mandok, and Aramot sailed along the south coast of New Britain to the Arawe Islands; the Malai Islanders did not. On the mainland, Tuam went only as far to the west as Sio. Malai, Mandok, and probably Paramot—the western-most groups—sailed beyond Sio to the villages of the Rai Coast.

Thus, the areal patterning of the trade connections of the five groups of traders exhibits considerable overlap. There is no evidence of competition, of the attempt of any one group to acquire or maintain exclusive trading rights within par-ticular areas. The principle is that trading voyages are di-rected to those places where the leader or members of an expedition have "friends." Where there are no "trade roads" (social connections) there is no trade. Therefore, it could happen that the usual itineraries of men of *different* Siassi communities might correspond more closely than those of men of the *same* community.

Some basis exists for speculating on the reasons why there was no inter-Siassi competition. First of all, only a small number of overseas traders was operating in a very large area—there was plenty for everyone. It is probable, in fact, that the more active the trade the better, for production is stimulated as the number and intensity of contacts increase. Secondly, the Siassi groups were themselves interdependent, for example, in the provision of sailing canoes. Attempts to hinder the activities of others, perhaps by warfare or other means, would be disruptive of trade and the interests of everyone concerned.

III

Canoes
and the Maritime Adaptation

THE ISLAND TRADERS—Bilibili, Tami, and Siassi—built their own ocean going canoes.[1] Within Siassi today, Aramot and Mandok are the canoe makers, and Tuam and Malai rely exclusively on them to maintain their fleets. Lacking local supplies of timber, however, Mandok and Aramot must acquire the materials needed for their industry in local trade with Umboi Island. Aramot and Mandok trade finished canoes—from single dugouts (with outrigger) to the large overseas craft—to Malai, Tuam, the outer islands, New Guinea, and New Britain, mainly for pigs.

Canoes of the Tami-Siassi style are manufactured elsewhere: at Sio, by some of the Rai Coast villagers, and by the

[1] The members of the Hamburg Expedition (1908–1910) concluded that Tami was the principal and the original center for the manufacture of large sailing canoes, and in their respective diaries the ethnologist Reche (1954, p. 50) and the artist Vogel-Hamburg (1911, p. 148) state that canoe making was supposed to have been learned by the Siassis from Tami. It is not clear whether this statement is based on informants' testimony, an examination of legend, or whether it is an inference from a comparison of Siassi and Tami workmanship. The fitting of the parts of the canoe and the carving of prows and prow-boards are performed with greater precision by the Tamis, and it is easy to understand how superiority might be translated into priority. Of course, such an inference is unwarranted.

Yabim and Bukaua of the Huon Peninsula. In addition, Friederici (1912, p. 269) observed that the Tami-Siassi style strongly influences the canoe making techniques of the Kalingi (Kilenge) of northwestern New Britain. The large sailing canoes of the Bilibili of Astrolabe Bay are structurally of the same type, differing in only one major detail of ornamentation: a long, curved, and elaborately carved S-shaped piece which is fastened to the prow-boards like a second bowsprit.

In their great length (up to sixty feet) and the depth of the hull (four to five and one-half feet), the Tami-Siassi canoes compare with the Murua-built canoes used in the Massim area (Seligman, 1910, p. 527) and the trading canoes of the Admiralties (see Haddon and Hornell, 1937, pp. 164–75, especially Fig. 106, p. 174). They have a greater cargo capacity and definitely seem better suited for ocean travel than the Trobriand *masawa* canoe used widely in the *kula* ring.

The canoe builders of the Vitiaz Strait generally make three types of canoes. At Sio, for example, simple dugouts (*kazalabu*), with single outrigger and platform, are used on the reef and lagoon. A second type (known as *wɔŋga pinora tetu*, "single-masted canoe"), the most common, is built up with a single plank or wash strake and can be fitted with a mast and sail. These canoes range between twenty and thirty-five feet in length. The third type (*wɔŋga ŋalai*, "big canoe," or *pinora rua*, "two masts") is between thirty-five and sixty feet in length, has two side planks (an over-all height of four to five feet), twin masts, and a two-tiered central platform.

It appears that Sio, the Rai Coast, Yabim, and Bukaua possessed few, and actually made fewer still, of the ocean going vessels. Only two such canoes have been in use at Sio in recent times. One of these was made on the Rai Coast by a Sio canoe-master, while a second was purchased from Tuam. This is to be compared with the trading groups who possess a large sailing canoe for every ten to twenty persons.

This ratio has probably changed little since aboriginal times. In the 1880's Bilibili had an estimated population of 200 to 250 and fourteen sailing canoes, one for every fourteen to eighteen persons (Finsch, 1888, p. 81; 1914, p. 477). Mandok informants say that in the old days (when the population was a little over one hundred), all the able-bodied seamen of the community could man only five canoes at a time.

The sailing canoes last for three or four years before requiring major repairs, but a good hull may endure for ten years or longer. Aside from normal maintenance, such as recaulking, a canoe may be completely rebuilt from the hull up once or twice before it is finally retired. The least perishable parts of the craft are the elaborately carved prow-boards—the hallmark of the Tami-Siassi style—which may be used successively in a number of canoes, or merely passed on as a family heirloom.

The large canoes are capable of carrying as many as twenty persons with cargo, but on trading voyages a crew of five or six men is normal. A full cargo for the large canoes might be two tons of taro or two hundred to three hundred clay pots.

The Gituans (Kelanoa), Sialum, and some Rai Coast people employ an extremely crude type of watercraft—in addition to the Tami-Siassi canoe. The hull of this craft is formed of a solid log that is merely shaped at the ends rather than being hollowed out. Into the top of the solid hull are driven two rows of upright stakes, to which are attached horizontal poles to form two parallel railings. A single outrigger and platform are attached in the usual way. When loaded, the hull—which resembles an oversized outrigger float—may be nearly submerged, and waves wash over, actually through, the "canoe."

The *saŋgiŋgi*, as the Sios call this type of craft, is adequate for travel and fishing in calm water, and for traveling back and forth between the mainland and the nearby island villages formerly occupied by the Gituan and Sialum people.

But the Gituans claim that large craft were fitted with masts and sail and were fully capable of voyaging across the Strait to Siassi. It seems possible, in spite of the extremely makeshift appearance of the craft, and Baron Maclay has left us a drawing of a *saŋgiŋgi* with a single mast and sail (1951–54, V, 53).

The Arop Islanders, liberally endowed with timber, constructed enormous dugouts without the addition of side planking, though they also acquired Siassi-built canoes in trade. The Arops paddled rather than sailed their canoes across the Vitiaz Strait to Sio (thirty-five miles away), a hazardous undertaking to say the least. Although large, the canoes lacked wash strakes and are said to have been easily swamped. If this happened, all but one or two of the dozen crewmen slipped into the water alongside the canoe while the others bailed it out. Bailing completed, the crew reboarded and resumed paddling.

Whether they build their own or sail in Siassi-built canoes, such groups as the Sios, Yabim, and Arop Islanders appear to be strictly fair-weather seamen. Their canoes, although of Siassi-Tami design, are inferior in workmanship, and as sailors they lack the skill of the Siassi and Tami Islanders. The reports of early observers confirm that this lack of craft and sailing skill on the part of the coastal peoples of the Strait does not represent recent "cultural loss." Vogel-Hamburg, one of the first Europeans to visit Sio (1909; Maclay was probably the first, in 1877), commented on the crudity of Sio canoes as compared with those of Siassi (1911, p. 258), while Baron Maclay contrasted the daring of the Bilibili Islanders—"the best seafarers in the whole region"—with the timidity of the coastal people around Astrolabe Bay (1875, p. 88).

The maritime capabilities of the inhabitants of the islands forming the northern side of the Strait—Karkar, Bagabag, Arop, Tolokiwa, Umboi, and Sakar—are about on a par with those of the mainland, or are even less developed. These high volcanic islands lack beaches and fringing reefs along

considerable stretches of their coastlines. With little potential for fishing, the interior uplands, which receive ample
rainfall and are favorable for taro cultivation, constitute the
most productive zone. It is quite possible that considerations
of defense also prompted inland settlement (cf. Scheffler,
1964, on Choiseul Island).

On Umboi Island most settlement is in the interior, where
taro is the staple crop. Areas below about five hundred feet
are subject to seasonal dryness and only varieties of small
yams seem to do well. The Kovai villagers of eastern Umboi
lay claim to strips of coastline which they visit for fishing,
collecting shellfish, and trading. They have no canoes. The
Kaimanga villages on the northeast coast of the island do
build canoes, while the southern villages of Gauru and
Yangla occasionally acquire old canoes from the Siassis (for
river transport).

On Arop and Tolokiwa Islands all settlement is on the
coast, but like the Sios and other mainlanders, these islanders are primarily gardeners rather than fishermen. Canoes
are built locally and are also purchased from the Siassis and
Paramot.

According to Kunze (1896, p. 194) all the coastal villages
of Karkar Island possess canoes, but he observed that the
canoes are smaller than those in New Guinea. The manufacture of large canoes is confined to the Mangar region (southwestern coast). Finsch saw three large sailing canoes on this
same coast in the 1880's, but they had been made by the
Bilibilis (1888a, p. 115).

In the 1870's Maclay wrote: "The inhabitants of Wag-
Wag [Bagabag Island] possess no canoes with which they
could come to the New Guinea coast, they are not visited by
anyone and live wholly to themselves" (1875, p. 88).

This review of facts relating to watercraft underscores a
significant distributional pattern: specialized and effective
mastery of the sea is confined to the three groups of island
traders located at the ends of the Vitiaz Strait. In between
are coastal and even island cultures (Karkar, Bagabag, Arop,

381.0995 H219 v

C. 1

Tolokiwa, Sakar, and Umboi) that exhibit a limited, in some cases extremely limited, adaptation to the sea.

Physical environment appears to offer the main clues to this distribution. The mainland coast has no barrier reef, and fringing reefs, which are not extensive in any case, occur only sporadically along the coast. Except for Sio Anchorage and Astrolabe Bay, there are few protected bays and inlets. Where fringing reefs are absent, fishing is poor, and along unprotected beaches canoes cannot even be launched on many days of the year. Environment thus affords no stimulus for an improved marine adaptation. If one supposes that the original colonists of the outer islands and the mainland coast were more effective seafarers and fishermen than their descendants, environmental conditions offer a reasonable explanation for the attenuation of such skills. I want here, however, to suggest a relationship between habitat and culture and not to construct a historical argument which the available facts cannot decide.

The possibility remains that intercultural relationships, in addition to physical habitat, have acted to limit the sea orientation of most of the Vitiaz Strait societies. That is to say, the overseas traders may have sought to preserve their monopoly of the carrying trade by attempting to curb the maritime activities of others. Of the Manus traders, Mead writes: "They serve as carriers for the southern region because they have almost entirely prevented other peoples from owning or operating canoes" (1961, p. 210). Whatever might have occurred in the past, the Siassis do anything but prevent other peoples from owning canoes; indeed, the Siassis are delighted to sell them. In addition, friends from Arop Island, Sio, Kalingi, the Arawe Islands, and elsewhere sometimes accompanied the Siassis on voyages. The Siassis thus provided the purchasers with opportunities to gain knowledge and confidence at sea along with the vessels themselves. But other things were not provided. The Siassis did not share their sailing, weather, and trading magic, which is deemed as essential as the purely technical side.

More important, the non-Siassi peoples lacked the overseas "trade roads"; without local friends to insure a peaceable reception for the voyagers, landing would likely be more dangerous than sailing.

It should not be assumed that other groups, such as the Sios, were striving to enter the overseas trade (or that Siassi interests would have been seriously harmed by the entrance of a few other groups). After all, the Vitiaz Strait presents an awesome blend of wind and current, with the added spice of unpredictability. The Siassi–New Britain route crosses the meeting place of the currents of the Dampier and Vitiaz Strait, where at times the sea is churned into boiling froth. "Round winds"—water spouts or tornadoes—form a recognized hazard to local shipping. In pre-European times, a canoe forced ashore where the party lacked social connections risked annihilation at the hands of the local inhabitants. Then there are numerous long and chilly voyages during which the sailors kill the pangs of hunger with tobacco and betelnut. Understandably, tales of hardship at sea, shipwreck, and drift voyages are common, and the loss of whole crews is also reported.

In the Vitiaz Strait, voyaging is not so much dependent on navigation, since these seafarers never sail out of sight of land. Rather it is a question of having the fortitude and skills necessary to cope under frequently perilous conditions of wind, wave, and current.

Environmental and a complex of social and cultural reasons impel the Siassi Islanders to undertake overseas voyages. The coastal peoples, on the other hand, have more room for choice. Before World War II, when a Sio canoe traveling home from Arop Island went down with all hands lost, the Sios made a choice: they discontinued overseas voyaging.

IV

The Economic Flow:
Products of Trade

THE TRADE SYSTEM sets in motion a flow of varied and specialized goods. There are seasonal and year-to-year fluctuations; during several months of the year, especially at the height of the Southeast Trade winds, the Siassi canoes are weather-bound, and the two sides of the Strait—mainland and archipelago—are temporarily isolated. Local trading, however, goes on constantly. The varied nature of the goods traded is impressive, yet they represent only a fraction of the total array of material goods produced by these societies. This fraction includes, however, the majority of those goods that are the most sought after and expensive, in terms of the time and labor required to produce them.

In this chapter I intend to break down the economic flow into its smallest units, to identify and describe the products which are traded; their provenience; the methods by which they are produced; their uses; the main directions in which they move; and the extent to which their production and distribution are conditioned by the availability of resources.

It is difficult to keep in mind the different combinations of goods that move between various points. A résumé of the main directions of movement of the principal items of exchange is given at the end of the chapter. Later chapters examine the significance of these movements, and present more concrete views obtained by scanning parts of the system, as well as the whole, from particular vantage points.

FOOD

The acquisition of vegetable food for festive as well as daily consumption is a prime objective of trade in a number of local trading spheres. In long-distance or overseas trade, food is less important than manufactured goods, but manufactured goods distributed by overseas trading find their way into local exchange for foodstuffs. The provision of food as a part of the general hospitality accorded to local and overseas trade-friends, though it does not form a part of exchange in the strict sense, is of considerable importance, and is mentioned in appropriate contexts in Chapters VI and VIII.

Food Areas

Within the Vitiaz Strait region, three types of areas can be distinguished according to their agricultural productivity:

1. *High Productivity*. Owing to a favorable annual distribution of rainfall, the mainland uplands, Umboi Island, New Britain, and the lowland rain forests of the Rai Coast are areas of relatively high productivity. In the highlands of the mainland, taro and sweet potato are co-staples. Taro and bananas are the chief crops on Umboi, while the Rai Coast produces taro, yams, and bananas. These areas are characterized by an absence of annual food shortages or "hungry times," more or less continuous year-round gardening activity, and sufficient food surpluses to allow export.

2. *Low Productivity*. The mainland coastal strip from the Kwama River delta in the west and extending beyond the Masaweng River to the southeast (about fifty miles) is subject to a long dry period corresponding to the season of the Southeast Trades (May to November). *Kunai* grass, extending several miles inland, is the prevailing vegetation. Small varieties of yams and *mami* are the staple crops, while

taro and bananas can be grown only in limited quantities. Annually the area is subject to periods of food shortage, during which people rely on fishing, famine foods, and the importation of taro and sweet potato from the mountains.

Meteorological data for this area are scanty[1] (see Fig. 2).

Figure 2. Rainfall Distribution at Opposite Ends of the Rai Coast

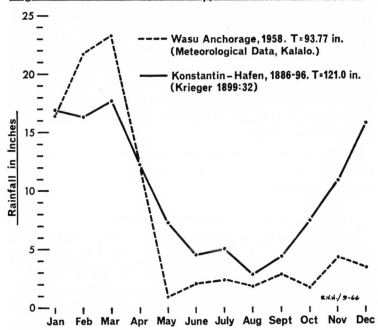

Rainfall figures for the eastern and western extremities of the Rai Coast—where rain forest predominates over *kunai* grass and taro and bananas are staple crops—show that this section of coast, too, receives little rainfall from May to November. While the entire coast is sheltered from the moisture bearing winds of the Southeast Trades by the Sarawaged and Finisterre ranges, it is possible that a varia-

[1] Rain gauges have only recently been installed at Sio and Gitua on the *kunai* coast.

tion of a few inches of rain during the dry period is critical in determining the marked differences in vegetation and production between the Rai Coast on the one hand, and the adjoining Kwama-Masaweng Coast on the other. It is possible, too, that the gardening and burning activities of the larger populations of the yam growing *kunai* coast are largely responsible for deforestation.

3. *Marginal Productivity.* The tiny raised or low coral islands of the Siassi Archipelago and the Tami Group have insufficient land to support their populations by gardening. The islanders devote land not taken up with coconuts and other economic trees to small gardens on Tuam, Malai, and in the Tami Islands; apparently Mandok and Aramot had no gardens whatever aboriginally. Coconuts are the islanders' main vegetable product, along with *Canarium* almonds, pandanus, and breadfruit.

Fishing is the chief subsistence activity, for although they lack land, the islands (except Tuam) are set amidst extensive reefs and shoals.

Taro and Other Staple Foods

Taro is by far the most important food item exchanged in local trading. The Siassi Islanders regularly exchange fish and mats for small lots of taro with the Umboi villagers, while at other times pigs, dogs, and other high-value goods are given for one- to two-ton loads of taro. On the mainland taro is the chief export of the uplands, moving to the coast villages in exchange for fish, coconuts, and earthenware pots. Sweet potatoes rank second to taro.

Singapore taro (*Xanthosoma;* N-M: *taro kongkong*), which is less subject to the depredations of the taro beetle than *Colocasia,* has been widely adopted in the highlands in recent years. In some highland localities, according to informants' testimony, it has become more important than taro. *Xanthosoma* is considered less palatable than taro by coast dwellers, but nevertheless it is readily accepted in trade. (It is not cultivated on the Kwama-Masaweng littoral.)

Other introduced vegetables now figure in the trade—white potatoes, corn, beans, cucumbers, cabbage, and onions, and also fruits such as papaya and pineapple. Like Singapore taro, these vegetables move from the interior uplands to the coast, but unlike the former, they are only given in small quantities, in addition to and never in lieu of staples such as taro, sweet potatoes, and bananas.

Yams (except for planting purposes) rarely enter into exchange. The food exporting regions produce few yams, while they form the staple crop in food importing regions. Owing to taro beetle, disease, or soil exhaustion, or some combination of factors, taro has all but disappeared from the Kaimanga area of eastern Umboi Island during the last fifteen years. Here yams have taken the place of taro in the local trade with the Siassi Islanders.

Sago and coconuts (see below) are the only foods regularly taken across the Vitiaz Strait by Siassi canoes, for in general food moves over shorter distances (the Siassis import taro and other foods from the mainland and New Britain, however). Sago is abundant in the low-lying swampy country of southern Umboi Island, where the Siassis obtain it in exchange for fish, in bulk quantities for pigs or cash, and sometimes by poaching. In the form of washed and dried flour, the sago is taken to the mainland coast where, especially on the Rai Coast, the sago palm is relatively abundant. The Sios explain the trade in sago thus: "Working sago is hard and we are lazy. It is easier to trade for it than to prepare it ourselves." The Sios maintain, however, that sago was less abundant in the past, local stands of sago palms having been greatly extended by planting in modern times.

Coconuts

One of the most striking changes to occur in the landscape over the last few decades has been the development of village coconut plantations. In aboriginal and early post-European times, the coconut palm was a comparative rarity on the coasts of northeastern New Guinea and of western New Britain. Today the coconut palm provides the coastal villagers with an abundance of readily obtainable food, fuel, materials for a variety of artifacts, and copra, the principal source of cash income.

When Groves visited Sio in 1933 the coastline was a barren, open expanse of *kunai* grass (1934, pp. 45, 48). Today Sio coconut groves stretch for eight miles along the coast. People here and in other areas owe their current wealth in coconuts to the plantings of their fathers.[2] Their grandfathers' holdings of trees, if they had any at all, can usually be counted on the hands. At present individual holdings of a hundred or more trees are common.

In the past, communities with a relative abundance of coconuts were confined to the small islands of the Siassi Group, Astrolabe Bay, and the Tami Islands—that is, the trading peoples.[3] When bad weather or perhaps warfare temporarily interrupted the local trade in foodstuffs, the islanders could fall back on coconuts and fish for their daily fare. Aside from subsistence, coconuts were an important stock-in-trade. On the coasts of New Guinea and New Britain, the coconut was a rare delicacy, and a community like Sio, which did have some palms of its own, was willing to exchange pots for Siassi coconuts. The Tami Islanders deemed their coconut monopoly so important that nuts taken across to the mainlanders were broken in two to prevent their being planted.

[2] Initially, plantings were made under government supervision. Forced planting was begun by the Germans, and annual planting quotas have been imposed occasionally by the Australian officers. Certain coconut groves at Sio are referred to by the name of the patrol officer who directed the planting.

[3] Of Astrolabe Bay, Maclay (1875, p. 67) observed that "the number of trees is very small in many villages, so that the inhabitants try to get coconuts from other villages. One finds coconuts only in a few mountain villages, compared with the coast of the neighboring islands where the trees appear to be numerous. . . ." (This and other translations from German articles and books are my own.)

Fish

Fish, smoked or fresh, and shellfish are exchanged against vegetable food in the local trading spheres. Rates of exchange have altered considerably in modern times, giving increasing advantage to the inland food producers over the fishermen. In many areas now there tends to be a one-to-one equivalence for taro and fish (allowing for adjustments for varying size and quality). The coastal people attribute the change to the influence of prices in the town markets (of Lae, Madang, Rabaul). The fishermen's lament is widely expressed in a statement of the kind: "In the old days we broke a fish in half. The tail bought one pile of taro, the head bought another. Now the bush people are very hard toward us."

Tobacco

Locally grown leaf tobacco is probably the most extensively and continuously traded article of exchange. In local trade tobacco moves from inland to coast, and in long-distance trade from mainland to archipelago.

Little tobacco is grown in the coastal belt. At Sio, where small amounts are planted, people claim that it does not grow well and point out besides that it is not worth the trouble to cultivate when a month's supply can be acquired from the interior for a clay pot. Tobacco is grown in the largest quantities by the communities on both slopes of the mainland coastal range, and while superior tobacco is supposed to be produced on Arop Island, in general the mainland people regard the people of the outer islands as perpetually tobacco starved.

Tobacco is everywhere regarded as an indigenous plant.[4] A Sio story relates that tobacco first appeared to the ancestors growing on a grave, the plant having been formed of the

[4] Local names include Sio *mundo;* Komba *mundo;* Gituan *momo;* Astrolabe Bay *kas;* Kovai *siau;* Barim *kas.* I do not know whether all of the tobacco grown in the Vitiaz Strait region is the American variety, *Nicotiana tabacum.*

blood and body fluids of the deceased. Tobacco has been used more widely among the population in European times, especially among women and children. Cigarettes, rolled in newspaper, and sometimes small cigars, are smoked universally. Native leaf tobacco is preferred to commercial twist or stick tobacco, and native trade stores are able to stock supplies of it through traditional trade channels.

Betelnut and Lime

Betelnut is extensively cultivated on Tuam and Malai, the largest of the Siassi Islands. The Aramot and Mandok Islanders receive betelnut in local trade with the Umboi villagers. Surplus nuts are taken to the mainland, along with lime produced by the islanders themselves.

Betelnut is abundant in many areas of the mainland interior and is traded within the interior as well as being taken to the coast.

On the mainland the inland villagers closest to the beach often produce their own lime from shells collected on the beach or from local fresh-water shells. The shells are heated in lengths of bamboo in open hearths, and several heatings are required for a full reduction to powder. Lime is traded further inland, and, curiously, several times while I was at Sio people traveled inland to purchase lime.

Salt

Salt is not an important item of exchange. Coastal and island housewives customarily cook vegetables in sea water, or a mixture of salt and fresh water. Occasionally coconut water bottles of sea water are taken to inland trade-friends. Interior villages obtain supplies of salt, either in the form of salt ash or sea water, by what the coast dwellers view as theft rather than through trade. Indeed, along the deserted stretches of beach on the mainland coast one frequently encounters small parties of bush people engaged in burning driftwood to obtain salt ash. According to Friederici (1912, p. 138) there was no trade in salt on the northwestern coast of New Britain, while Maclay observed that in Astrolabe Bay pieces of driftwood and wood chips cut from drift logs were carried to the interior as gifts to friends (1875, p. 71).

Pigs and Dogs

Pigs represent the supreme value of all objects of wealth. Dogs are a close second. Although the sentimental attachment to dogs is not expressed to the same, almost pathological, degree that it is in American society, the animals are, relatively speaking, much more highly valued in an economic sense than in America. Dogs are occasionally eaten (in some locales), and on the mainland coast, especially, good hunting dogs spell the difference between successful and unsuccessful pig hunts. On the whole, however, they are about as useful or useless as our pets.

Pigs appear to be raised in the largest numbers in the interiors of New Britain and New Guinea. They often move in local trade from inland to coast, but not in the reverse direction. Most overseas Siassi voyages are aimed at securing either pigs or other goods that may eventually be exchanged for pigs. Generally, the animals are under one year of age, because not only are they cheaper, but they are easier to transport and are more likely to survive long trips.

Pigs are exchanged against dogs, wooden bowls, pots, valuables (see below), canoes, and—nowadays—cash. On the New Guinea mainland, where pigs appear to be more expensive than in the archipelago, the more-or-less standard equivalents are five pounds for a one-year-old, ten pounds for a two-year-old, and fifteen pounds for a three-year-old.[5] Females are more highly valued than males (except for boars with curved tusks).

Like pigs, dogs appear to move mainly from inland to coast in local trading. In overseas trade they are carried from various parts of the archipelago to the mainland. A

[5] Prices or equivalents of native commodities are quoted in Australian pounds and shillings. In 1963–64, the Australian pound was valued at U.S. $2.24, while a shilling had an approximate value of 11.2 cents.

grown dog is equivalent in value to a six-month- to one-year-old pig.

CRAFT GOODS

Earthenware Pots

Three groups of pottery making communities of the New Guinea mainland supply cooking ware to the peoples of the Vitiaz Strait. They are the villages of Siboma, Laukanu, Lababia, and Buso on the south coast of the Huon Gulf; four neighboring communities on the north coast of the Huon Peninsula—Sio, Nambariwa, Gitua, and Sialum (producers of "Sio" pots); and the island villages of Bilibili and Jabob in Astrolabe Bay (producers of "Madang" pots). All three types of ware are plain cooking pots, simply decorated, and each tends to be made in a single form, though with a considerable range of sizes or capacities.[6] Aside from their use in cooking, pots are widely treated as wealth-objects, and on Umboi Island and in western New Britain they customarily form a part of bridewealth payments. In fact, in such areas more pots are likely to be found among a man's store of valuables than among his wife's cooking utensils.

The wide distribution of pottery is effected by the three groups of sailor-traders, as well as by hand-to-hand movements both within and beyond the range of their voyaging. Tami canoes formerly brought Huon Gulf pots to the southeastern portion of the Huon Peninsula, to the south coast of New Britain as far to the east as Möwehafen (Parkinson, 1907, p. 54), and to the Siassi Group. Sio pots are distributed to the Rai Coast and its hinterland via the local coastal and inland trade, while at the western end of the Strait the "Madang" pots are distributed from their source by the Bilibili traders. The Siassis deliver pots to the outer islands

---

[6] The Sio pot makers distinguish three named sizes of vessels (*kulo*); *kulo katuŋa* are the standard cooking pot, *kulo tabageri* are oversized, *kulo ŋgaŋga* have capacities of one or two quarts. In earlier days, at least, Bilibili potters made pots in two forms, a wide-mouthed cooking vessel (*bodi*) and a water jug (*io*) (Finsch, 1888a, p. 83).

and to New Britain. Though they concentrate on the Sio type of pots, which are manufactured closest to home, the Siassis sail to Tami and the Finschhafen area for Huon Gulf ware, and they also acquire the "Madang" pots—which move eastward by local trading—along the Rai Coast. In recent years canoes from Malai have sailed to Madang itself to procure these pots.

Although Huon Gulf ware enters from the south and the "Madang" pots (which are more finely made and are most valued) come from the west, the "Sio" pot remains the main stock-in-trade within the Vitiaz Strait. Until recently pottery manufacture was restricted to the Sio group of villages (including Nambariwa) and Gitua, fifteen miles to the east. According to local accounts, the industry was introduced about twenty-five years ago at Sialum by two Sio women who had married there and by a Sialum girl who grew up and learned pot making at Gitua. In spite of the fact that many Sio and Gituan women have left their villages in marriage before, this is the first breach of the Sio/Gitua monopoly, which has always been closely guarded. Sio women are not permitted to make pots away from home, even though supplies of clay are available. In recent years Gituan relatives of Tuam Islanders, taking supplies of clay with them to Siassi, have made pots there, but I cannot say whether this was done in the past.

The question of the Sio ban on pot making away from home has been raised a number of times in the last few decades. Many Sio families have gone to the Rai Coast as Lutheran evangelists, and wives who found local sources of suitable clays have, at times, desired to make pots. In all cases they were restrained from doing so. Maintenance of the monopoly of manufacture is considered to be important by both Sios and Gituans. Though the Sios are less involved now in the Siassi trade than the Gituans, pots are the chief means by which Sios acquire tobacco, taro, and other goods from the interior. There is, however, a difference in the attitudes of the Sios and Gituans with regard to the Sialum "theft" of pottery, and no doubt this reflects their differing economic involvements. The Sios, more concerned with exporting pots to the inland areas and the Rai Coast than to Siassi, seem relatively unconcerned about Sialum's new industry. The Gituans, on the other hand, must now compete with Sialum's exports to Siassi.

In the history of Pacific peoples, pottery has often been a "lost art." Sialum provides an example of the extension of the art, and the circumstances surrounding its adoption are interesting for the light they may shed on factors determining diffusion. Sialum has close ties with the communities of the Siassi Group (it also lies nearer Siassi than Gitua and Sio), and it is reasonable to suppose that these pre-existent trade relationships provided a prime motive for adopting pottery manufacture. Sufficient pots for home use could have been acquired from Gitua, as in the past. The development of a home industry, on the other hand, places Sialum in a very advantageous position vis-à-vis the established pot makers.

The Huon Gulf pottery industry has been described by Hogbin (1947), while Bilibili pottery making techniques are summarized by Schurig (1930). Sio techniques are described in Chapter V, under "Pottery."

Wooden Bowls

Two types of wooden bowls, manufactured in the Tami Islands and on the western Rai Coast respectively, figure prominently in trade. Both types are distributed throughout the area, though the Tami-style bowls are more common in the eastern Vitiaz Strait while the Rai Coast bowls are found oftener in the west. The Tami bowls are hardwood, with expertly carved designs that place them among the most outstanding artistic products of New Guinea. The Rai Coast bowls, most of which are manufactured in the interior,[7] are

[7] Schmitz lists the upper Nankina Valley (central Rai Coast) as one center for the manufacture of these bowls (1955, p. 306), but it appears that they are widely manufactured in the hinterland of the Rai Coast and

generally small (less than twenty-four inches in length), ovoid in form, and are adorned with simple incised designs. Because they are often made of softwoods, they deteriorate rather quickly. Both types of bowl are used as food mixing and serving dishes, especially in ceremonial distributions, and furthermore both are used widely as wealth-objects. Their relative values are indicated by the cash payments they may command: five to ten pounds for the largest Tami bowls, only five to ten shillings for the Rai Coast product.

Tami bowls are produced in three basic forms: zoo-morphic (bird, fish, and turtle), rectilinear, and oval. The oval form is the most common and ranges in length from about ten inches to four feet. Characteristic of the ovoid bowls are reptiles and other motifs carved in high or low relief just below the rim. Often a stylized crouching figure is carved in high relief just below the rim on both sides. The surface of the bowl is stained black and polished.

In aboriginal and early post-European times, the Tami Islanders were the sole manufacturers of the large and ornate hardwood bowls,[8] which they distributed within the Huon Gulf, to the opposite mainland, and exchanged for boars' tusks and other goods with the Siassi Islanders. Sometime in the first decades of the twentieth century, however,

---

the western Strait. Sio informants distinguish two types, one oval in form, the other eye-shaped with a slight keel. I was unable to establish whether the two types stem from distinct regions, as some informants said.

[8] Parkinson concluded that these bowls were also manufactured in southern New Britain from the fact that he observed bowls in various stages of manufacture at Möwehafen (1907, pp. 212–13). Todd, who spent a year doing field work on the islands off Möwehafen, makes no mention of bowls being manufactured locally, but specifically states that they came from Siassi via the Arawe Islands (1934, p. 198).

At times in the past, groups of Tami Islanders camped for extended periods on Mutumala Island (just off the southern tip of Umboi) in order to make canoes from local timber (see Chap. VI). During these visits they made bowls, fished, and traded for foodstuffs with the Umboi villagers. The Tamis also visited Möwehafen for trade, as Parkinson records, and it is possible that the unfinished bowls that he saw were made by the Tamis during an extended visit. A protracted stay might be intentional or, as sometimes occurs, caused by weather sufficiently bad to prohibit sailing.

the production of Tami bowls apparently declined to the point that the Siassis could no longer rely upon obtaining sufficient numbers. Whatever the specific factors affecting the supply, they must have stemmed from the involvement of the Tamis with the early European community at Finschhafen. (This is discussed fully in Chapter IX.) Because of the fundamental importance of Tami bowls in the Siassis' trading for pigs (see Chap. VI), the shortage amounted to an economic crisis, and had it not been remedied, the Siassi trading regime in the archipelago might have been seriously crippled. About 1930—perhaps somewhat before—the Mandoks and Aramots, the canoe builders and wood carvers of the Siassi group, began to duplicate the Tami bowls, usually in the ovoid form. The Siassi copies are inferior to the Tami originals. They lack the symmetry, precision of detail, and durability achieved by the Tami carvers.[9] Nevertheless, the Siassi product is highly regarded, and it is exported to the mainland and to all parts of the archipelago, particularly to Umboi Island, Cape Gloucester, and the Arawe Islands in southern New Britain. Throughout the Vitiaz Strait the large, black, Tami-style bowl has come to be known as the "Siassi bowl" (N-M: *plet bilong Siassi*).

The Tamis presently derive much of their cash income from the sale of carvings intended to be more appealing to European tourists than the traditional forms. The traditional bowls are still made, however, and occasionally they are acquired by the Siassis. For the most part the Siassis must rely on the carving industry of Mandok and Aramot.

The Rai Coast bowls move along the coast toward the east to such places as Sio and Gitua. The Siassis obtain them in the various beach villages of the mainland, and dispose of them in the archipelago. Although these bowls are relatively

[9] According to Tami carvers, the critical differentia is that the Siassis cut the length of the bowls along the grain. Because of this, bowls which are dropped or loaded with hot puddings sometimes split down the middle. Tami bowls, on the other hand, are stronger and aesthetically more pleasing because they are cut at an angle across the grain.

common on the mainland, I saw very few of them in the Siassi Islands or on Umboi Island in 1964.

Hand Drums

Hand drums, cylindrical or more usually of hourglass form and varying between twenty and thirty inches in length, are used throughout northeastern New Guinea. The drums are almost always black, with a polished finish, and are ornately carved. The drum cover consists of a piece of lizard skin, which is glued and tied to one end of the drum.

The waist of the drum is ornamented, while the slightly flaring end portions are left plain. Bodrogi may be right when he suggests that the geometric designs carved around the middle portion are an imitation of turtle-shell bracelets (1959, p. 77).

Drums are probably manufactured over a wide area, but the Tami Islands, Arop and Karkar Islands are recognized centers for the manufacture of superior hardwood drums.

The Bilibili traders distributed drums from Karkar Island in the western Strait (Kunze, 1896, p. 194). The Siassis had their supply for trade purposes near at hand in Arop Island, and Tami served as a second source. All of the finest drums at Sio are Arop-made and were acquired directly from Arop (with which Sio has close relations), often for cash payments of one to two pounds.

The Tuam Islanders currently purchase drums from Arop and Tolokiwa Islands for cash (ten shillings to two pounds) and *laplaps*. They are then exported to New Britain, where a drum brings a dog, and to the mainland, where a drum is equivalent to a dogs'-teeth headband.

Obsidian

Obsidian was supplied to northeastern New Guinea from a single region in the south of the Willaumez Peninsula of New Britain. Modern informants name Garuwa, near Talasea, as the point of origin. From there, obsidian was traded westward along the north coast to Cape Gloucester, where the Siassis obtained it. The Siassis traded obsidian all along the mainland coast and also supplied the Tami Islanders, who distributed it throughout the Huon Gulf.

Friederici investigated the trade in volcanic glass as carried on around the turn of the century. The coastal and island dwelling Kombe peoples acquired obsidian from the Walupai (to the east and inland) for fish and coconut palm leaves, to use in making baskets. The Barriai, neighbors to the west, gave shell money and pigs to the Kombe for obsidian, which they then exchanged with the Kalingi of Cape Gloucester for earthenware pots from the mainland. The Kalingi are in direct relations with the Siassi Islanders, and they received more pots for the obsidian (1912, pp. 138–39).

As obsidian moved farther from its source, the size of the pieces traded progressively decreased and the relative value increased. Thus, a cubical piece the size of a coconut, exchanged for a single pot in northeastern New Britain, might command a dozen or more pots at Sio (it is hard to say which increased more in value, pots as they moved to the archipelago or obsidian as it moved in the opposite direction). In turn, the Sios exchanged several small and roughly shaped blades for small pigs in the interior.

There appears to have been no regular blade industry (i.e., flaking from prepared blocks or pressure flaking) associated with the use of obsidian. Small blades were obtained by simply smashing a large block with a stone, while in time blades were broken into smaller fragments to obtain newly sharp edges. Judging from the numerous fragments around village sites—mostly micro-blades and waste chips—straight-edged blades and scraper and burin-like forms could be produced by this relatively crude knapping technique.

The blades were used for hair cutting and shaving, and in surgical operations, such as male circumcision, the cutting of ear lobes, and removal of the umbilical cord. Probably because of its rarity, obsidian was not used for the manufacture of spear and arrow points. According to Friederici (*ibid.*), the Barriai sometimes produced adze blades out of suitable pieces, and it is probable that, in spite of its brittleness, obsidian would hold up for the light woodworking for which adzes are frequently used. According to modern Sio informants, however, obsidian was not used for carving or woodworking.

Stone Adzes

The extent to which chippable stone or stone adzes were exchanged in aboriginal times can no longer be reliably established. Polished and ground stone adzes came north across the Sarawaged Range from the Wain and Naba peoples to the Komba area, where they were exchanged for pigs and *tambu* shell. Siassi-made clam-shell adzes were traded to the Umboi villagers and perhaps farther afield. Of the Astrolabe Bay region, Maclay recorded that "Stone for hatchets (a kind of agate) is received from the mountain-dwellers and it is not found in great quantity, so that each adult possesses only *one* good axe . . ." (1875, p. 75).

Paints

Red and black earth pigments, from two widely separated localities, are distributed throughout the area by the Siassi traders and through local exchange. Black paint from the region of Malalomai on the Rai Coast is used mainly to blacken the hair and face (canoe planks, masks, and other artifacts are painted with charcoal in a resin binder). Red ochre mixed with water is used to paint canoe planks and other artifacts. It is also used as face and body paint. In dry form it is rubbed into the carved designs of drums, wooden food mortars, and stirring paddles. Tricolor designs in red, black, and white (lime), painted on wood, bark cloth, and coconut bast are characteristic of the entire area.

Red ochre comes from several localities in or near stream beds in the vicinity of Tarawe village, on the eastern side of Umboi Island. The Tarawe villagers dig and wash the pigment, and trade it in small or bulk quantities to Barim

(Paramot), with which Tarawe has close relations, and to the Siassis. On Umboi a hard-packed ball of the pigment, about three inches in diameter, is exchanged for a clay pot or a basket of betelnut. Large lumps (fifty to sixty pounds) are equivalent to a pig or dog. The Siassis take the red ochre to the mainland in the form of small lumps or balls wrapped up in pandanus leaf.

Bark Cloth

Bark cloth went out of general use long ago, and it is difficult to establish the precontact patterns of exchange. The Rai Coast is known for the manufacture of bark cloth for loincloths, while the interior mainland (Komba, Selepet, Timbe, Uruwa, and the Yupna peoples) manufactures painted bark-cloth blankets or capes. Formerly, the Sios relied on both areas for the bulk of their bark-cloth apparel, and Sio still imports tapa from the Rai Coast for use on ceremonial occasions.

The Siassis regularly acquired bark cloth along the mainland coast for export to the archipelago. It appears also that the Siassi voyagers and the Bilibili traders redistributed bark cloth along the mainland coast.

Net Bags

The well-known New Guinea *bilum* or woven net bag is a common article of exchange as well as being a main carrying device. Manufacture is restricted to the mainland, the best ones being made in the interior where the vines used for thread grow in the greatest variety. Thus, Sio often acquires *bilums* from the inland Komba and Selepet, even though many are made locally. The Siassis get net bags all along the coast of New Guinea for export to the archipelago. Both the large woman's *bilum* (Sio *kɛta*) and the smaller man's bag (*toŋa*) are traded.

Woven netting was formerly an item of apparel. Komba men wore hair nets, and the customary mark of widowhood in the Siassi Islands is a net head covering.

Pandanus Products

Sleeping mats constructed of previously sewn strips of pandanus leaf are a chief manufacture and article of trade of the Siassi and Tami Islanders. They are about six feet square and are usually folded double for use as a mattress. Their manufacture is exclusively women's work. The sleeping mats are also manufactured by the Umboi villagers, but the testimony of the Siassi mat makers, as well as the inferior quality of the Umboi mats, indicates that the Umboi craft may have been acquired recently. Pandanus rain hoods, used mainly by women, are manufactured in the mainland interior and are sometimes traded to the coast.

A mat is exchangeable for a cooking pot or a net bag of food. At the recently established weekly market at Barang, Umboi Island, the best Siassi mats are sold for six to eight shillings (sixty-seven to ninety cents).

Square pandanus sails, woven of pandanus-leaf strips an inch or more wide with the aid of long wooden needles, also figure in trade. When the Siassis sell sailing canoes, sails are furnished as part of the vessel's equipment, and they may provide replacements for worn out or damaged sails. Groves (1934, p. 58) reports that Sio sails were mostly acquired from Siassi. These would have been used mainly on the single-masted canoes manufactured by the Sios.

Pandanus is abundant on the small islands and in the mainland uplands, but it appears that only within the latter area is the fruit an article of exchange. In the Komba-Selepet region the seed stones are cooked with vegetable food, boiled, and served as a treat (in this context pandanus fruit is regarded as the highland equivalent of the coconut), and the fruit is often brought by visitors to their hosts, relatives, and trade-friends.

Bows and Arrows

The bow and arrow (along with the stoneheaded club) is the traditional weapon of war and hunting implement on the mainland. In the archipelago, and also in the Tami Islands, slings and spears are the chief weapons. The Umboi Islanders hunt pigs with heavy nets and spears.

Bows and arrows are manufactured chiefly in the interior of the mainland and are traded to the coast. The Sios, who do not make bows, acquire them from the Komba and Selepet villagers and from the Rai Coast. The Sio domain lacks both the palm from which bows are made and the tree (Selepet *hipau*) which produces the resin used in hafting arrow tips. Bows are an important article of exchange for the highlanders in their dealings with the coast, though all beach villagers may not be ignorant of bow making. Furthermore, the Siassi traders acquire bows and arrows on the mainland for export to the archipelago, where they are used to some extent in hunting and fishing, and formerly in warfare.

The bows are about six feet in length (unstrung) and are fashioned from the outer layers of the black palm. Once the material is at hand, it takes about a day to fashion a bow with steel tools (a machete is used), though the work may actually be spread over a number of days. After fashioning, charcoal is applied and rubbed out with a bunch of fresh leaves, producing a dull black satin finish. A strip of bamboo about three-eighths inch wide serves as a string. The ends of the strip are flayed and tied in loops. The bamboo retains its strength only while fresh, and strings must be replaced frequently.

The arrows, which are about five feet long, consist of a cane shaft three-eighths inch in diameter and unfletched, with a tip about eight inches long. Tips are made of bamboo and hardwood and in a great variety of forms: broad-bladed, multipronged, barbed, and plain. Quivers are not employed, bow and arrows being carried together in one hand or over the shoulder.

In exchange, a bow and a half-dozen arrows, their tips carefully wrapped in leaves, are given as a unit worth about two shillings.

Today bows and arrows are used universally for hunting,

and on the coast for fishing as well. Sio men frequently carry them along when they leave the village, especially during the early period of gardening work when there is a good chance of flushing a wild pig. Perhaps, too, this habit is a holdover from the not too distant past, when no one ventured very far afield unarmed. In the old days, say the Sios, men slept on top of their wooden armor, their bows and arrows at their side, while the use of carved wooden headrests kept the warrior from sleeping too soundly for his own good.

VALUABLES

Boars' Tusks

Abnormally curved boars' tusks used as wealth-objects and ornaments—distributed widely from New Guinea to Samoa (Finsch, 1887, p. 156)—occur throughout northeastern New Guinea. The tusks are valued according to their size and the extent of curvature. Tusks that have grown to the point where the "eye" of the tooth nearly meets the base, thus forming a circle, are considered to be the most valuable. The values of particular tusks, then, may be determined according to the degree of closure or recurvature.

Usually a pair of tusks is bound near the base to form a breast pendant that is suspended from a string around the neck; this ornament is worn mainly by men. Boars' tusks are most often exchanged in the form of such oversize pendants.[10]

The paired tusks are known as *saŋiri* at Sio, where they enter into the most important classes of payments—brideprice, indemnification, payments to sorcerers. Nowhere do the boars' tusks seem to be more esteemed than among the Tami Islanders, who consider them an indispensable item of brideprice. According to modern informants, the custom-

[10] According to Finsch, it is customary along the whole north coast of New Guinea to suspend single tusks from a cord. He did observe the paired tusks at Astrolabe Bay and in New Britain (1887, p. 158).

ary payment of bridewealth includes, among other goods, five pairs of tusks.

It takes five to six years for a pig to produce a perfect pair of tusks, by which time the animal has grown to enormous size. At an early age the upper canines are removed to allow unimpeded growth of the tusks, and when the desired degree of recurvature has been attained, the pig is slaughtered and the tusks removed.

Unfortunately, information on the distribution of the pigs producing these abnormal tusks, or rather the techniques by which they are induced to grow, is meager. In all places visited, I queried people regarding tusk bearing pigs, but with regard to past distribution the results were inconclusive. I actually saw boars bearing curved tusks at one village, Gomlongon, on Umboi Island.

It seems clear, however, that boars' tusks move mainly from the archipelago to the mainland, via the Siassi traders, while dogs'-teeth valuables move in the opposite direction. Thus a typical transaction between Sio and Siassi trade-friends would be the exchange of a *saŋiri* or boars'-tusk pendant for a headband composed of one or more rows of dogs' teeth. The Tami Islanders exchanged their beautifully carved hardwood bowls for the tusks. According to them, three bowls, two large and one small, are equivalent to a boars'-tusk pendant. The two large bowls are payment for the two tusks, while the smaller one is said to "cut the rope joining the tusks." Mandok informants, however, say that a large pair of tusks sometimes commanded as many as a dozen bowls at Tami in the old days.

Imitation Boars' Tusks

In aboriginal times imitation tusks were made from giant clam shell (*Tridacna*), and although the most influential men are said to have monopolized the genuine tusks, lesser men could hope to acquire the imitations. According to Finsch, "the natives hold them in extraordinarily high esteem," and he adds that "Understandably, they occur more frequently than the genuine article" (1887, p. 158). Earlier, Baron Maclay wrote that they were "greatly valued everywhere on the Maclay coast" (1951–54, II, 358–72).

Maclay designated the village of Singor on the eastern Rai Coast (near the modern village of Singorokai) as the main place of manufacture, where he observed that "Everywhere were lying about large shells (*Tridacna*), from which are turned *syual-boro;* here there were also lying large whetstones, on which these decorations were turned" (*ibid.*). Bilibili traders regularly visited Singor, and it is likely that the Siassis also acquired imitation tusks there for purposes of trade.

Dogs' Teeth

The canine teeth of dogs, worked into elaborate ornaments, rank with boars'-tusk pendants as valuables and articles of exchange.[11] There are three main classes of dogs'-teeth valuables: (1) woven headbands and belts to which

[11] Finsch sought to convey the great esteem in which dogs'-teeth and pigs'-tusk valuables are held, as well as their relative values, by comparing the former to silver and the latter to gold (1887, p. 158). While a dog's canine is much less valuable than a boar's tusk, the most elaborate dogs'-teeth valuables outrank boars'-tusk pendants. When exchanged for cash, either an average pair of tusks or a dogs'-teeth headband (about forty teeth) is currently worth £2 ($4.50).

In another way, the great value of these ornaments to their owners is revealed by the difficulty Finsch (and also Maclay) had in inducing people to part with them. I encountered the same difficulty almost a century later. For example, one man would not even discuss my offer of £50 ($112) for a very elaborate dogs'-teeth ornament. Finsch also commented on the rarity of these ornaments in museum collections.

Baron Maclay was the first European to live in these parts, where he was known as "a big big man, a man from the moon, a Russian man" who was deserving of great gifts and respect. Even so, he resorted to cajoling as well as handsome payments in order to acquire specimens of the ornaments. Some examples of his transactions are:

At Singor (1877)
One clam shell replica of = Two knives and "a great
boars'-tusk pendant   number of various trinkets"

At Sio (1877)
One boars'-tusk decoration = One good steel knife
(1951–54, II. 358–72).

are attached rows of dogs' teeth, often in combination with parallel rows of *tambu* (small cowrie) shell; (2) V-shaped breastplates of dogs' teeth, the larger specimens having two hundred to three hundred teeth; and (3) woven net bags one side of which is covered with dogs' teeth, often several hundred of them.

The Sios refer to valuables of dogs' teeth by the collective term *panair,* and rank them in value as follows: headbands and belts are the least precious, breastplates are more valuable, and net bags (*toŋa panair*) rank the highest. The criteria of value are the number of teeth composing the ornament, to some extent its age and history, and the designs formed by the rows of teeth and subsidiary pendants of teeth and shell worked into or suspended from the ornament. The number of teeth ranges from as few as twenty in a small headband to several hundred in the *toŋa panair.* In the case of the *toŋa panair* and the larger breastplates (termed *ŋgoa melamela,* "pig's tongue"), the number of teeth is too great to count. The headbands and belts, however, may be compared by counting the number of rows of teeth and the number of teeth in each row. Frequently, the accounting unit used is a group of four, that is, the number of canines possessed by a single dog, so that a "twenty dog" headband contains eighty teeth.

Ornaments containing roughly equal numbers of teeth are differently valued according to their designs. For example, in the case of headbands, distinctive designs are achieved by the arrangement of varying numbers of rows of dogs' teeth and *tambu* shell in parallel. Breastplates may be distinguished by the arrangement of teeth and shell on embroidered appendages suspended from the lower tip. Whatever the distinguishing design or design element, the right to duplicate them belongs to the male patrilineal descendants of the original designer. Rights of ownership and inheritance of finished valuables, as distinct from rights to reproduce specific designs, are not limited to men or to groups of related agnates. Indeed, valuables most esteemed for their designs frequently pass from a man to his sister's son.

From the Sio point of view, the criterion of design cross-cuts the classification into types of ornaments—headband, *toŋa panair,* and so on. Valuables bearing distinctive familial designs are withheld from external trade—rarely, if ever, would they be given to a Komba or Siassi trade-friend. Headbands, valuable for the number of teeth they contain, are given to Siassi friends in exchange for boars'-tusk pendants, but they are second-class valuables. First-class *panair* circulate only internally, as bridewealth, payments of compensation, and especially as gifts of inheritance to children and sisters' children. It may be added, however, that from the point of view of an outsider unfamiliar with the designs and sentimental-historical values of particular ornaments, *panair* of the second class often do not appear to be inferior in any way.

Villagers throughout the Vitiaz Strait keep dogs, yet dogs'-teeth ornaments move mainly from the mainland to the archipelago, while live dogs go in the opposite direction. Wild or semiwild dogs are reputed to occur in large numbers on Arop Island, where they are hunted. Domestic dogs, even those enfeebled by illness, are not killed for their teeth. Allowed to die a natural death, they are placed in shallow graves with half coconut shells under the muzzle to aid in the later recovery of the canines.

It is apparent that here dogs' teeth are used more in the manner of *kula* valuables than "currency." Mead writes that "The value of every object sold or exchanged in the Admiralty Islands can be expressed in terms of dogs' teeth" (1930, p. 122). Thus, one large dog's tooth can be exchanged for ten taro, ten coconuts, or forty betelnuts, while a lime gourd is rated at two dogs' teeth, a lime spatula at five or six (*ibid.,* pp. 121, 122). I know of no comparable rates of exchange in the Vitiaz Strait. The teeth are incorporated into ornaments, and as such have a limited exchangeability (or "liquidity"), moving against boars' tusks, drums, pigs, and (nowadays) cash in some cases (one to five pounds for the less elaborate ornaments).[12]

Tambu Shell

Small cowrie (*Nassa*) or *tambu* shells, in the form of strings of shell or more elaborate ornaments, are as highly prized as boars' tusks and dogs' teeth. The Komba of the Huon Peninsula recognize five types of *tambu* shell valuables or *dasɛn* (Sio *jana*). Headbands (*matin*) and belts (*bukawa*), which consist of rows of both shell (with the backs removed and ground down) and dogs' teeth have already been described. Incidentally, people frequently wear the "belts" as headbands wrapped twice round the head. The most highly valued *dasɛn* consist of a rectangular piece of coconut bast (burlap is sometimes used today), eight by ten inches, which is heavily embroidered with shell. The open field between the designs formed by rows of shell is painted red, green, yellow, or blue. If made in a single piece, these are known as *senam* (Sio *sapu*). Somewhat larger and more valuable ones are made in two pieces, which are sewn together and may be folded like a book (*kınsa*). The *senam* and *kınsa* are equipped with tie strings and are worn suspended from the waist in front, on the buttocks, under either arm, or even on the forehead.

Strings or spans of *tambu* shell were formerly important articles of exchange, brought to Sio by the Siassis and traded inland by the Sios, but today the shell is relatively unimportant except when contained in larger ornaments. Wicker armlets embroidered with *Nassa* are found throughout the

[12] It is evident that dogs' teeth must be exchanged in small quantities at some time in order to permit sufficient accumulation for the manufacture of the ornaments. Of course, old worn-out ornaments are cannibalized to make new ones.

If fake and real dogs' teeth were imported by German traders in quantity as they were in Manus, there was no lasting effect on the value of the ornaments (but cf. Groves, 1934, p. 57). The Manus people rejected the fakes, but accepted the real ones (from Turkey), with the result that the teeth were reduced to one tenth of their original exchange value (Mead, 1956, p. 99).

Vitiaz Strait, and they must have been widely exchanged in the past.

The rectangular embroidered *tambu*-shell ornaments belong to the elite class of wealth-objects, which includes boars' tusks, dogs' teeth, and pigs, and it is unfortunate that so little can be said about the distribution of their manufacture. They are definitely made by the Umboi Islanders, the Sios, Gituans, and Komba and Selepet (I actually saw ornaments being made or repaired at the Komba villages of Sambori and Tipsit; see Map 3). In general, *tambu* shell was carried from the archipelago to the mainland, although supplies are available in New Guinea. The elaborate ornaments exhibit a great variety of embroidered designs, and the Sio strictures on the export of valuables bearing familial designs apply to those of *tambu* shell as well as to those of dogs' teeth.

Additional Ornaments

Turtle-shell bracelets and strings of yellowish disc-shell beads, both women's ornaments, are valued highly and are widely exchanged. The disc beads—known as *namatawuk* in Siassi, *patawuku* in Sio—are reportedly manufactured by the Kombe. The Siassis acquire *patawuku* for export to the mainland from the Kalingi of Cape Gloucester, west of the Kombe. At Sio, for example, spans or necklaces of *patawuku* are given in brideprice, and a single necklace is considered to be equivalent to a small pig.

Turtle-shell bracelets, worn on the upper arm and two to eight inches in width, are widely manufactured and traded. According to Bodrogi (1961, p. 128), the finest specimens come from the Tami Islands. The plates from the sides of the shells of two large turtles, *Chelonia mydas* Lin. and *C. imbricate* Lin., are used for the bracelets (*ibid.*, p. 125). When softened in boiling water, the plates can easily be cut into wide strips and molded into bracelets. Finely incised geometric designs adorn the entire outer surface of the bracelets.

Ring bracelets of turtle shell, of relatively little value, are manufactured in northwestern New Britain and reach the mainland via Siassi. Examples at Sio had been purchased directly from Talasea. From the same area come incised trochus-shell bracelets which, according to Parkinson (1907, p. 222), "are found in great numbers on the opposite coast of New Guinea, where they arrive via the trade route over Rook [Umboi] Island."

White or eggshell cowries are also made into ornaments. Of particular interest is a type of breast pendant that Finsch called "war-ornaments" because they are held by warriors in their teeth. These are used throughout the area of the Vitiaz Strait—"from Huon Gulf to Astrolabe, eastward to Willaumez" (1888b, p. 36). The ornament "consists of a cross-piece or stretcher . . . at both ends of which a large or smaller white shell (Cypraea or Ovula) is fastened, besides this a leaf-shaped finely plaited appendage, which is gayly painted and trimmed with cowry-shells (Nassa) . . ." (*ibid.*) is suspended from the stretcher.

The Sios, who currently use these ornaments in dances, acquired eggshell cowries from Siassi, although the shell can be collected on the Sio reef. Like the clam-shell imitations of boars' tusks, I suspect that white cowrie pendants are also poor men's substitutes for the tusk pendants.

PATTERNS OF EXCHANGE, MONEY, AND CATEGORIES OF GOODS

It is evident that the exchange of vegetable food for products of the sea, the foundation of much of local trading, derives from environmentally determined differences in production. Overseas trading, on the other hand, rests far more on the distribution of technical skills and established exchange patterns than on environmental variation, including the distribution of natural resources. (For example, Sio lacks neither the resources nor skills required to produce mats, ornaments of cowrie shell, and *tambu* shell and sago. Why import these goods from Siassi?)

An interest in importing specific goods guides the overseas trade, but exchange is often much less direct than might be assumed. To anticipate the chapters which follow, the Siassis are narrowly intent upon the accumulation of pigs and vegetable food. Dozens of transactions involving a variety of goods from various parts of the Vitiaz Strait may be required to attain this objective. The Sios, on the other hand, seek a wide variety of goods. Imported from Siassi are canoes, dogs, boars' tusks, disc beads, *tambu* shell, white cowries, wooden bowls, hand drums, red ochre, mats, obsidian, sago, coconuts, *Canarium* almonds, betelnut, and lime. With the exception of canoes and consumables, all of these goods might be re-exported at a later time. Sio acquires the Siassi goods for pigs, clay pots, dogs'-teeth ornaments, black pigment, net bags, bows and arrows, and bark cloth. Now, all of these goods, even pots (Bilibili-made pots which have come along the Rai Coast) might have been initially imported and held for trade. The conversion of one kind of good or whole constellations of goods into other desired goods may thus be quite complex. A particular trading event often represents the culmination of a protracted series of prior exchanges.

It is apparent that the mainland and archipelago form complementary regions with respect to a large number of goods. Thus:

Mainland Exports	Archipelago Exports
Pigs	Boars' tusks
Dogs' teeth	Dogs
Bows and arrows	Mats
Net bags	Disc beads
Pots	Obsidian
Tobacco	Betelnut
Black paint	Red ochre
Taro	Sago

The movement of pigs and dogs' teeth in one direction and the countermovement of pigs' teeth and dogs may seem rather curious. Pigs actually move from both the mainland and archipelago to a central point—the Siassi Group. Some of the incoming pigs are exchanged for vegetable food and other goods on Umboi Island, and, within Siassi, pigs are exchanged for canoes. But unlike pots, dogs' teeth, net bags, and other goods from the mainland, the Siassis do not re-export pigs to distant points within the archipelago. Most pigs that come to Siassi have reached the end of the line.

It is very unlikely that dogs are more numerous on a per-capita or per-village basis in the archipelago than on the mainland. Nevertheless, both the statements of informants regarding the general pattern of exchange and records of transactions show that dogs are first collected within the archipelago by the Siassis and then forwarded to the mainland, not the reverse.

There is no doubt that boars' tusks are produced on the mainland as well as in the outer islands. In the western Strait the Bilibili traders carried on traffic in these valuables, and they may have come into the central Strait from that direction. The Siassis, however, are the main carriers linking the two sides of the Strait, and they carry boars' tusks to New Guinea and dogs' teeth to the archipelago.[13]

Earthenware pots, bows and arrows, and net bags are manufactured only on the mainland, while red ochre and obsidian come from single localities on Umboi Island and in New Britain, respectively.

With regard to tobacco and betelnut, it should not be thought that the voyages of a few hundred traders supply more than a minute fraction of the daily needs of the thousands of villagers on both sides of the Strait. Insofar as the Siassis traffic in these items, betelnut is carried to New Guinea and tobacco is brought back. The Siassis also buy tobacco from Arop Island, Umboi, and New Britain.

[13] In regard to the islands off Möwehafen, Todd writes: "Dogs' teeth come to the natives of these parts from the mainland of New Guinea *via* Siassi and Arawe" (1934, p. 199).

In describing the products of trade, cash equivalents of many items were noted. The traders are thoroughly familiar with the use of Australian currency (a few have bank accounts), and monetary units may be used in the evaluation of transactions. Cash equivalents for most products have become more-or-less well established, and money is commonly used in transactions involving traditional trade goods. Money in the amount of more than one pound, however, tends to be treated like a valuable, as if it were indivisible. Thus, goods may be exchanged for one, two, five pounds and so on, but not for one pound, five shillings, and six pence. Five pounds' worth of shillings, termed *pus* (fuse) in Neo-Melanesian because the roll of coins resembles a stick of dynamite,[14] is an especially common unit. Cash equivalents for the more important goods are listed in Table 1.

These equivalents reflect agreement among the statements of a large number of informants checked against records of transactions. In no case are the figures deduced, for example, from the fact that if A is worth two B's or one pound, then one B must be worth ten shillings. I believe that the traders themselves rarely make this kind of calculation.

Finally, I should explain why I have avoided the often used distinction between utilitarian and nonutilitarian goods in listing the products of trade. In the first place, the distinction is absent among the traders themselves. Nonconsumable manufactured goods constitute wealth, which is differentiated according to comparative worth, but not "utility," that is, the capacity of a good to satisfy material or technical needs. An important distinction, evident in both trade and internal exchange, is made between food and consumables (betel, tobacco, lime) on the one hand, and durable, manufactured goods on the other.

Secondly, goods that would naturally fall into the utility

14 Formerly, unscrupulous European traders sold dynamite to natives for fishing. In spite of the terrible accidents that have occurred—involving Europeans as well as natives—dynamiting fish would be widely practiced today if it were not outlawed.

TABLE 1

RATES OF EXCHANGE

Boars' tusk (pair of average quality)	£1 to £2
Bow and six arrows	2s.
Canoes	
no cash purchases reported, but the usual payment of three to six pigs implies a minimum value of £15 to £20.	
Disc-bead necklace	£1
Dogs	
puppy	£1 to £2
hunting dog	£5 and up
Dogs'-teeth headband	£2
Hand drum	10s. to £2
Net bags	2s. to 6s.
Pandanus mats	4s. to 8s.
Pigs (mainland)	
under one year	£1 to £2
one-year-old	£5
two-year-old	£10
three-year-old	£15
Pots ("Sio" type)	
small	5s.
medium	10s.
large	£1
Tobacco (packets vary greatly in size)	2s.to £5
Wooden bowls (vary greatly in size)	
Tami-Siassi	10s. to £5
Rai Coast	5s. to 10s.

category, particularly wooden bowls and clay pots, are highly valued quite apart from their utilitarian qualities. It can be said of pigs, too, that the least important thing one can do is simply to eat them.

Third, in discussions of primitive trading, the utilitarian-nonutilitarian dichotomy comes close to being the same as the distinction between "economic" and "ceremonial" aspects of exchange, and thus implies a definition of economy in terms of utilities (cf. Tueting, 1935; Uberoi, 1962). Such a dichotomy is consistent with the notion, apparently held implicitly by many anthropologists, that identifies objects or processes as "economic" exclusively by their relevance for human biophysical necessities. However, a broader concept of economy as the provisioning of society (Sahlins, 1965) is more in line with both the views of professional economists and ethnographic fact.[15] Clearly, goods employed in transactions that establish or maintain social status—transactions that will receive special attention in later chapters—are to be rightfully regarded as economic, as are any material processes which sustain a sociocultural order. Accordingly, it is proper to refer to the intercommunity movement of goods strategically important in the above sense as "trade," rather than to limit the term to traffic in "utilities."

Finally, the utilitarian-ceremonial dichotomy is linked with a functional perspective that should be revised or amplified in light of data from the Vitiaz Strait. In discussing the *kula* ring, Fortune distinguished between "utilitarian exchange" or the "trading aspect" on the one hand, and the "[economically] useless exchange" of the *kula* proper on the other; and in commenting on the function of the exchanges of *kula* valuables, he suggested that they were "like an annually repeated peacemaking ceremony" (1932, pp. 200–210). For comparative sociologists, surely, the maintenance of the "peace of the trade" is one of the most interesting facets of regional trading networks linking politically acephalous societies. In the present case, however, it would be a mistake to restrict attention to those transactions in ornaments that most resemble the *kula*. The fact is that transactions involving *any type of good*, depending on the

[15] In a critique of anthropological concepts of economy put forth by Bunzel and Herskovits, the economist Knight wrote: "Of all the fallacious and absurd misconceptions which so largely vitiate economic and social discussion, perhaps the very worst is the notion . . . that an interpretation of utility, or usefulness, in biological or physical survival terms has any considerable significance at the human level. A discussion of human society, even if restricted to 'economic' life in the narrowest meaningful interpretation, must unquestionably relate as much or more to what may be called the 'higher values' as to 'subsistence' in the sense of physical nutrition and protection from the elements. As all anthropological data themselves clearly show, such a conception of 'subsistence' in connection with man is meaningless to the extent that man is human" (1952, pp. 520–21).

manner in which goods change hands and the contexts of exchange, may serve peacemaking (i.e., social) functions. Moreover, adopting Fortune's perspective, one can say that most of the transactions described in this study simultaneously embody economic and peacemaking aspects.

V

The Mainland:
Sio and Its Hinterland

Sio is a large Melanesian speaking community of yam cultivators, fishermen, and traders located on the north coast of
the Huon Peninsula. With an estimated population of eight
hundred people in 1910, the Sio population has steadily
expanded to nearly fifteen hundred in 1964. Prior to World
War II the Sios occupied a small island, less than three acres
in area, situated a few hundred yards off an extensive grassy
and wind-swept cape known as Teliata Point.[1] They now
live in four villages on the opposite mainland. These are,
from east to west: Lambutina, Basakalo, Laelo, and
Balambu.

Within the trade system the main importance of the Sios
is their role as manufacturers and suppliers of earthenware
pots. Sio is centrally located on the southern shore of the

---

[1] Sio was known to early European explorers as the island-village or
Dorf-insel. Its original name, Sigaba (or Sigawa) was changed by the
Administration—the name Sio being suggested by the people themselves—
apparently to reduce the confusion caused by the fact that there are two
other locations in the Morobe District with the same or similar names—
Sigaba, the original name of Kiari village, fifteen miles west of Sio, and
Singaba near Lae. Teliat or Teliata is probably the Bilibili name for Sio,
and appears on one of Maclay's maps made in 1877. See Chapter IX,
note 10.

Strait and is a main port-of-call for the Siassi overseas traders. Inland and to the south and southwest are the Komba, Selepet, and Timbe villages, mountain tribes with a present combined population of twenty-five thousand, which constitute the Sio hinterland. Sio is the most populous community in the trade system and its hinterland is the most densely settled inland region.

This chapter is concerned with Sio and its hinterland regarded as a local trade sphere, one of a number of similar units which make up the larger trade system. After presenting a brief description of trade, and a sketch of Sio society and of some indigenous economic concepts, the discussion turns to local trade viewed against the background of environment and local production.

TRADING

Trade between Sio and its hinterland typically involves the exchange of pots, fish, and coconuts for taro, sweet potatoes, and tobacco. Less frequently other products change hands. Sio sends inland obsidian (formerly), dogs' teeth, boars' tusks, *tambu* shell, red ochre, black paint, Rai Coast and Siassi bowls, and more recently has sent tomahawks, knives, plane irons, *laplaps*, and money. Besides staple foods and tobacco, the inland exports pigs, dogs, dogs' teeth, bows and arrows, net bags, pandanus rain hoods, and betelnut. To these exports, introduced foods have been added: Singapore taro, white potatoes, cabbage, beans, onions, papaya, and pineapple.

Exchange takes place in one of two ways, either between trade-friends—usually bush people visit Sio—or at markets (*naw*). The Sios distinguish further, however, between prearranged and unannounced visits by trade-friends. Meetings of trade-friends or markets can occur at any time of the year, but trade is most frequent between August and December, when supplies of food at Sio are apt to be short. During the rainy months of January to April the Kwama River is at times impassable, so that trading trips to the west are rarely

undertaken during this period. Even after heavy rains, however, the water level of the river often rises and falls within
twenty-four hours, and people who must travel simply wait
by the banks until a crossing can be made.

Exchange at market sites between a group of Sios and
people from an interior village is aimed at securing food.
Fish, coconuts, and pots are given for taro and sweet potatoes. The meetings are generally prearranged by a Sio and
a bushman who are trade-friends and who serve as leaders of
the trading parties and supervisors of the market. Prior to
the meeting, these men traditionally exchanged knotted
cords, each knot standing for a day. When three knots
remained, the bush traders went to their gardens for produce. With the removal of the penultimate knot the trading
party set out for the market.

There are at least seven recognized market sites, most of
them located near streams that seasonally provide drinking
water. Five of them are located on or near the beach, while
two are between the coast and the front range. The farthest
site is about fifteen miles west of Sio, but they are generally
less than six miles away.

According to one aged informant, the Kombas were
greatly feared as sorcerers, and for this reason holding markets with them was considered unsafe. Most trade with the
Komba was conducted between trade-friends (as it is now)
rather than in meetings where one confronted a large number of comparative strangers. The Selepet villagers, on the
other hand, are regarded as "good men" and more markets
were conducted with them. This seems to be borne out by
the distribution of the traditional market sites, five of the
seven being located for trade with the Selepet region.

At the old-time markets the two groups of men and
women, one to three dozen people on each side, sat down in
two rows facing each other. The bush people normally
initiated the transactions by pushing forward a net bag of
food and taking back the goods—fish, coconuts, and pots—
which the Sio had in front of him. The *bilums* of food differ

greatly in weight (ten to thirty-five pounds), and the Sios could adjust the amount of goods they were willing to give for a particular *bilum* beforehand. Thus, a man who was carrying two pots and some coconuts, and who judged that the taro held by the bushman opposite him was worth one pot plus coconuts, would remove the second pot and place it behind him.

The exchanges were conducted largely in silence, without haggling or bargaining. Aboriginally only the most rudimentary kind of communication would have been possible anyway. Following the main exchange, surplus Sio goods were traded for betelnut, tobacco, bows, and net bags.

Two middle-aged men of Basakalo village currently have reputations as arrangers of markets, and some were held in September and December, 1963. Sio women frequently travel to Kiari village (on the coast) or to meeting places between Sio and Kiari to exchange pots for bananas. Under the dry, exposed conditions of cultivation at Sio, bananas do poorly, while the Kiaris regularly produce a surplus—they are known as "banana eaters." Markets today are more informal and sociable gatherings than in the past, and in the opinion of informants they are held less often.

A SKETCH OF SIO SOCIETY

The principal social units of Sio society are moieties, the village, men's houses, patrilineal lineages, personal kindreds, and the household consisting of monogamous conjugal families.

In legend the island community in which the Sios lived, until they were forced to move by the events of World War II, was founded by the leading men of two of the several mainland villages. These villages had been established by seaborne migrants from the west—we may call them the "canoe ancestors"—who were the original Sios. The two men, Pasa and Mburu, divided the island between them, Pasa taking the smaller seaward portion while Mburu established himself on the larger landward section. The descendants of the relatives and associates of the two ancestral cofounders make up the two broadest social divisions of the Sio community, Latoa and Lambutina. The Lambutinans (Pasa's section) now reside in a large compact village to the east of the Sio lagoon; the larger Latoan group (Mburu's section) is divided into three settlements to the west.

The two divisions, Latoa and Lambutina, resemble moieties, though they are not exogamous (a majority of marriages are intramoiety) nor are they descent groups in a strict sense. More than mere residential groupings, however, Latoa and Lambutina are communities within the community, and their semi-independent status within the body politic was recognized by the German Administration, which appointed a set of village officials for each of the two divisions. Latoa is the larger division, and probably for this reason enjoys the status of "number one place." No formalized difference of rank or rules of ceremonial precedence, however, are associated with the dual division. In some contexts, Latoans and Lambutinans assert the superiority of their respective groups, but at other times they emphasize relations of equality and interdependence. Intermoiety rivalry was formerly expressed in ritualized (nonlethal) combat, of short duration, while today it is expressed in informal joking, in brawling among school children, and less frequently in adult softball competition.

Each of the moiety divisions (of the island village) was divided into named residential sections or wards. Most of the male residents of a ward, or in some cases part of a ward, were close agnates. Their houses were grouped around a men's clubhouse (*mbawnza*). The agnatic residents of a ward were organized in two ways: as a patrilineage—a property managing group—and as a men's clubhouse—the principal political and ceremonial unit.

An ideological emphasis on patriliny is expressed in prevailing ideas of land tenure and inheritance, succession to political positions, recruitment to the men's house, patrilocal residence, and the patrilineal bias of personal kindreds, but the Sio patrilineage is not a highly visible action group. The lineage holds collective title to bounded tracts of arable land and formerly to a number of scarce and highly valued house sites (ŋge) on the island. The lineage head, termed "father of the land" (*tono tama*), is the senior male descended in the senior line from the founding ancestor (two to four generations removed). He is supposed to serve as spokesman for his group in the event of disputes over ownership or boundaries, but he does not necessarily direct the gardening activities of junior lineage mates (see below under "Horticulture"). There is no generic term for lineage, but in appropriate contexts it is possible to identify specific patrilineages by combining the word *se*, meaning "blood" or "kin," with the name of an apical ancestor—as in Mburu *se*, "Mburu's lineage." The lineage as such does not arrange marriages, it is not a vengeance unit, nor does it form an exclusive group in gardening. Furthermore, the patrilineages are unsegmented and are not embraced in a sib or totemic organization.

In contrast to the weakly structured lineage, the men's house or *mbawnza* emerges as a sharply defined and highly solidary unit in competitive feasting, blood revenge, and ancestral cult ritual. The men's house took its name from the residential section where its members lived and where their clubhouse was located. There was not, however, a one-to-one correlation between named section and clubhouse group, for some sections contained two, sometimes three clubhouses. The term *mbawnza* refers to both the clubhouse and its membership. Each group owned, in addition to the clubhouse, a raised platform (*korokoro*) for the display of ceremonial presentations and also various ritual paraphernalia, which included, principally, carved wooden masks representing the main *barɔwe* or ancestral ghosts associated with the group. Boys were initiated into their fathers' *mbawnza*. The male initiation ceremonies of the various groups were timed to coincide, and new clubhouses were erected in anticipation of these ceremonies.

The central figure of the men's house was the *koipu,* a term which is best translated as "leader" (the statuses of *koipu* and "father of the land" are combined in the same men). "Big-man" refers to any senior male, but may be added to *koipu* for emphasis: *tamɔta ŋalai koipu,* "big-man leader." He is also referred to as *maro,* "great" or "great one," a term since appropriated by the Lutheran Mission for God. Second in command to the leader was the *dumui,* usually a younger brother, who acted as the leader's administrative assistant and spokesman. The remaining members of the clubhouse are called *skoŋa tamɔta* or supporters (a *skoŋa* is a transverse brace, of the kind used, for example, to support the main posts of a house). The position of leader was acquired through primogenitural succession and rested on the control and use of hoards of teeth and shell valuables, and most important, the provision of large-scale distributions (*weŋa*) of pigs and food on a variety of occasions. Thus, political status and social pre-eminence in Sio society depended chiefly on the superior control and deployment of the most important forms of wealth.

While the lineage persists, the men's house organization was in an advanced state of decay by the 1930's. Traditional leadership, clubhouses, competitive distributions of yams and pigs, and male initiation no longer exist. The Sios were quick to embrace Christianity, and this acceptance impelled the abandonment of initiation ceremonies, the carved masks representing the ancestral ghosts and other ritual equipment, and the ancestral cult itself. The disintegration of the traditional system of politics and ceremonial exchange in which the men's house was the fundamental unit followed in the wake of these changes. Most of the clubhouses had disappeared by the time of Groves's visit in 1933, and men now aged forty-five or under were not initiated in traditional ceremonies. The raised platforms associated with the old men's houses were preserved in the island village, but they were not rebuilt in the mainland villages established after the war. Thus, the last physical symbol of the *mbawnza* disappeared two decades ago.

The demise of the *mbawnza* organization is typically expressed by Sios when they say: "Today we eat in a disorganized fashion." This reflects the role of the men's house in the traditional large-scale competitive distributions of food (described below). Today large-scale distributions are noncompetitive and are associated with housebuilding, the funerals of eminent members of the community, village meetings, marriages, and homecoming parties (for returning or visiting wage workers). In such distributions the men's house group often emerges in vestigial form under the name ŋ*gu*. The word means "group," any collection of persons or things. As a social term and unless otherwise specified, ŋ*gu* equals "congregation," the Sio community as a local Lutheran congregation. In appropriate contexts, however, ŋ*gu* denotes any level of organization above that of the family or household up to and including the community as a whole. The levels are the moiety, village,[2] and the residential section—groups of neighboring agnates and their families together with those of affiliated kin, which coordinate their activities in distributions of food. Eighteen of these small ŋ*gu* are recognized as the descendants of the old men's house groups. These are important groups. Composed of an influential man, his close patrikin as well as affiliated affines and cognatic kin, they form the residential section of the modern village, their members cooperate in gardening, and they emerge as the principal political factions. When specifically mobilized for the collection, preparation, and dis-

[2] The four modern villages—Balambu, Laelo, Basakalo, and Lambutina— are derived from Sigaba or Sio Island. The small Sio speaking community of Nambariwa (population 150) three miles to the east never formed part of the island community, but today it is regarded as part of Sio in a political sense. Sometimes Nambariwa is grouped with Lambutina as a single ŋ*gu*, at other times it is treated as an independent village ŋ*gu*.

There are no other Sio speakers in the Sio Census Division, which stretches along the coast from Gitua to Roinji, and includes a number of speakers of non-Melanesian languages of the interior.

tribution of food on festive occasions, the group is known as ŋ*gu*.

Marriage, mourning rites, housebuilding, and associations for gardening and other productive tasks are largely kindred affairs. In general, a majority of a person's effective kindred are both neighbors, at least village mates, and patrikin.

The kin terminological system is generational in emphasis ("Hawaiian" in Murdock's terms, 1949, p. 223). All consanguineal relatives of one's own generation are siblings, distinguished by age or birth order and optionally by sex. There are separate terms, however, for mother's brother and sister's child, father's sister, and brother's child. The address terminology is incomplete: four of eleven consanguineal terms lack distinctive vocative forms. Neo-Melanesian kin terms, especially *kandiri* (maternal relative), *barata* (sibling of the same sex), and *tambu* (affine), are frequently used in address, but generally, personal names are more often used than kin terms. A complete list of Sio kin terms is given in Appendix I, and additional material on Sio kinship is presented in Chapter VIII.

Independent conjugal families are the rule in Sio. Polygyny, formerly frequent, has not been practiced by the senior generation of men. Widows and widowers, allied with other households in gardening, usually maintain separate dwellings and hearths.

Residence after marriage is patrilocal. Typically, at marriage an eldest son built a new dwelling next to that of his father. If house sites (ŋ*ge*) were not available, younger sons lived with an older brother or with their father, while the youngest son might eventually inherit his father's house site. The extremely crowded conditions on the island, however, forced alternative patterns of residence. A nonrandom sample amounting to about one third of the 172 dwellings composing the island village just prior to its abandonment in 1943, reveals that twenty-seven married sons were living with their fathers, married brothers shared a house in twenty-three instances, while there were nine cases of uxorilocal and three of avunculocal residence.[3] During the island period and in the modern villages there are many dwellings which accommodate two or more conjugal families—a man and a married son, for example. Such a residential unit is not, however, an extended family. Each family is lodged in a separate compartment and has its own hearth and stores of food.

The household is the principal unit in trade. Trade links households of different communities. Production for exchange is performed by the household, although, in satisfying economic obligations at any particular time, people frequently call upon kinsmen for aid. Relations with one's trade-friends tend to be extended to close kin on both sides. The trade-friendship thus allies the restricted personal kindreds, especially coresiding kin, of the two partners. Just as the physical mobility of Sio villagers on the island was restricted by the boundaries of moiety and residential section, so the movements of visiting traders are confined to the main thoroughfares and the residential section of their trade-friends. Male visitors are housed in the men's clubhouse, while women and children are dispersed among the dwellings of the residential section. The visit of a trading party thus involves the meeting of two groups of relatives, defined by two trade-friends who are the principal agents in exchange. The setting for exchange is domestic, the principals stand in the relation of protector-host and privileged guest, some of the goods given and received are in the form of hospitality and gifts acknowledging hospitality. Trade takes place in and through the friendly intercourse of social visiting, and it is often an occasion for minor festivities.

Relations between the sexes are characterized by equality. The Sio system of land tenure recognizes the secondary claims of cognatic kin, with the result that wives often are owners, even if in a remote sense, of their husbands' lineage

[3] Based on census materials gathered with the aid of a village map drawn from a low-level aerial photograph of the island village taken in 1943, just before it was destroyed by Allied aircraft.

land. (For this reason, one man told me, it is impolitic to bring up questions of land in wrangles with one's spouse.) Women have a restricted role in gardening. The heavy tasks—cutting, burning, cultivating, fence building, and the planting of yams—are performed by men. In production for trade, on the other hand, women bear the main burden. They produce the bulk of the goods moving to the interior— fish and pots—and pottery is the main overseas export.

SOME ECONOMIC CONCEPTS: WORK, WEALTH, AND ECONOMIC OBLIGATION

Indigenous economic concepts, such as work, wealth, and debt, help to illuminate the nature of economic activity, trade included. The data are most complete for Sio, but it seems likely that equivalent concepts are present in other societies of the Vitiaz Strait region.

In Sio and the neighboring societies of northeastern New Guinea, the notion of work is broadly conceived. There is no clear-cut distinction between work and leisure-time activities. Physical productive labor is not more highly regarded than tasks involving mainly mental effort, artistic expression, or the performance of social services. Lawrence, with the societies of northeastern New Guinea in mind, offers these perceptive comments on the indigenous concept of work:

. . . as a person's productive role is not relegated to a single field but impinges on nearly every field within the socio-economic system, so work cannot be regarded (and is not regarded by the people themselves) as any narrow specialized activity. It is rather a very large part of everyday living—any general activity which serves to perpetuate the total system. It includes not only major occupations such as agriculture, house-building, making tools and weapons, and so forth, but also accompanying a relative on a journey, helping him retrieve an errant wife, or cooking at a feast. As everyone is likely to engage in these activities at any time, no terminological distinction is made between them, as with us, on the basis of, say, craft proper, social chores and hobbies. This emphasizes the essentially co-operative nature of native society. Work, as it is defined here, is its basic currency for, in the absence of a cash economy which permits a man to buy himself immunity from unpleasant physical labour, it alone enables him to fulfil his social obligations. Co-operation at every level is essential for survival but it can be paid for only in kind—by counter co-operation on a personal basis. Thus work is seen as the physical expression of a man's important inter-personal relationships—his membership in a local community and his association with other such communities to which he is connected by marriage and kinship [1964, pp. 30–31].

Not only social services, but also the public performance of dancing festivals (N-M *singsing*) are conceived as work (*rota*). Sios have two types of *singsings*. *Kiniŋa* are public dances which customarily include mimetic performances involving the impersonation of animals and supernatural beings. The costumed participants act as drummers, dancers, and singers. *Jombe* (magic) are specifically magical in function, are reserved to men, and consist of singing and chants without drums and dancing. The performances of *jombe* and *kiniŋa* associated with initiation and other social rituals constitute work, while some other *singsings* are regarded simply as entertainment. The significance of dancing festivals in overseas trade is discussed later (see "Siassi Dancers" in Chap. VI).

Wealth

The Sio concept of wealth is expressed in the word *mbaliŋa,* which designates durable manufactured goods, valuables, and money. Most of the principal articles of trade as well as some goods not usually exchanged are *mbaliŋa:* canoes, paddles, bailers, stone adzes and hafts, bows and arrows, pots, wood bowls, red ochre, obsidian, lime gourds and spatulas, food pounding mortars, fish nets, drums, bark cloth, shell and teeth ornaments, and most European goods and money.

In the Sio view *mbaliŋa* goods exhibit at least one of three qualities: (1) considerable labor is required to produce them; (2) they are durable; and (3) they are given and received in payments for other like goods or services or to satisfy important social obligations. The ornaments are perhaps to be regarded as wealth par excellence, since they qualify on all three counts of labor, durability, and convertibility. Yet the ideas underlying the concept of wealth are variously expressed, and it is likely that no one criterion is more fundamental than the others. For example, woven net bags do not qualify as *mbaliŋa* because they wear out quickly, though their manufacture involves substantial labor and they are used in payments of various kinds. Red ochre is consumed in use and only a small amount of labor is involved in its initial acquisition. It is "wealth," however, since large payments (e.g., pots) are given for it.

Because of the role of *mbaliŋa* goods in payments and exchange they acquire a commodity-like character. Thus, pigs and dogs, not ordinarily regarded as *mbaliŋa*, are so regarded when they form part of a payment. Since the development of cash economy based on copra, coconuts also have become *mbaliŋa*.

Wealth is broadly differentiated as major wealth (*mbaliŋa ŋalai*) and goods of less value (*kerimɔta* "small"). Earthenware pots, for example, are "small wealth," while the Sios know well that in Siassi and New Britain they are very highly valued.

Opposed to *mbaliŋa* are perishable manufactured goods, things quickly worn out, and slightly modified or unmodified implements, all of which are referred to as *kano*, "nothing." Leaf mats, bamboo forceps, coconut-shell cups and pot covers, drying rings for pots, anvil stones, pot making paddles, shell spoons, and woven net bags—mostly women's goods— are *kano*.

Debt

The obligation to assist others by providing goods and services is strongest among people who count themselves as close kin (*se laiti*, "close kin," or *se tetu*, "one blood"), particularly coresiding agnates and their families. All consanguineal relatives of one's own generation, however, are "brothers" and "sisters" (*tata*, "senior sibling"; *tɛŋgu*, "junior"), and the tendency, especially on the part of men of rank, is to emphasize the close relations which these primary kin terms imply rather than to distinguish degree of obligation on the basis of genealogical distance. Correspondingly, economic obligations between kin, own and classificatory, are phrased as *generalized* ones—i.e., both the interval between gift and countergift, or between help rendered and help repaid, and the equivalence of returns are left indefinite to a marked degree.

In view of the wide extension of primary kinship[4] and the general economic reciprocity associated with kinship, it is not surprising that the Sio concept of debt—the obligation to repay precise equivalents or specified amounts—is limited to a special class of transactions. In fact, these transactions represent the antithesis of the social ethic guiding the main run of economic dealings among kinsmen.

In the Sio view, the root of the notion of debt (*jili*) is anger. A gift presented out of anger creates *jili*, which is canceled only by a countergift of equal or greater worth. If the *jili* is not canceled, the debtor incurs a burden of shame, while the reputation of the giver is enhanced. To illustrate: A fights with B, and B is injured. With the help of his kinsmen, the injured man B acquires an enormous pig which he presents to A. A is shamed, and though he tries, he is unable to raise or otherwise obtain a pig equal in size which will cancel the *jili* resting with him. After the death of the principals, A and B, the debt passes to A's descendants, though their shame (*mai*) as well as the social advantage enjoyed by B's descendants are much dissipated with time.

In the main, debt producing transactions take the form of large-scale competitive distributions of food and pigs among men's house groups. These distributions express status rivalry between opposed *koipus* or big-men and their sup-

---

[4] "Primary" refers here to the conventional rather than the actual or biological gradient of kinship. Relatives outside of the nuclear family, who are assigned the same terms and social qualities of own parents, siblings, and children, are primary kin.

porters. The production and redistribution of food involved in the inter-*mbawnza* distributions are the fundamental activities of the society-wide or political economy.

A typical *weŋa* might be initiated and conducted like this: A has impugned B's abilities as a gardener and has implied that B is a man of no account. B carries the tale of this insult to the *koipu* of his men's house and asks that the *koipu* aid him in gaining redress by sponsoring a *weŋa*. The *koipu* agrees, and a small feast is held in connection with planning the *weŋa*. At this time portions of cooked food are sent to all the other men's houses, which informs them that a big feast and not some mischievous plot is being discussed. The *koipu* later makes a public announcement of the feast. Meanwhile, coconuts are tabued, pigs are earmarked for distribution, and special yam gardens are planted. After many months, when sufficient food has been accumulated, rectangular enclosures (*sopi*) are built atop the raised platform of the sponsoring *mbawnza*. An enclosure is erected for each receiving group, and each is equipped with a central mast from which ripe coconuts are suspended. The *sopi* are filled with taro and yams, the largest prize yams being placed on top. Pigs for each of the *mbawnzas* are tied around the base of the platform. In the presentation the name of each recipient men's house is called and the members of that group carry away their gifts. Careful records of the length and shoulder height of the pigs and the girth of the largest yams presented are kept, for cancellation of the *jili* that each receiving group has incurred depends on returning pigs and yams of equal or greater proportions at a later time. The prestige of the *koipu* of the sponsoring men's house and of the group as a whole is enhanced by a successful presentation. If any of the recipients are unable to reciprocate at a later time, they suffer a permanent loss of prestige. In addition, B's reputation has been publicly vindicated, and he may have the satisfaction of saying to A: "Look at all of these pigs, look at those huge yams, look at all of this food! Where do you think all of this has come from?"

Labor services are always recompensed with cooked food by the household for which the work is being done. There is no other payment for help in housebuilding, gardening, canoe building, pot making, and net making. The provision of food (also tobacco and betel) to workers on the job, and even to onlookers who are said to keep the workers alert with their conversations, is considered natural and inevitable. Never would it be viewed as a *jili* obligation. The same is true of feasts provided for special services: the *jere*, which is given to midwives and grave diggers, and the *mawŋgu* feast, marking the end of a mourner's period of seclusion and given for kinsmen who have fed him during the seclusion.

In its narrowest sense, *jili* is primarily a political notion rather than a concept of everyday economics. It springs from "anger," that is to say, the rivalrous behavior of big-men and their supporters in intergroup distributions. Considerable disagreement—no doubt enhanced by the introduction of the wider and essentially European concept of debt (N-M *dinau*)—arises over the applicability of the concept to other kinds of transactions. Some maintain that *jili* is "group-debt." On the other hand, on the principle that "where there is anger, there is debt," *jili* develops ex post facto out of transactions that were originally and properly of a generalized kind. For example, A, the classificatory brother of B, contributes a pig to the bridewealth payment of B's son. B incurs no debt. Later, however, A becomes angry with B and demands the return of a pig. *Jili* is now said to rest with B, though many would question the propriety of A's demand.

The question of the applicability of *jili* to exchanges between trade-friends exhibits further disagreement. Trading frequently involves delayed reciprocity. The interval between gift and countergift consists of a day or two, a season, a year, or perhaps an even longer period. Informants who maintain or suggest that debt-relations exist between trade-friends refer to this delayed character of the transactions. If exchange is immediate there can be no debt (as in markets). In view, however, of the specific institutional context of *jili* and its ascribed psychological basis or concomitants, it seems quite likely that such evaluations are influenced by the Neo-Melanesian and European-like concept of *dinau*. To anticipate the later discussion of the social basis of trade, the ideology of trade relationships on the one hand, and the descriptions of these relationships in terms of the obligations of creditor and debtor on the other, are contradictory. Exchanges between trade-friends are phrased as general reciprocity, though in fact trade often involves the nearly immediate and balanced exchange of equivalents. To discuss trade in terms of debt relations exposes realities which expressed ideals customarily play down.

The concepts of work and wealth are closely related, though only some kinds of work—craft labor—are productive of wealth. Wealth of this sort is the stuff of local and overseas trade, in which, therefore, labor is necessarily a criterion of value.

Debt, on the other hand, seems only remotely related to work and wealth. Normally, the rendering of productive labor and social services does not create debt. Nor is debt engendered in transactions of wealth goods, but rather in competitive distributions of food. Indebtedness is more a statement of the temporary political condition of individuals and groups rather than a simple economic obligation.

The concept of work as "the physical expression of a man's important interpersonal relationships" is shared by the societies of the trade system (obviously it is not expressed in these terms), if not by primitive societies generally. Notions of wealth similar to the *mbaliŋga* concept of Sio appear to be indicated for Siassi, Gitua, and Umboi Island. Siassi, Gituan, Kovai, and Kaimanga terms are offered as equivalents of the Neo-Melanesian *dinau*, but my information on the meanings of these terms and the social contexts in which they are used is too limited to permit any comment.

PRODUCTION

Habitat

The Sio domain is an extensive grassland, bounded on the east by a low mountain spur jutting out to the sea, and on the west by the swift flowing Kwama River. From the coast, the grassy plain rises gently to a height of several hundred feet, where it meets the slope of the coastal range and where *kunai* grass gives way to rain forest. Within the coastal plain a series of low terraces, apparently old beaches, run from east to west parallel to the present beach, and these are transected by ravines and watercourses. Between the main expanse of grassland and the broad delta of the Kwama River, the country is broken into a series of low bluffs and hills.

Three of the four communities stemming from the prewar island community are located on the Sio cape (Teliata Point on most maps), which forms the forward part of the coastal plain. A fringing reef several hundred yards wide runs around the shores of the cape. There is no barrier reef. At its northern tip, the cape is bisected by a narrow channel which leads into a large lagoon-lake. The shores of the lagoon are fringed with mangrove; the low lying ground south of the lagoon supports stands of sago palm and patches of forest.

Land is abundant: Sio territory encompasses about forty square miles.[5] The crude population density is twenty-five persons per square mile. Less than two hundred acres of land are cultivated annually,[6] and plots are cultivated for only one year with a minimum fallow period of three to five years. Thus, if only a half of the total is considered arable—

[5] A land survey made in connection with the sale of a small plot of Sio land for a government school estimated forty-three square miles (report on file, Kalalo Patrol Post). Although this estimate was based on a more accurate map than the one I used, I believe that the western boundary of the Sio domain was placed too far to the west.

[6] This estimate does not include coconut lands and land planted to other tree crops, such as breadfruit and *Areca* palm, nor does it include old gardens in which bananas continue to grow.

12,800 acres—yearly horticultural needs demand, at the most, one sixty-fourth of the available land.

Rainfall, rather than land and soils, appears to be the most important limiting factor imposed by the environment. There is marked seasonal variation. A long dry season corresponds to the months of the Southeast Trades (*mbuera*) from May to November. The season of the Northwest Monsoon (*wora*), from November to March-April, is the rainy period. There are no rainfall figures available for Sio itself, but Wasu Anchorage, twelve miles to the west, received close to ninety-four inches in 1958, 78 per cent of the rainfall coming during the four months of January to April (see Fig. 2, Chap. IV).

Horticulture

The production of food in Sio means primarily yam growing. Horticulture demands more time than any other productive activity, but it would be incorrect to characterize the Sio gardener as wholly committed, in a moral sense, to his necessary calling. Though industrious gardeners are admired as "strong men," a deeply felt reverence for the land is lacking. Rather than extolling the virtues of life on the land, people are more apt to express a sense of captivity to the toilsomeness of farming. They seem to take more pleasure in fishing, crafts, pig hunting, and trading.

In part, these attitudes may represent the loss of old values through acculturation. Expecially the loss of gardening magic seems to have evoked or added to a sense of futility in the face of the uncertain conditions of food production. In any case, while the Sios may be known to others as "*kunai* men"—grassland farmers—they conceive of themselves as "men of the sea" who have been rather cruelly fated to toil and sweat in the sun-baked savanna.

A type of small yam known as *goka* (*mami* in Neo-Melanesian) is the preferred staple, sometimes amounting to 80 per cent or more of the plantings of individual households. Both *goka* and large yams (*dewa*) are planted in hills, which are arranged in neat rows. The *goka* hills produce seven tubers on the average, while the *dewa* produces two or three. Planted among the yam hills are sugar cane (*ŋgosa*), bananas (*mbole*), sweet potato (*yabi*), winged beans (*mbute*), edible *pitpit* (*taumbwa*), and a green termed *wesi lau*. Maize (*sæŋgo*), pumpkins (*waru*), manioc, and green beans have been added to these indigenous crops. Separate gardens are devoted to taro (*dɛŋa*).

Gardening activities begin in late March or April when the rains of the Northwest Monsoon diminish. Burning of the *kunai* grass advances over larger areas as gardening proceeds. Localized burning is sufficient for the first yam gardens, the *tono gale*, which are made close to the village, generally less than an hour's walk away. The second garden, the *tono luwatu*, and the final gardens, *tono ŋalai* (big garden), which are planted between June and August, are farther out in the *kunai*. Yam planting extends over about five months, from April to August. Taro gardens are made last, after the yams are in, on the slope of the coastal range or in the forested tract west of the Kwama River delta. Planting thus extends from late March until early October, about seven months.

The first step in gardening is to remove the *kunai* grass by burning, or, if this is impractical, the grass is cut and allowed to dry before burning. This is men's work, while women sweep up and remove debris of ash and incompletely burned material (little ash is allowed to remain). After the burning is completed comes the most difficult task for these grassland farmers, breaking up the earth, which remains interlaced with the tough *kunai* roots. The aboriginal Sio method is quite remarkable for its effectiveness and the dexterity with which it is performed. It appears that the same procedures were followed at other localities of the Kwama-Masaweng littoral, for Stolz's description (1911, p. 252) of Sialum tillage is identical to the methods described and demonstrated by the Sios. Four to six men stand or sit in a row, each of them equipped with a pair of heavy mangrove digging sticks five to six feet long. The men jab their sticks into the sod by working them up and down in quick succession, one after the other. Holding the left-hand sticks in place, they jab the right-hand sticks into the earth across and in front of the left-hand ones. Then, using the right-hand sticks as levers, they disengage large pieces of sod and quickly flip them over. All of these operations are performed in unison and with great speed.

The next operation is performed by women. They break up the large clods of earth with small digging sticks and remove grass stubble and roots by hand. Later the men work up the earth more finely when they scoop out and then pile up the soil forming the yam hills.

The Sio gardeners stress the efficiency of their method of tillage, emphasizing particularly the incentive to work provided by the team of men working in unison. The initial and most heavy task of breaking up the ground for one man's garden or plot was accomplished in one, at the most two days, while the gardens of the team were prepared within two weeks (i.e., the first set of gardens). With the introduction of hoes, spades, and crowbars, the teams have disappeared—as the Sios say, these are one-man tools. Still, men seldom work alone in preparing the ground for planting. Other workers are called in and are fed by the owner of the garden on the days during which they work. Other phases of gardening—planting, fence building, the erection of yam poles, and weeding—are not considered to require labor beyond the household.

As the gardening cycle proceeds, gardens are located farther from the village, and the population is progressively dispersed over a wider area. Corresponding to this dispersion is a progressive increase in the size of the gardening groups, which is predicated in part on the requirements of the old digging stick technology.

The first yam gardens are sometimes made by single households. Frequently, however, two households combine to plant a joint garden. A large rectangular plot is prepared and divided initially by stakes, later by planted rows of maize, sugar cane, bananas, and shrubs. The activities of the two gardeners and their families are carried on quite independently, though they are coordinated in time. Newly planted yams must be protected from marauding pigs, so that each gardener is compelled to complete his portion of the fence once a number of yams are in. Joint gardens represent a saving in fencing labor, but this is not the main reason for joining with others. An industrious gardener or a man known to be a skilled garden magician is apt to attract gardening associates, but on the whole social rather than technical considerations determine these partnerships.

The *tono luwatu* are generally joint gardens involving at least several households. When digging sticks were still in use, the teams of tillers prepared each member's plot in turn. It was therefore convenient to have these plots adjoining one another, rather than scattered over a wide area. It makes less difference with regard to the *tono gale,* since these gardens are closer both to the village and to each other.

A larger group, a half-dozen to a dozen or more households, join in making the final *tono ŋalai.* These gardens are larger because of the increased number of individual or household plots, not because the plots themselves are larger. As in the case of the second gardens, the size of the cooperating group is partly dictated by the requirement of teamwork in tillage combined with the distance between garden and village. In that the number of cooperating households often exceeds the labor requirements of a team, however, it is probable that considerations of defense have been added to those of technology.

Aboriginally, Sio had little fear of direct attack on their island stronghold (*sio* is the third person plural form of the verb *-o,* "to put," "place," "take up position," "wait in ambush"). They were most vulnerable when dispersed in small gardening groups over the *kunai* plain, and recent accounts of warfare recount the ambush of gardeners by mountain raiders. An outer territorial limit was thus imposed on

Babwa, a prominent Sio trader, and his granddaughter, Muri

Ornaments of dogs' teeth, boars' tusks, and *tambu* shell (Sio)

A Siassi trading canoe

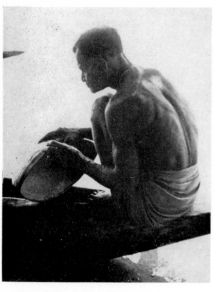

A Mandok carver working on a bowl

Nimbako man carving a palm-wood bo

Washing red ochre, Tarawe village, Umboi Island

gardening by considerations of defense; to venture beyond those limits was to invite attack by the mountain people. There was an increasing gradient of danger as one proceeded outward from Sio. Correspondingly, as the Sios move from the nearer *tono gale* to the distant *tono ŋalai,* the size of the gardening group increases.

There is a tendency for people to associate with close patrilineal kin in gardening, and to work with the same people year after year. On the other hand, a man annually engages in planting several gardens, and he is likely to work with affines and matrikin in some of those gardens.

The latitude of choice apparent in forming gardening partnerships corresponds to a considerable flexibility in the system of land tenure. There are two main types of land (*tono*). An irregular strip of land, several hundred yards deep and running along the beach, is divided into named, rectilinear blocs. These blocs are bounded by low mounds of stone and rubble (*dɔŋgu*), the debris swept up by many generations of gardeners. This land is known as *tono dɔŋgu,* and sometimes the blocs themselves are loosely referred to as *dɔŋgu.* The blocs are associated with particular ancestors and patrilines, and primary rights of ownership and cultivation are limited to a relatively narrow patrilineal group—the lineage making up a residential section of the village. These rights are concentrated in the senior male descendant of the ancestor who reputedly established the original claim. With reference to particular blocs of land, this man is variously known as *tono tama,* "father of the land"; *katonɔŋa,* "trustee" (from *-katona,* "guard," "care for"); and *koipu,* "leader" or *tamɔta ŋalai,* "big-man," over the land. Accepted Neo-Melanesian equivalents help to clarify the nature of this status. The *tono tama* is the "face" (*pes*) or he is "first" (*nambawan long graun*), but it is not appropriate to speak of him as the "boss" (*bos bilong graun*). In a purely titular sense, the *tono tama* is first among a large number of claimants. He does not, for example, assign gardening plots within the bloc, and though people intending to make gardens on the land should ask his permission beforehand, they frequently do not do so.

Traditionally, the *tono tama* was the rallying point for a group of land owners who sought to defend their rights in the event of infringement. The "father of the land" would thus figure prominently in land disputes as the chief representative and spokesman of a group. In fact, land disputes are rare, and informants could provide no cases involving gardening land in recent times (disputes have to do with coconut lands).

The patrilineal emphasis of Sio society is expressed in the prevailing ideas of land tenure. The titular owners or supervisors of the land are the direct patrilineal descendants (in the senior line) of the original ancestral owners. Still, both in theory and practice, cognatic descendants have legitimate, though secondary, claims. Informants sometimes illustrated these rights by suggesting a hypothetical debate between a group of lineage owners and their fathers' sisters' sons. The latter emphasize their claim to the land by saying: "We issued from the testicles of your fathers, our mothers' brothers. Therefore, we are the real owners of this land." In fact, the cultivation rights of sisters and sisters' sons are both undisputed and frequently exercised.

The *tono dɔŋgu*, land divided into small named blocs, makes up no more than about one tenth of the Sio domain. A large part of this land is now taken up with coconuts. Remaining land is partitioned into much larger named blocs that are also associated with particular ancestors and patrilines. Their boundaries are defined by watercourses, outcrops of rock, trees, and the like. Group ownership of this land, however, is more diffuse than in the case of the *tono dɔŋgu*. Individual ownership is said to be established by cultivation, and land so claimed is known as *tono pweoŋa* (from *-pwea*, "innovate," "combine old and new," in this case to combine labor with the land in cultivation). Henceforth the primary rights to such land are in the hands of the cultivator's patrilineal descendants. Trees growing on the land belong to them also, and others wishing to cultivate or merely cut timber must get their permission.

Currently a man plants an average of five gardens annually. The first is a sweet potato plot in a large communal or village garden in which traditional boundaries are ignored. The remaining plots, three of yams and one of taro, will be found on both *tono dɔŋgu* and *tono pweoŋa*, land which is likely to be owned by matrikin or affines as well as patrilineal relatives.

People often cultivate the land of affinal and cognatic kin, but this does not mean that the land of their own agnates is in short supply. Land, in general, is abundant, and it can be suggested that the flexibility of the system of land tenure owes in part to this abundance. The changing constitutions of particular groups of gardening associates may reflect the current alignments and cleavages within the kindred organization, but these are conditioned to a minor extent, if at all, by the availability of land.

Pig Hunting

Large-scale pig hunts are associated with the burning of the *kunai* grass in preparation for gardening. During April, however, it is normally too wet for the grass to burn well, so that in making the first gardens small areas are cut and allowed to dry before burning. During this time men take their weapons and dogs to the fields, as pigs are frequently encountered in the gardening areas. The cries of the dogs when they flush a pig sound the call to action. Gardeners hastily grab whatever weapon is handiest and rush toward the scene, meanwhile calling out to one another in an effort to surround the pig or cut off its retreat. Unaided, the dogs frequently kill or bring down small and medium-sized pigs. On the other hand, if the animal is a large boar, the hunters are apt to be more concerned for their own safety and that of their dogs than killing the pig. Pigs killed are butchered and shared out to all of the gardeners in the immediate vicinity.

Large hunts, in which men of all the villages participate,

take place in May. Traditionally, the hunters painted themselves with black war paint and performed a rite of augury in which coconuts were smashed on a rock. If the nuts broke into many pieces a bountiful hunt was predicted. Nowadays a brief ceremony involving a Christian prayer and the sharing of coconuts, betel, and tobacco among the assembled hunters precedes the hunt.

Fanned by the brisk winds out of the east that are characteristic of this season, the *kunai* grass burns fiercely. Restricted areas of the grassland are burned on different days, the fires being confined by ravines, watercourses, and the setting of back fires. (A substantial amount of preliminary work is necessary: fire brakes are cut around garden fences, yam vines are removed from poles and laid on the ground to prevent their being seared by the heat.) Hunters encircle the fire and move in behind its path, while others station themselves on pig trails along which animals are likely to attempt escape. Sometimes pigs are caught by the flames, younger animals may be downed by the dogs, and invariably many slip through the cordon of hunters. If the dogs can bring a pig to bay or at least slow it down, the hunter is afforded the surest shot for his arrow. Following the main hunt, tracking parties search for wounded animals that, temporarily at least, have succeeded in escaping. Piglets, if they are not dispatched by dogs, are taken alive and raised as domestic pigs. Bound and tied, fed and handled, their "redomestication" takes only two weeks.

For a period of about six years during the 1950's, the Administration imposed a ban on extensive burning of the *kunai* grass at Sio. Burning was to be restricted to the areas needed for planting. The Administration apparently assumed that the grasslands are anthropogenic, but whether the ban was intended merely to limit further destruction of timber or to foster reforestation on a large scale, as the Sios were led to believe, is not clear. After incessant petitions, and after three men had been jailed for infractions, the ban was eventually lifted.

The Sios objected to the prohibition on a number of grounds. The annual firing of the *kunai* is an ancient privilege with which the government had no right to interfere. Communal pig-hunting associated with burning was highly productive as compared with hunting at other times of the year. Most important, extensive burning has an important relationship to cultivation. Through firing the grassland over its entire extent and the associated hunting, wild pigs are either killed or driven far away from the gardening areas. Planting and fence building can then proceed apace with less risk of depredations by pigs. Normally, a great deal of planting is done before fencing is completed, since gardeners are anxious to have part of the yams in as early as possible. With burning restricted to the gardening plots alone, the pigs remained in the area and foraging raids on newly planted crops became frequent.

Fishing

The fishermen employ a variety of techniques, depending on whether they fish on the fringing reef, beyond the reef, or in the lagoon. Spears, bow and arrow, hook and line, large nets, small handnets, and poison are used.

The usual method of men's fishing is carried on at night by means of spears and torches. One man paddles the canoe while the spearman, who stands in the bow, holds the torch of coconut fronds (sometimes a pressure lamp) as well as his spear. The spear consists of several lengths of heavy steel wire fixed to the end of a long bamboo pole.

More productive than spear fishing from canoes, but seldom practiced today, is the use of large nets (sixty to one hundred feet in length). Net fishing is carried on in the same way as currently practiced in the Siassi Islands. The net is dropped from a canoe and is laid out in a semicircle in the shallow waters of the fringing reef. Fishermen, in other canoes or wading, drive the fish toward the open mouth of the net. The net is then closed in a circle. The surrounded fish are speared, while those entrapped in the mesh of the

net are caught by hand. About a half-dozen men are required for this type of fishing.

Men also fish individually with bow and arrow (smaller
versions of the spears) on the reef or throw lines off the
outer edge of the reef into deep water. The poisoning or
stunning of fish with *Derris* root in tidal shallows is also
men's work, but women and children eagerly help in gathering the stunned fish. Seasonally (toward the end of the
Northwest Monsoon) some men take their canoes into deep
water to troll for tuna and mackerel.

Women fish by means of a pair of triangular, framed
handnets, hook and line, and by hand, and they collect
shellfish on the reef at low tide and in the mangrove fringe
of the lagoon. The handnets are used individually, and
sometimes two to three dozen women combine to form
surrounds.

It is probable that the daily fishing and collecting activities of women contribute more to the diet than the poten-
tially high-yield but discontinuous and more uncertain male
fishing. The largest catch of fish recorded during my stay
was that of two men who worked from about 10:00 P.M.
until dawn. It consisted of sixty fish, about twenty to twenty-
five pounds. This was considered a successful but not an
unusually large catch.

Turtles are not hunted, though they are sometimes
caught. The Sios occasionally gather turtle eggs at nesting
sites along the stretch of beach near the mouth of the
Kwama River. Crocodiles are neither hunted nor eaten. The
Sios are familiar with the palolo worm and the fact that the
worm is eaten by neighboring peoples such as the Gituans.
They do not gather palolo, however, and explain that they
consider their odor to be offensive.

The impending or actual arrival of trade-friends prompts
fishing activities, though in general older men do little
fishing if any. Supposedly, one of the main reasons bush
people come to the beach is to eat fish, and it is therefore
incumbent on Sio hosts to provide some. Bush trade-friends

could possibly receive more fish as a part of hospitality than through exchange. In this way "trade" frequently takes the form of the pooling of inland vegetable food and fish, which is consumed jointly by hosts and guests during the course of one- to two-day visits.

Pottery

All phases of manufacture of pottery—digging and transporting the clay, cleaning and kneading, shaping and firing —are female tasks. Finished pots (*kulo*) are roughly spheroid in form, with narrow mouths and flaring lips. They range in capacity from a quart to about three gallons.

The pots are made by the paddle-and-anvil technique, which is widely distributed in Oceania. After kneading, the clay is aged for ten days to two weeks. Then it is formed into discs seven to eight inches in diameter and an inch or more thick. Holding this disc in the left hand, the potter begins by driving the anvil stone (a smooth beach pebble) into the center of the disc. With the clay folded about the stone she then begins beating out the walls of the pot with a wood paddle. The vessel is smoothed with the hands and paddle and decorated with a small stick. Simple designs consisting of zigzag parallel lines, rows of indentations, and hatching are applied to the interior of the lip, the neck, and upper two fifths of the body. With decoration complete, the pot is placed on a pandanus-leaf drying ring for two weeks or longer, after which it is fired on its side in an open fire. Firing takes twenty to thirty minutes, during which the original gray color turns to a brick red. Since new pots are immediately tested, however, they quickly acquire their characteristic covering of black soot. A woman typically makes three to six pots on a pottery making day, but she often fires only one or two at a time, combining firing and testing with the normal preparation of an evening meal. On completion of firing, the fire is built up and the pot is returned to the heat. A small amount of vegetables or some shellfish is then placed dry in the pot and water is slowly added, small quantities at a time. If no leaks or cracks develop the full amount of water is added. Pots are always tested in this way before they are traded.

Pots are most often transported in the large women's *bilum* or net bag. For long-distance transport by ship or sailing canoe, four to six pots are packed with banana leaves in long coconut-leaf baskets.

Pottery making involves no organization beyond the household—frequently a mother and daughter cooperate. Often, however, a larger group of neighbors or perhaps all of the women of a village coordinate their activities through such phases as digging the clay, shaping, and sometimes firing.

Many but not all Sio women make pots. Of the twenty-eight adult women in Basakalo village (population 125), thirteen are potters (but six of the nonpotters are non-Sio). Women who do not know the craft have pots made for them by kinswomen. The nonpotter digs and prepares the clay and on the day her pots are made she provides the potter's household with cooked food. No other payment is required for this service.

Men whose wives do not make pots appear to be in no difficulty when it comes to satisfying obligations to trade-friends, for they can call upon a wide range of female kin. For example, one man, who is active in trade and whose wife does not make pots, had at the time of a household census nineteen pots, thirteen of which were being held in reserve for trading. In a society in which pots are so important as objects of external exchange, one might expect some special rules limiting internal circulation in order to allow households to accumulate sufficient reserves. Pots circulate freely, however, in generalized reciprocity—as part of the general assistance given by women to their male kin—and except for explicit short-term borrowing that sometimes occurs, a man who calls upon his kinswomen for pots incurs no specific obligation to repay.

Large numbers of pots are often, but not necessarily,

produced in anticipation of visits by trade-friends. Production is a household matter. People generally know when to expect the arrival of inland trade-friends, and they prepare accordingly. The unannounced visit of more than one bush friend at a time would be rare, and normal household supplies suffice. The arrival of several Siassi canoes places a sudden and heavy demand, but there is the expectation that the normal stocks of Sio's two hundred households are sufficient to meet the demand. (The Sios cannot know in advance the precise time of arrival of the Siassi canoes, or how many there will be, or whose friends will be on them.) Even when large-scale transactions are planned well ahead of time by the Sios themselves, there is apt to be reliance on other households. Thus, in 1964, a man who intended to buy pigs at Barim collected twenty-seven pots, only one of which was made by his wife.

THE FOOD SUPPLY

In the Sio view, inland trade is linked to yearly variations in the supply of food. Trade increases as available food decreases. Food is moderately plentiful during the rainy months of December, January, and February when the yams of the first gardens become available. Yams mature in eight to ten months so that plantings made in early April produce some edible tubers by late November. Food is abundant from April through July. Then for a period of about two months from late August to November there is a "hungry time." The food shortages of the hungry time are said to occur every year, though it is likely that they vary in duration and intensity. During a "normal" hungry time, people rely on sago, coconuts, fish, and collection of wild yams, as well as imported foodstuffs from the interior (taro and sweet potato).

Older informants say that when seasonal hunger was at its worst, and fish and game were unobtainable, people were forced to cut into the stocks of seed yams, and sometimes children were killed and eaten (they hasten to add that

Figure 3. Seasonal Variation in Food Supply, Production, and Trade

Northwest Monsoon (Wet)			Southeast Trades (Dry)						Northwest Monsoon (Wet)			
Houses and Canoes built			Yam Planting									
	Harvesting					Taro Planting						
			Food Abundant					Food Shortage				
Little Trade		Occasional Trade					Active Inland Trade					
Jan	Feb	Mar	Apr	May	June	July	Aug	Sept	Oct	Nov	Dec	

hunger cannibalism is probably "only a story"). During a particularly severe famine which is supposed to have occurred late in the last century, a number of people were forced to migrate to the Rai Coast and to Siassi. In modern times, increased production of root crops and the purchase of rice and other foods with cash earned from the sale of copra have done much to alleviate seasonal shortages (see "Changes in Production and Local Trade," Chap. IX).

The yearly variations in food supply, productive activities, and trade are shown in Figure 3. It may be noted that in one respect, at least, Sio is better off than some other societies that experience seasonal hunger. The period of abundance and the expenditure of the greatest physical energy in gardening coincide at Sio, whereas in many African societies the shortages occur at a time when extra effort is required in constructing new gardens (Miracle, 1961, p. 278; Johnston, 1958, p. 207).

As the title of a recent essay suggests, seasonal hunger is "a vague concept and an unexplored problem" (Miracle, 1961), and caution is necessary in evaluating informants' statements in the absence of long-term measurements of yearly food supplies and household consumption patterns. In a critique of African data, Miracle observes that "The degree of hunger is questionable. . . . It is entirely possible that people often say they are hungry when they are not short of calories so much as calories from a preferred staple." Furthermore, "It remains to be established that people actually suffer a regular seasonal shortage of calories" (*ibid.,* p. 279).

There is also something to be said for the view that people may become adapted to a feast-and-famine regime without suffering adverse effects from periods of low food intake.[7] It has been argued, for example, that if seasonal hunger "is regular and not sporadic, and is characterized by no decline in body weight from one year to the next, it may be mode of life, 'a peculiar way of ingesting calories' " (Miracle quoting M. K. Bennet, *ibid.;* cf. Johnston, 1958, pp. 206–7).

It may be noted in this connection that if the Sios are underproducers they are also light eaters, at least compared with the prodigous appetites evidenced by some other Oceanic peoples.[8] Mealtimes are rather haphazard affairs.[9] Families often do not sit down together to eat, and there is no special etiquette associated with the serving of food. After preparing the food, the wife sets aside portions for

[7] In evaluating a statement of this kind, it is important to realize that differences in patterns of consumption during periods of food shortage as opposed to times of plenty may have markedly diverse effects on various segments of the population. Children, for example, the most expendable members of the community, may suffer the most during shortages (Stanley Garn, personal communication, 1964).

[8] This judgment is impressionistic, since I did not determine the Sio daily food intake by weight. Sio daily consumption may equal, but certainly does not exceed, the average intakes of New Guinea peoples for whom figures are available. Hogbin estimates four pounds, eight ounces of taro and twelve ounces of bananas per person per day for Wogeo (1938–39, p. 290), while adult and adolescent Kapauku males consume 2.89 kilograms (over six pounds) of root crops daily (Pospisil, 1963, p. 376). Sahlins, who was able to compare Sio eating habits with those of Moalans (Fiji), points out that Moalans regularly eat two or three times more yams at single sittings than the Sios (personal communication, 1964).

[9] "Nowadays we eat in disorganized fashion" (see "A Sketch of Sio Society," above). The disorganized mealtimes may be the result of the loss of etiquette and ceremony formerly associated with male dining in the clubhouse. In everyday dining, as in other things, however, there is no male-female segregation as found in other New Guinea cultures. Sio life is strikingly family-centered.

each adult and older child, and they eat when they arrive and where they please—in the house, on the veranda, or outdoors. The use of betelnut and tobacco to stave off hunger when it is inconvenient to eat or when supplies are short should also be noted.

The actual extent of seasonal hunger at Sio in aboriginal times cannot be established at this late date. Nevertheless, it was and is considered a real enough problem to motivate trading in foodstuffs. Informants' descriptions of seasonal shortage will be accepted in this light with the proviso that the shortages were probably not so regular in occurrence or so uniform in degree as direct testimony often suggests. That is to say, there were probably substantial year-to-year variations in the duration and severity of the hungry times.

Current patterns of consumption are at least indicative of aboriginal ones as well as of the contribution of local trade to the food supply. Detailed records were kept of the foods consumed by a Sio household at two different times of the year, the first during the traditional period of shortage, the second in the time of abundance. The results are presented in Table 2.

TABLE 2

FOOD CONSUMED BY A SIO HOUSEHOLD*
DURING TWO FIFTEEN-DAY PERIODS

Type of Food	Period I November 19– December 3, 1963		Period II May 5–May 19, 1964	
	Number	No. of times	Number	No. of times
Yam	13	5	50	23
Sweet potato†	92	10	19	4
Taro	3	1	13	5
Singapore taro‡	21	6	2	1
Coconuts	17	6	9	9
Bananas	87	7	79	14
Fish	23	5	20	7
Rice	?	10	?	7

    * Two adults and three young children.
     † Some sweet potato in Period II imported from the inland.
     ‡ All Singapore taro via trade.

In Period I, small quantities of pumpkin, beans, greens, melon, onions, manioc, cabbage, eggs, mangoes, pineapple, bully beef, tinned fish, tea, sugar, and hard biscuits were eaten. In Period II pumpkin, beans, greens, *pitpit*, onions, eggs, tinned fish, tea, sugar, biscuits, wheat flour, chicken (one), shellfish (seventy-two), and pork (eaten six times) supplemented the staple foods.

The amounts of food consumed in both November-December and in May appear to be roughly equal. During Period I sweet potato and Singapore taro were the staple tubers while, as expected, there was a shift to yams in the second period. About the same amount of bananas and fish were eaten in both periods. Rice meals were eaten slightly more often in the first period. There was no difference in the number or the frequency (two, often three, per day) of meals between Periods I and II.

There was, however, a widespread feeling of shortage in Period I (especially earlier, in September)—many people said that their supplies of yams were very small or had been exhausted—and this may be reflected in the changing frequency of food sharing. For the same household, the rate of extra-household sharing more than doubled in Period II. Most of the presentations given and received (68 per cent) consisted of cooked food (see Table 3).

TABLE 3
EXTRA-HOUSEHOLD SHARING

	Given	Rec'd	Total
Period I	9	11	20
Period II	34	18	52

There is a theoretical expectation that, in general, a sharp increase in the rate of interhousehold sharing will coincide with the maxima and minima of the food supply (Sahlins, 1965). Increased sharing in times of shortage is a Sio ideal. Failure to share food in lean times is regarded as evidence of bad character. (It is said, furthermore, that there are always some people who exhibit this character, people who are generous enough when food is abundant, but who "throw you away" when it is scarce.) If other households had as much food as the one surveyed, there was only a felt shortage in Period I, and the data suggest that given an adequate amount of food, sharing will increase as food becomes more abundant.

Today Sios produce more yams, taro, and particularly sweet potatoes than in aboriginal times. Yam gardens are larger, and new lands suitable for taro cultivation—e.g., the slope of the coastal range—have been brought under cultivation. Sweet potatoes, especially, have helped to eliminate former seasonal hunger. Large communal sweet potato gardens—totaling twenty to thirty acres—are planted at the beginning of the gardening cycle, whereas in the past only small amounts were interplanted with yams. At neighboring Sialum, at a time when steel tools had not yet had a great impact on gardening, Stolz observed that there was almost no taro, bananas were not plentiful, coconuts did not produce good yields, and sweet potatoes did not last through the year. He adds: "Therefore, more months of the year would be hungry months if it were not mitigated by trade with the inland" (1911, p. 254). This corresponds to the picture given by Sio informants.

With this in mind, it becomes relatively easy to correct Table 2 for aboriginal conditions. All of the Singapore taro (an introduced crop) listed for Periods I and II, and some of the sweet potatoes in the second period, were supplied by inland trade-friends directly to the household head or indirectly via other Sios. Since Singapore taro is nonindigenous, it and the purchased rice would be eliminated. Assuming trade, the high figure for sweet potato, the staple during Period I, could be retained. Thus, either the amount of food consumed in both periods would again be about the same, or lacking trade, there would be a pronounced shortage in Period I.

The causes of yam shortage were in the past as they are today: underproduction combined with unfavorable variations in rainfall. The productivity per se of the staple *goka* yam compares favorably with other yam growing areas. In Melanesia as a whole the average yield for yams ranges from three to eight tons an acre (Barrau, 1958, p. 45). In West Africa the gross yield is about 3.2 tons per acre (eight tons per hectare), while under favorable conditions five to eight tons can be expected (Johnston, 1958, pp. 115–16). At Sio an acre of yams contains fifteen hundred hills, each producing an average of seven tubers weighing ten pounds. The gross yield per acre is thus about seven and one-half tons.

The problem is not the productivity of the crops themselves, but the fact that too few yams are planted. The Sio household (5.2 members) plants about six hundred yam hills on four tenths of an acre of land annually, giving a gross yield of three tons. About a third of the yams are withheld for planting (two to three of the average of seven per hill), so that the net yield is only two tons, or about eight hundred pounds per capita per year.

Barrau (1958, p. 24) estimates that the average area of garden land per person in savanna localities in Melanesia is about 0.15 to 0.2 acres, or 0.75 to 1.0 acre per household. Sio acreages of 0.4 (taro plots must be added to this) may also be compared to those of the Yäko of Nigeria, who farm under broadly similar conditions. According to Forde, the average Yäko household (polygynous, 7.5 members) annually plants nearly 2,500 yam hills on 1.4 acres. Though 40 per cent of the households plant only 0.5 to 1.0 acre, much less than the average, seasonal shortage is not a problem (1937, pp. 32–33).

Sio production would appear to be aimed at minimum or slightly below minimum requirements. This, combined with irregularity in the amount and timing of rainfall, produces shortages. Planting begins after the rainy period, and a protracted dry spell during the ensuing Southeast season can result in low yields. The *tono ŋalai* planted far out in the *kunai* are most vulnerable, since soils there seem less capable of retaining moisture than soils nearer the coast.

Factors other than rainfall would appear to have only

sporadic significance. No extensive crop damage due to insects or disease is indicated by informants. Storage losses, too, are negligible. Because of the dry conditions at Sio, yams store well in the ground. The planting of the three gardens is usually staggered as well, so that portions of the crop mature at different times. This permits harvesting in small amounts as daily or weekly needs require. Harvesting must be completed, however, before the onset of the rains in November or December.

The food problems and the seasonal patterns of consumption and trade characteristic of Sio are probably substantially the same along the entire *kunai* coast of the Huon Peninsula. To the west, along the Rai Coast with its more extensive bush lands, taro cultivation, and reserves of sago, seasonal hunger and trading in foodstuffs do not occur, or occur only sporadically. To the Sios the Rai Coast is food-rich, and during previous hungry times, voyages were made to nearer villages such as Malasanga and Singorokai to trade pots for food.

It seems reasonable to suggest that the pattern of production of the Kwama-Masaweng littoral is geared to coast-inland trade, even as it also represents a response to physical conditions.

THE HINTERLAND

Sio's hinterland, consisting of the interior drainage of the Kwama River, is inhabited by the Komba and Selepet peoples, mountain agriculturalists who live in large communities located at altitudes of 4,000 feet and above. The Selepet number 7,450 (1963), and the average size of their communities is 392. The Komba population is 7,700, with a village size averaging 265. The Komba and Selepet consider themselves to be one people in culture and origin. The distinction between them is based on geography (the Kwama Gorge is the main boundary), language (the languages are related but not mutually intelligible), and predominant ties of kinship and marriage.

The Kwama River and its two main tributaries, the Puleng and Pumene, have cut deep gorges along their northerly courses to the sea. The valleys are narrow and steep-sided. Typically, the valley side descends sharply from the bounding ridges, levels off over a broad terrace, and then drops almost vertically to the valley floor. Human population is located mainly on the terraces or shelves, which provide extensive stretches of level or undulating country.

The interior drainage of the Kwama is almost completely deforested in its upper reaches where human settlement is concentrated. Patches of forest cling to the uppermost portions of steep ridges, while there is extensive forest on the face of the main range and in the Puleng Valley. Komba and Selepetland constitute a large pocket of savanna within the otherwise heavily forested Huon Peninsula. The predominant vegetation is *kunai* and *pitpit*. ("Komba," applied to all the peoples east of the Kwama River, means *pitpit* in Dedua, and the name was introduced by native missionaries from that area.) Timber for construction purposes is in short supply; bamboo, which is extensively planted, is used in housebuilding and for garden fences, while dry *pitpit* stalks are the usual fuel. Today house walls consist of split or pit-sawn planks laboriously cut and transported from remote forested tracts. The houses are roofed with *kunai* grass.

The staple crops of the Komba and Selepet are taro and sweet potato; other indigenous foods include yam, bananas, pandanus, sugar cane, and winged bean. Singapore taro has been widely adopted and has tended to replace taro in some areas. European vegetables—maize, potatoes, beans, cabbages, and onions—thrive over most of the region.

Population over the entire area has a density of about 50 per square mile, but there are extreme variations. In the case of the small Komba village of Balup located in the front range, each household has access to a square mile of land. In the upper Pumene Valley, with a population of 2,700 (Selepet), a survey in connection with the purchase of 180 acres of land for the Kabwum Patrol Post revealed that there is

only about one acre of arable land per person—barely sufficient if fallowing requirements are taken into account. The
planting of coffee plantations, generally placed on the most
fertile soils, further aggravates the shortage of arable land in
the upper Komba and Selepet regions.

The indigenous social organization consisted of patrilineal
lineages and clans. Sixteen years ago, Schmitz found that the
clan and lineage system had largely disintegrated, leaving a
kindred based social organization in its place (1960, pp.
155f.). Undoubtedly, there were several "levels of segmentation": lineages which were local land holding groups and
which maintained a men's ceremonial house; subclans and
clans, which occupied a settlement; and linked clans, which
formed a tribe or confederation. One of the most potent
factors of change has been the shifts in the pattern of
settlement induced by the Lutheran Mission and later reinforced by the Administration. Schmitz, who has done ethnographic work both among the Komba and in the Wantoat
Valley to the west, describes the changes in settlement in
Wantoat:

. . . the people were accustomed to live in small villages, usually
only numbering some 60 to 80 persons, and so arranged that the
villages belonging to the same lineage were closer together. In this
matter contact with Government and mission led to a change of considerable consequence, as both institutions impelled the population to
move together into larger villages. In this way, the European work
of administration became easier. As a rule, those who belonged to the
same lineage moved into a new village together. It also occurred,
however, that subdivisions of a lineage which had quarreled with one
another, made use of the opportunity to separate for good. This forci-
ble modification, . . . diminished the number of local groups by two
thirds within two years . . . [1963, p. 21].

In the Kwama Valley, insofar as it can be established,
aboriginal settlements consisting of a subclan or clan were
composed of two hundred people or less. Several neighboring settlements were linked by ties of kinship and marriage
and by joint participation in the annual pig festivals, and

they formed an alliance group in warfare. The Lutheran Mission began working in the area in the 1920's, while the Komba and Selepet were subject to only infrequent patrols by the government until after World War II. Patrolling European missionaries and resident native mission workers encouraged the formation of large, compact villages. To a great extent these new settlements were—as they remain today—"front villages" where people assembled for church meetings and for government census and taxation. Thus, the people of the upper Pumene Valley formerly assembled at Konindo, where it was common for several families to share a house. Iloko informants list six pre-mission hamlets which the mission brought together at Iloko (population 545), though there has been a redispersal in more recent times. Gilang (population 425) was selected by the mission for grouping together the surrounding hamlets, and consists of four previous hamlets.

Today the large villages serve as centers for church and school—people come in on week ends for church services— for medical treatment, ceremony, and for recreation and craft activities during the slack season of January and February. Much of the time people are dispersed over the countryside in household or family groups, living in "pig houses"—proper dwellings surrounded by pigpens—within or adjoining their gardening land. At the same time, however, living in the large villages has acquired a value of its own, despite the difficulty of traveling to distant gardening areas. Life in the "big place" is more exciting.

VIEWS ALONG AN INLAND-COASTAL ROUTE

The "trade route" from Sio to Iloko (see Map 3) ascends from sea level to about fifty-one hundred feet and penetrates inland about twenty miles. Because of the ruggedness of the terrain, the distance actually traversed is probably more than twice that (under good conditions the total walking time is about twenty-five hours). Sixteen inland communities, ranging in population from eighty-five to over twelve hundred, lie along this route.

The Sio-Iloko track is significant for a number of reasons related to the investigation of trade, but it is not a mainline trade route from the coast to the mountain face of the Sarawaged. Travel from Sio to Iloko is somewhat like climbing a tree, in that the lower portion—from Sio to Sambori— constitutes the trunk line, while beyond, within the densely settled regions, there is a branching out—a single route gives way to a network of intervillage tracks presenting many alternatives for travel. Previous to pacification, villages along the route would not have used more than local segments of it. For example, between Sambori and Nimbako the route crosses the Kwama River, the boundary of the Komba and Selepet peoples. Formerly, Nimbako and other Selepet traders would have stayed within Selepet country, moving to the coast along a route lying to the west of the Kwama. Depending on local political conditions at the time, other groups of traders, too, would take circuitous paths in order to avoid contact with hostile communities. In a sense, each group may have sought its own route to the sea. Judging from accounts of prewar travel to the coast, trips to Sio had the character of forced marches. Traders often began walking before dawn, they moved as fast as possible considering their heavy burdens, they walked as much as twelve hours in a day, and they avoided intervening communities. From various points in the more remote interior, the first and hardest day brought the party to the base of the coastal range (inland side), where there are camp sites along the Puleng River. On the second day the traders crossed over the front range and were able to reach Sio by dusk.

Also, of several alternate routes, the Sio-to-Iloko is the most difficult to traverse. It is much easier to stay east of the Kwama Gorge and to move south and up through Komba-land, or to travel twelve miles along the coast to the west and then inland. The track chosen for study runs south, then west, then south again. The western segment crosses the gorges of the Puleng, Kwama, and Pumene rivers, and thus one is traveling across or against the grain of the country. I chose this more difficult route, however, for these reasons: (1) It includes both Sambori and Nimbako, important groups of middlemen for the coast-inland trade; (2) it crosses the Selepet-Komba border twice, and by moving along this track one encounters the maximum variation in terrain, features of production, and community size; (3) it runs through the government station at Kabwum, which, since its establishment in 1960, has become the economic as well as the administrative focus of the hinterland; and (4) Iloko, the last community, is the terminus of one of the main trans-Sarawaged trade routes connecting the southern and northern halves of the Huon Peninsula.

The route was constructed on the basis of advance knowledge of these features just listed. Rather than being a natural trade route, it is more a route of investigation—an arbitrary connection of points within and cutting through a complex network of intercommunity relations.

This route can be most conveniently described from the point of view of an observer walking along it from the beach to the mountain wall. One moves south for several miles through grassy coastal plain and a short stretch of wooded savanna to the base of the front range, where the track turns sharply upward and savanna gives way to rain forest. From this point about two hours of walking and climbing bring us to Balup, the first Komba village, located at an altitude of about twenty-five hundred feet. Balup is a small community with a population of eighty-five, including absentee workers. In 1964 there were about sixty-five residents living in nine dwellings, which are arranged in an oval surrounding a central cleared place. The country surrounding Balup is heavily forested, and the chief garden crop is taro. In addition to gardening, however, Balup acts as a principal intermediary for coastal and overseas products moving to the interior—it is the first and one of the most important links between Sio and the hinterland.

Balup's history during the last half-century has been one of movement back and forth along a section of the inland route. The earliest remembered settlement of Mula (termed hereafter Old Mula)—attracted by the Sio Mission established in 1911—moved to the base of the coastal range, where it was known as Munau. The people did not fare well at Munau. The area of the village is unsuited for taro cultivation, infant mortality was high, and the mosquitoes were bothersome. Before World War II the community moved back to the mountains to Lembanggando, between Old Mula and the present site of Balup. After the war, and encouraged by a government officer, who suggested that they concentrate on coconut production at lower altitudes, the people moved again to Munau. Sometime after 1956 Balup was established, and it is here in the mountains where people say they wish to remain. The soil is suitable for taro, the preferred staple, and visits from friends and kinsmen from the more remote Komba occur oftener than at Munau. Indeed, if Komba villagers must travel to Munau to trade, they may as well go on to Sio—being useful middlemen depends on being somewhere in the middle.

Partly because of the ruggedness of the coastal range, which here rises to six thousand feet, it is generally an unfavorable area for human settlement. In addition, people like those of Balup who frequently travel to the coast to trade, are continuously infected with malaria. Through the postwar period the population of Balup has increased only slightly; indeed, the population has only been maintained by immigration. Nine of seventeen household heads are outsiders or descendants of outsiders who currently garden on land belonging to matrikin or affines.

Both Sio and Komba legends record the previous existence of subcoastal communities in the high *kunai* plain. Balup informants pointed out an old village site near Munau—known in Sio as Triwasoko—where their ancestors were nearly wiped out by the dawn attack of a Sio war party. According to Sio informants, most trading with the Komba

in the past (as it is today) was conducted among trade-
friends rather than at market places, and Komba men said
that the Sios sometimes called markets which they turned
into ambushes. The Sios feared Komba sorcery, and Sio big-
men sometimes hired Komba men as sorcerers or assassins.
Elder Sios today emphasize the value of the *tambu*-shell and
dogs'-teeth ornaments by pointing out that one of the elaborate ornaments is equivalent to a man's life—the fee for a
Komba sorcerer. It seems apparent, then, that temporarily
the link between Sio and the interior along this route might
be broken because of hostilities.

The second Komba community of Mula (population
ninety-eight) is a two-hour walk from Balup. Mula is an old
settlement site, but this community was formed after the
war. Government census records reveal a migration of fifty-
three males and fifty-seven females to Mula from Tauknave
—in the Puleng Komba—in 1948. New Mula occupies territory claimed in part by Balup and partly by Sambori, the
next community, which is located beyond the front range.
The Sambori people have vociferously objected to the settlement of the Mula people on their former hunting grounds.
This area is too far from Sambori to be used for gardening,
though small sweet potato gardens are made near the main
track to provision hunting parties and traders traveling to
Sio. In 1964 informants indicated that Mula might break up,
that some people would move to Balup while the rest would
return to the parent community of Tauknave. The leading
man of Mula, however, told me that he intended to hold the
community together.

From various observation points near Mula one catches
glimpses of the sea and the coast. In the opposite direction,
to the south, looms Mount Bangeta (over thirteen thousand
feet), appearing as a small hump on the continuous ridge of
the Sarawaged Range. Looking down the valleys of the
Kwama and its tributaries, one can make out many of the
Komba and Selepet villages below. The nearest of these is
Sambori, located on the ridge top flanking the Puleng River,

and about four hours away. Sambori (population 158) is one of the most important nodes of the inland trade network, and this was especially true in pre-European times when more remote Komba communities did not have direct relations with Sio. The residents of Sambori and Old Mula (Balup) were the middlemen of coast-inland trade for the Komba.

Interlocal trade in the interior follows channels established by marriage. The pattern of intermarriage revealed in genealogies shows that there is, generally speaking, a three-step movement in coast-inland trading. Balup exchanges wives with the communities of the Puleng Komba (current marriages with Sambori, Kumbip, Puleng, and Tauknave). The Puleng Valley villages, in turn, exchange wives and coastal products, such as pottery, with the densely settled upper Komba region further south.

From Sambori roads lead to the Puleng Komba country and beyond, and across the Kwama River to Nimbako, the next village of the route. The Kwama is too swift to ford, but there are several spots with large boulders that can be spanned by bridges. These are often washed away when the river floods after heavy rain, but a dozen men can replace the bridges in about two hours. Nimbako (population two hundred) is the first village of the Selepet along this route, and like Balup and Sambori, it comprises an important group of middlemen for pots and other coastal products. From Nimbako it is a long day's walk to Sio for men carrying only lightweight tobacco, while it takes two days for women carrying *bilums* of food. There were several Nimbako-Sio marriages in the previous generation, one of which led to what was probably the last raid made on Sio by the mountaineers (it occurred sometime after the Sio Mission was founded in 1911). Shortly after the marriage took place, the Sio husband died. Sorcery was the presumed cause of death. When two close kinsmen of the dead man's wife later visited Sio, the blame was fixed on them, and they were both killed by the Sio man's brothers before they could escape. In retaliation, the Nimbako people raided Sios in their gardens; one Sio woman was killed and others on both sides were wounded by arrows.

Nimbako is known for the manufacture of superior palm-wood bows, and during one of my visits in the slack season in February, men were spending most of each day around the men's houses fashioning new bows. Formerly, the bows were exchanged on the coast for a hand's length of *tambu*. Nowadays, if they are sold for cash rather than being given as gifts to trade-friends, a bow with a half-dozen arrows commands from two to five shillings.

Of the interior villages of the Komba and Selepet, Sambori and Nimbako are closest to the coastal range, near the confluence of the Kwama and its two tributaries. In this area rain forest is the predominant vegetation, though on the ridge tops inhabited by the Sambori and Nimbako people there are extensive patches of *kunai* and of secondary re-growth. Looking south from Nimbako, into the Pumene Valley where the route leads next, forest gradually gives way to savanna. Taro is the chief crop for the lower villagers, but as one passes into the core of the savanna country in the upper valleys, sweet potato cultivation increases relatively, and in some areas surpasses taro in importance. This eco-logic threshold corresponds to the approximate boundary of the lower Komba and Selepet peoples and the *kumboi kalawe,* the distant bushmen, with whom Sio had no direct relations until European times.

From Nimbako the track descends to the Pumene River and then up to the village of Wap (population 220). From this point onward the villages are larger and closer together. An hour's walk along a track sloping gently upward brings us to the joint village of Kabum-Sarong (population 800) and the government patrol post of Kabwum. At Kabum one first encounters wet taro cultivation. The valley of a small tributary of the Puleng River has been converted into an extensive system of low terraces for the growing of irrigated taro. Retaining walls, two feet high or less, are flimsily constructed of bamboo and *pitpit* stalks with earth thrown up behind. In old portions of the system the earth walls have been compacted and solidified by the growth of grass and planted shrubs. Irrigated plots produce for three or four years, and then require only a brief fallow of one to two years.

Further along the route, at Gilang, one recently constructed garden consisted of four tiers or terraces fed by two channels leading off a spring-fed stream. It contained 275–300 taro. At Tipsit village there was a larger terrace system being dug into the side of a hill. Fan shaped and fifteen yards across at its lower end, it consisted of about twenty separate levels, and would accommodate about three thousand taro on completion. The villages of Upat and Erendengan also have some wet taro gardens, but only at Kabum is the irrigated area extensive.

People claim that wet taro cultivation is a recent technique. Irrigation protects taro from taro beetles, and informants give the impression that their most recent ancestors devised the terrace systems as the outcome of a trial-and-error approach to the problem of insect pests. No extensive stonework is involved in terracing, and I saw no evidence of old or abandoned terraces.

Leaving Kabum the track proceeds to Selepet village (population 362), Indum (population 1,258; a village cluster of three settlements), then out of the Pumene Valley to Wekae (population 225), Erendengan (population 723), Gilang (population 425), Upat (population 289), Tipsit (population 609), Bamurofto (population 272), Sanon (population 256), and Iloko (population 545). Generally, less than one-half hour's walking time separates these villages. For government census purposes, Tipsit is taken to be the last of the Selepet villages. Locally, however, Wekae is regarded as the last group of Selepet-speakers, from Bamurofto on is Komba, while the communities in between are linguistically mixed.

Iloko (with its outlying hamlet of Kiraro, population

150), the last village, is the starting point for a trans-Sarawaged route linking the Komba-Selepet and the Naba peoples on the south side of the main range. Iloko-Naba marriages provided the basis for trade links which brought greenish-black polished stone adzes to the Komba-Selepet region in exchange for pigs, dogs, and *tambu.* Though trade in stone adzes ceased long ago, this route has been used a great deal in post-European times. Government officers visiting Iloko and patroling the "top of the Naba" have noted a considerable amount of movement, in connection with visiting and intermarriage, over the Sarawaged Range (Worsley, 1964). For migrant laborers from the "top Komba," it takes two days to scale the range and reach the first Naba villages, and then three more days through Naba and Wain country to Lae.

TRADE WITH THE HINTERLAND

Traditionally, Sio received imported foodstuffs and tobacco from the nearest inland villages—Old Mula, Sambori, and Nimbako. In addition, these bush traders brought pigs, dogs, net bags, bows and arrows, stone adzes, painted barkcloth robes, and dogs' teeth. For food and tobacco they received Sio pots, fish, and coconuts. For other goods they acquired Tami and Rai Coast bowls, *tambu* shell, boars' tusks, obsidian, and red and black pigments. From the densely settled upper Komba and Selepet, the bush middlemen received sweet potatoes, yams, bows, net bags, stone adzes, and pigs and dogs in return for such coastal and overseas products as pots, boars' tusks, *tambu,* wooden bowls, and lime. In spite of the fact that locally produced food is sufficient, the middlemen accept sweet potatoes and yams for pots and other goods. They explain: "They don't bring taro, which we have plenty of. We don't need more food, but they are our kin and we accept what they bring." The Sios also, of course, frequently accept goods which they do not need at the time. When I asked one Sio man why he had four bows (most men have more than one), he replied:

"If a bush friend comes with a bow, you have to help him."

To provide an idea of modern trading between Sio and its hinterland, we may examine a number of recent transactions reported by Sio and Komba informants:

(a)	4 pots, 8 coconuts	=	2 *bilums* Singapore taro, 3 packets of tobacco
(b)	1 large pot, 12 coconuts, 1 *laplap*, 2s.	=	1 *bilum* Singapore taro, 1 bunch of bananas, 4 stalks of sugar cane, 1 bundle of greens
(c)	1 large pot, 1 small pot, 8 coconuts, 1s., 1 piece women's clothing (6s.), 2 *laplaps* (8s.), 1 pair short trousers (3s.)	=	1 *bilum* Singapore taro, 1 bundle of lettuce, 3 packets of tobacco
(d)	1 pair trousers (£1)	=	6 packets of tobacco
(e)	1 s.	=	1 bamboo container of lime
(f)	1 pot, 4 coconuts, 1 *laplap* (12s.)	=	5 packets of tobacco
(g)	1 small pot, 1 large pot, 16 coconuts, 1 *laplap*, 1 pair short trousers	=	5 packets of tobacco, 20 Singapore taro, 5 large taro, some bananas
(h)	5 coconuts	=	1 *bilum* of Singapore taro
(i)	5 coconuts, some fish	=	2 *bilums* of taro
(j)	1 pot	=	1 packet of tobacco
(k)	(no return gift)	=	1 *bilum* of taro and Singapore taro, 3 packets of tobacco
(l)	1 pot, 8 coconuts	=	3 large packets of tobacco (200–350 leaves)
(m)	(no return)	=	2 packets of tobacco
(n)	£1	=	1 female piglet

(o) 3 pots, 2 *laplaps*,   = 1 two-year-old pig
     £5

(p) 1 large machete   = 2 *bilums* of sweet potato,
                            taro and Singapore taro,
                            4 packets of tobacco

All of these transactions except (e) occurred between trade-friends at Sio. It is apparent that informants' statements regarding rates of exchange offer only the roughest guidelines, and that no series of transactions of this kind will illuminate any implicit rates of exchange. If a balance, according to some standard, exists over the long run, it could only be shown by examining a number of series of transactions between particular sets of trade-friends extending over a period of years. The manner in which exchanges are made and the social ethic guiding exchange (see Chap. VIII) combine to make informants' memories of past transactions of the run-of-the-mill sort rather hazy. Transactions involving pigs, dogs, and ornaments, however, are remembered well.

Many of the transactions outlined above are incomplete, that is, they are but an episode in a continuing series. In the case of (c), the Sio man explained his generosity as follows: "The bushwoman's husband died recently and I felt sorry for her. Besides, I thought of all the food that she will bring next time." In (h) it was conceded that five coconuts were only part-payment for the *bilum* of food received. In (k) the bushman had an expectation but received no specific promise of a future return. Transaction (m) illustrates the common practice whereby a bushman sends tobacco to a Sio trade-friend via another trader along with a message as to what he wants in the future. By resorting to a third party, the man may make a specific request, something he is loath to do when he meets his trade-friend face to face. In (n) the bushman was dissatisfied with the one pound received for the pig—this is the stated rate of exchange—and this combined with other unsatisfactory transactions caused him to break off the relationship. A Komba trader reported trans- action (p) as evidence of the generosity of his Sio trade- friends.

Transaction (l), one pot and eight coconuts for three large packets of tobacco, is unbalanced in favor of the Sio side of the exchange. A small pot is worth three to six shillings while one shilling is the widely recognized equiva- lent for one "rope" of coconuts (four). The Sios regard an ordinary packet of tobacco containing at least several dozen leaves to be worth one shilling, while a large packet is worth three or four shillings (sometimes tobacco is made up in packets three feet long, which are worth five pounds or a pig). In these terms, the goods exchanged were of unequal value—five to eight shillings' worth of pots and coconuts for at least ten to twelve shillings' worth of tobacco—and the Komba partner was highly dissatisfied. Increasingly, younger men feel that prices for tobacco, in particular, should correspond more closely to town market prices, where six leaves may be sold for one shilling. In this case the Komba man did not calculate values on this basis, but regarded the three packets of tobacco together to be worth eighteen shillings, while he put the cash value of the pot and coconuts at five shillings. This comparison was made in the course of illustrating the general point that the Sios are unfair when it comes to paying for tobacco. His dissatisfac- tion in this particular case, however, stemmed mostly from the fact that he wanted not pots or coconuts but a *laplap*. In general, people travel to Sio with specific needs in mind, but sometimes they receive as gifts things which they do not want at the time. Similarly, Sio people are generally more pleased by a gift of taro than of sweet potato, or of tobacco rather than bows or net bags, of which they may have plenty. Thus, dissatisfaction may arise on both sides even though—unlike transaction (l)—the exchange is objectively balanced.

DIVISION OF LABOR RELATED TO TRADING

Most trade between Sio and the hinterland is conducted between trade-friends, and most exchange between trade-friends takes place at Sio. Therefore, the transport of goods, one of the main burdens of labor in trading, is borne by the inland people, especially the women. A comparison of the activities performed by the different groups, and men as opposed to women, indicate that Sio men do the least, while Komba and Sio women do the most. The various trade-related activities are distributed as follows:

Komba women: The bulk of transport; taro planting and weeding, harvesting for trade; manufacture of net bags.

Komba men: Heavy work in gardening; cultivation of tobacco, curing and wrapping of tobacco leaf; bow making; on trading trips men carry their personal belongings and the lightweight packets of tobacco; sometimes a man carries a single *bilum* of food while his wife carries two.

Sio women: Pottery making, fishing, transport to markets, cooking; collection and grinding of *tambu* shell for ornaments; cleaning of coconut groves, preparation of sun-dried copra (cash from copra sales used in trade).

Sio men: Fishing; cleaning coconut plantations and processing of copra.

The position of Sio men, in particular, seems enviable. When a trade-friend arrives, the Sio becomes a gracious host. His wife cooks the meals, brings down pots from their overhead storage racks, and if any fish are to be provided she probably catches them. Children are dispatched to collect coconuts. Meanwhile, the head of the household fulfills his obligations by sitting in the company of his friends on the veranda.

At the same time, as money, bush knives, and *laplaps* have become more important in local trading, the burden of Sio men increases. The cash returns of hard labor as a wage worker or in copra production must be diverted from other uses to sustain trade relationships.

COMPARISONS WITH GITUA

Moving east from Sio along the *kunai* littoral, one finds that the coast is sculptured into a remarkable series of grassy terraces rising in regular tiers to heights of several hundred feet. The terrace land is visible from Siassi, thirty to forty miles away, as a yellowish swath. The heart of the swath is barren, dry, and oppressively hot. It is this protruding part of the mainland coast, from Fortification Point to Cape King William (named by Dampier who in March, 1700, saw the "smokes" of the pig hunters from the other side of the Strait), which helps to produce the "funnel effect" of the Vitiaz Strait that is noted by European seamen during the Southeast season. On land, too, the winds reach high velocities, and gardens near the beach are walled off with wind screens to protect the yams against salt spray. The three large communities of Sio, Gitua, and Sialum all formerly lived on small offshore islands, as if they intended to dissociate themselves somehow from the inhospitable character of the coastal strip itself.

Gitua (population 415) is twelve miles east of Sio, closer to the heart of the terrace land, and in major respects environmental conditions are less favorable than at Sio. Timber and building materials for houses and canoes are in short supply; the fringing reef is small; wild pigs are few; extensive stands of sago palms are lacking; there are much fewer coconuts than at Sio; and bush areas favorable for taro planting are very restricted. Finally, the terms of the inland trade are much less favorable than at Sio.

As at Sio, local trade takes place both at markets and through visits of trade-friends. A much larger proportion of trading at Gitua, however, is performed in markets. According to the market rate, the Gituans say, a clay pot currently brings three to four taro, while in dealing with trade-friends a pot is worth five to ten taro (more comparable to Sio). The difference between Sio and Gituan rates of exchange may be largely a matter of geography. The hinterland villages of

A hamlet of Indum village, Selepet country

The Saturday market at Barang, Umboi Island

A Sio potter at work

Mandok Islanders and Kovai housewives exchange fish and taro

Gitua—Kumukio, Kinalakna, Bambi, Gitukia, Sikikia, Wetna, Ezanko, and others—are all a walk of two hours or less from the beach. Meeting places for trade are therefore convenient to both the Gituans and mountain villagers. A trading trip that begins in the morning can be concluded well before midday—and much of the exchange of inland for coastal products takes place at these midway sites. From Sio, on the other hand, the nearest inland village of Balup is three and one-half to four hours away. Sometimes Balup people visit Sio and return in a day, but more often they stay overnight. Traders from Mula, Sambori, Nimbako, or more remote villages must plan on spending at least one night at Sio. The traders therefore require hospitality—food and lodging—and for this reason most trade is conducted on the much more sociable lines of trade-friendship.

Coast-inland exchange at Sialum, twenty-five miles east of Sio, probably closely resembles the situation at Gitua. Stolz, who lived at Sialum between 1907 and 1911, states that fish was the main item moving inland (Sialum did not manufacture pottery at this time) in return for taro, sweet potato, tobacco, betelnut, and bows. He observed that "Strange to say, the trade is carried on only by old women" (1911, p. 254).

THE TRADE SYSTEM VIEWED FROM SIO

Before leaving the mainland of New Guinea for the archipelago, we can appropriately scan the trade system from this vantage point. Looking out over the waters of the Strait from the Sio beach in early morning, or late afternoon, the outer islands stand out in bold silhouettes. Arop Island, Tolokiwa, Umboi, and beyond Umboi the two great mountains which stand guard at the western tip of New Britain, appear much closer than they really are. Beyond Sio to the south loom the towering ridges of the Sarawaged Range. Prior to the advent of Europeans, the Sio world was bounded by these ranges, the outer islands, and the lines of clouds visible on the horizon. This world, corresponding approximately to the territory of the trade system, was not necessarily or inherently hostile, for it was interlaced by social connections radiating from Sio. The Sios found their enemies closer to home, the nearby communities of Gitua, Kumukio, Kiari, and the Komba. People from afar were friends.[10]

To the people of the hinterland, Sio is known as *amaŋ topŋe*, the source of pots. In return mainly for their clay pots, the Sios receive all the specialized products that the Vitiaz Strait has to offer. From the interior comes food when it is most needed—taro, sweet potatoes, and bananas. Also from the interior come bows and arrows, net bags, pigs, dogs, bark cloth, pandanus rain capes, dogs' teeth, and tobacco. From the Rai Coast come wood bowls, black pigment, bark cloth, dogs' teeth, *Canarium* almonds, and, when required, yams, taro, and bananas. Arop Island provides the finest hand drums and betel mortars. In addition to pots, some of these goods—such as tobacco, Rai Coast bowls, bows, net bags, pigs, and dogs' teeth—are passed on by the Sios to the Siassi traders in return for pandanus mats, coconuts, boars' tusks, disc beads, sago, red ochre, obsidian, and wooden bowls.

Trade was often the occasion for gala festivals, or the two events were timed to coincide. When the members of the Hamburg Expedition visited Sio Island in 1909, a festival—an inter-*mbawnza* distribution and *singsing*—was about to get under way. Present as guests were Arop Islanders, Siassis, and small, timid men from the interior, probably Kombas (Vogel-Hamburg, 1911, pp. 258–61). At such crossroads of trade as Sio, then, people from different parts of the "world" met face to face, and there is nothing to suggest that such mixed gatherings were unusual.

[10] Describing native trade in eastern Melanesia, Belshaw writes: "The peoples of adjacent areas were often enemies, though friendly to the inhabitants of areas further away. Thus people of the southern and northern parts of San Cristoval were friendly, but on visits they were careful to keep away from the central villages of the island, since murder or fighting would have resulted from contact" (1954, p. 11).

The regular voyages of the Siassi Islanders bring them to the Sio Coast once or twice annually, during the change of seasons. For example, in November they take advantage of the tag end of the Southeast Trade winds to make the crossing, and return by the first winds of the Northwest Monsoon. These intrepid seafarers and traders are the subject of the next chapter.

VI

The Archipelago:
The Siassi Traders

"God gave us two occupations—
making canoes and making fish nets."

THE SIASSI ARCHIPELAGO consists of over twenty small islands
and sandbanks, together with numerous coral reefs, lying to
the south of Umboi Island and bounded by latitudes 5° 48′
S. and 6° 01′ S., and by longitudes 147° 52′ E. and 148° 22′
E. At present six of the islands are inhabited. Mandok and
Aramot Islands, lying close to the southern shores of Umboi,
are little more than wooded sandbanks, yet the populations
of the villages on these islets are 343 and 398, respectively.
The largest of the islands is Tuam, lying about ten miles out
in the Strait, south of Umboi. It is about one and one-quarter
miles long by one-half wide, and rises to about 250 feet at its
highest point. The population of Tuam village is 496. Malai
Island, like Tuam, is a raised coral island, and is located
about seven miles to the southwest of the southern tip of
Umboi. The Malais number 448. These four islands are the
homes of the Siassi traders.

Because of overcrowding on Aramot, some of the islanders
have recently established a colony on the islet of Mutumala,
between Aramot and Mandok. The sixth inhabited island,

Aronaimutu, lies off the southwest coast of Umboi. The Aronaimutus, a small group of fishermen who garden on the adjacent mainland, do not speak a Siassi dialect and are not overseas traders.

The Siassis make up approximately one quarter of the population of the Siassi-Umboi area, while they occupy only about one three-hundredth of the land area. Measures of population density for the islands themselves are not meaningful, since a large part of subsistence is founded on exploitation of the extensive reefs of the archipelago by fishing. Malai has the largest reef area; Tuam is surrounded mainly by deep water. Unlike the three other groups, Tuam does not utilize large fish nets which are designed for reef fishing. In addition to fishing, each group of islanders uses the smaller islets and sandbanks in their immediate vicinity, chiefly for growing coconuts. Mandok, for example, owns Pore and Mutumala Islands,[1] both of which support coconut groves. One of the islets belonging to Tuam is a seabird rookery, which seasonally provides large quantities of eggs.

The larger islands, Malai and Tuam, have sufficient land to permit a limited amount of gardening, the staple crop being a small variety of *mami*. Most of the gardens viewed at Tuam in 1964 were planted to manioc and sweet potato, neither of which were planted in aboriginal times. Malai garden crops are *mami*, sweet potatoes, manioc, sugar cane, edible *pitpit*, corn, beans, and melons. Areas not under garden cultivation are given over to coconuts, pandanus, betelnut, and *Canarium* almonds. Timber is scarce, and a large part of the building materials used in house construction—timber and sago leaf for thatch—is transported from mainland Umboi. The Mandok and Aramot Islanders have no land on their islands for gardens; indeed, all available space on Aramot is taken up with dwellings and canoes. The Aramots were gardening in a limited way on the opposite

[1] The way was cleared for the Aramot colony on Mutumala Island by the Administration. There is a Catholic Mission station on Pore Island, which is only several hundred yards from Mandok.

mainland as early as 1925 (Chinnery, n.d., p. 36) and probably before. The Mandok Islanders, also, began to garden before World War II. The main crops are *mami,* manioc, and sweet potatoes.

The four Siassi groups are dependent on local trade with the Umboi villagers for the bulk of their vegetable food—taro; sago, consumed at home and traded abroad; bananas; tobacco; extra supplies of betelnut; timber and other materials for canoe building; sago leaf and timber for houses; and fibers for the making of fish nets. The Umboi people receive in turn fish and shellfish, pigs, dogs, carved wooden bowls, clay pots, and various kinds of wealth-objects.

It is evident that local trade in food, combined with net fishing, the collection of shellfish, local production of coconuts, and limited horticulture, adequately meet the subsistence needs of these island populations. If one considers in addition that the flow of wealth controlled by the Siassis produces frequent dividends in the form of surplus pigs and taro, and that the traders annually spend several months living on the hospitality of host communities, their economic position seems enviable.

Nevertheless, certain recurrent conditions create hardship and even famine. Most commonly, an extended period of bad weather may prohibit the Malai and Tuam Islanders from sailing. (Faced with the same situation, the Tami Islanders smoked and cured taro peelings, which served as emergency rations.) Less common, warfare arising perhaps out of sago poaching by the Siassis on southern Umboi or out of trade itself could result in the suspension of trading. And with less readily calculable effects, a sailing crew of five or six men might be lost at sea.

Past generations of islanders may have considered their economic position to be more precarious than people do today—certainly the physical hazards were greater in the past. In any case, informants maintain that population limiting techniques were regularly employed. The size of families was limited by infanticide—males as well as females were

killed—abortion (reportedly by means of herbal prepara-
tions), and a prohibition on sexual intercourse between the
birth and subsequent weaning of a child. In addition, genealogies suggest that a smaller proportion of men married in
the past than at present. Mandok informants explain that
men remained bachelors because some had no canoes or fish
nets, and were thus permanently relegated to the status of
"rubbish men." Adult men in Mandok now number about 75
in a population of 343, and they own 49 canoes and 108 fish
nets.

Judging from the descriptions of early European visitors
and extant photographs, the general appearance of the Siassi
Island villages has not changed over the years. The compact
groups of dwellings have a shanty town appearance, which
is due to the scarcity of building materials and resulting
makeshift methods of construction. House walls are pieced
together from small irregular planks cut from driftwood[2]
and waste lumber from canoe construction, while old canoe
wash strakes, with their painted designs faded but intact,
provide larger planking. The houses are raised on pilings six
feet or more in height, so that many dwellings are two-story
affairs. The upper story, the house proper, is reserved for
sleeping and storage. The lower level, which may be only
partly enclosed if at all, consists of a platform built above
ground, and is the setting for domestic and craft activities.
Long drying racks draped with the large fish nets and
dozens of canoes of all sizes—beached, moored, and under
construction—are the other prominent features of the
village.

To the north and overshadowing the islands of Siassi is
Umboi, a large volcanic island about thirty miles long and
sixteen miles wide at its broadest point. The island is largely
mountainous—the highest points are about forty-five hun-

---

[2] Considerable use is made of driftwood. Aided by high winds and the
reversal of current that sometimes occurs during the Northwest Monsoon,
the Siassi Archipelago is a trap for the flotsam and jetsam disgorged by
such large mainland rivers as the Kwama and Timbe. Logs large enough for
canoe hulls are sometimes recovered.

dred feet—and rain forest is the predominant vegetation. The southern tip of the island is level and is covered with extensive areas of swamp. The rugged interior of the southwestern portion of Umboi is uninhabited.

Rainfall varies seasonally and with altitude. On the western coast rainfall is heaviest during the Northwest Monsoon; the wet season on the east coast comes with the Southeast Trades (May to November). At Gizarum Plantation on the west coast, rainfall is about 90 inches per annum, while a few miles inland the average is about 180 inches (AGS, 1943, p. 59).

The bulk of the population is made up of the fourteen villages of the Kovai people, who are settled in a series of valleys in the interior of the western part of the island. The six villages of the Kaimanga people, occupying less rugged terrain and closer to the coast, are located on the eastern side. The most important coastal community (settlement is largely in the interior) is Barim on the west coast. As mentioned previously, the Barim people were formerly overseas traders who made large ocean going canoes.

The Kovai villagers, living at altitudes above five hundred feet where rainfall is ample, produce the majority of the taro that is acquired in exchange by the Siassi Islanders. Most of these villages control routes to the sea and claim sections of the eastern coastline where they collect shellfish, engage in limited reef fishing, and hold markets with the Siassis. In recent years these beach trading sites have grown into establishments consisting of copra sheds, pig enclosures (keeping pigs near the coast and away from the villages eliminates the necessity for protective garden fences), and dwellings of the families charged with pig tending.

There are four main language groups in the Siassi–Umboi Island area. The Siassi Islanders of Mandok, Aramot, Malai, and Tuam speak closely related dialects of the same language. The name Siassi for this language and the islanders as a whole is apparently a European innovation (*sisi* is a Siassi word for island; in the Sio language *sia* means "island" and *siasia* is "archipelago"). To the Umboi mainlanders the Siassis are known simply as "islanders" (e.g., Kovai *mutu*) and the mainlanders in turn are known as "bushmen" (*kumbwai*). Umboi Island itself is commonly referred to as *"bik Siassi."*

A second linguistic group is made up of Barim, Mantagen, and Aronaimutu on the west coast of Umboi, together with the dialects of Arop Island and Tolokiwa (a volcanic cone forty-five hundred feet high, sixteen miles northwest of Umboi).

The villagers of eastern Umboi, along with the two hundred inhabitants of Sakar Island (eight miles northwest of Umboi) speak a third language named Kaimanga. The Kaimanga, Siassi, and Barim-Arop language groups are Melanesian and appear to be closely related to each other and to the mainland languages of Sio, Gitua, and the Rai Coast. The fourth language, Kovai, with the largest number of speakers, is apparently non-Melanesian.[3]

THE STIMULUS TO OVERSEAS TRADING

As trade-dependent communities, the Siassi Islanders are not unique in the western Pacific. Such trading-manufacturing groups as the Amphletts, Ware (Teste Island), and Tubetube within the *kula* ring, Mailu Island in Papua, Alite in the southern Solomons, Langalanga in the central Solomons, and the Manus traders of the Admiralties come to mind (see Malinowski, 1915, 1922; Belshaw, 1955; Codrington, 1891, pp. 297, 327; Hogbin, 1939; Mead, 1930, 1956, 1961). To a remarkable extent, however, the economic position of the Siassis in aboriginal times was based on the carrying of goods rather than manufacturing; what the Siassis themselves produced for exchange—mats and coco-

[3] It is interesting to note that in physical appearance the mountain dwelling Kovai correspond to the physical stereotype of "sea people" (they are tall and have refined facial features), rather than of bushmen, a judgment which is made by the Sios and others. Irrespective of physical traits, however, they are regarded as bushmen by virtue of their mountain habitat, their lack of canoes, and their inability to swim.

nuts—was a small part of the economic flow sustained by their overseas voyages.

The ultimate objective of trade is revealed in the nature of the goods accumulated and the uses to which they are put, and it is articulated by the influential Siassi men who are principal actors in overseas voyaging. The numerous transactions separated geographically and spread over periods of months or even years, form characteristic sequences at the end of which lies surplus wealth in the form of dozens of pigs and tons of taro. Under the direction of traders-become-big-men, the amassed food and pigs are prepared, distributed, and consumed as the material side of status building ceremonials.

However distinctive the economic system of the Siassis, in a socio-political sense Siassi society is typically Melanesian. The operations of big-man political systems, of the kind found from one end of the Melanesian island chain to the other, provide the rationale of overseas trading. Motives of prestige, of social climbing and the enhancement of political status, and not profit in any narrow or pecuniary sense, impel the Siassis to undertake overseas voyages.

The social and political life of the neighboring societies of the Strait depend equally on the accumulation and large-scale distribution of pigs and food. But, as horticulturists, surplus production for them is more readily accomplished. The Siassis tap this surplus production for themselves, but not without the expenditure of what they regard as labor: voyaging, trading, and, in addition, the performance of dances, for which they are famed, as part of the festivals staged by the big-men of the various host communities of the trade system.

If Siassi political life depends on surpluses amassed by means of trade, overseas trading also contributes to the social as well as the material side of life in the communities touched by trade. The demand for much of the goods—wealth-objects and valuables—imported by Siassi traders stems from the requirements of the social systems and institutions of the importing societies. To describe these institutions in organizational terms means also to describe the internal transactions in which such Siassi imports as wooden bowls, clay pots, and the valuables of teeth and shell find a constant role. For many Siassi customers—in New Britain, Umboi Island, and the Tami Group—overseas trade supplies the stuff of developed bridewealth institutions. In other importing societies, overseas trade provides the material trappings and wherewithal of political status. A mainland big-man, for example, relies on his hoard of imported boars' tusks not only as a mark of his rank, but as a means of gaining followers and sometimes the services of sorcerers.

The trade system rests on a regional distribution of resources and intercommunity specialization of production. At the same time, it is predicated upon the organizational needs of particular local institutions, apart from which the trade system is not intelligible. The tasks of this and the following chapters are to examine the nature of overseas trade and its relationship to local institutions.

INTRA-SIASSI RELATIONS— PAST AND PRESENT

In the past, each of the four Siassi groups and Paramot manufactured pandanus mats and produced coconuts which were traded overseas and also, together with marine products, were exchanged locally for Umboi taro and other foods. Malai and Tuam were dependent on the other three groups for large sailing canoes, the traditional payment for a canoe consisting of three pigs. The acquisition of red ochre, traded widely overseas, appears to have been mediated to a large extent by Paramot. The source of supply is Tarawe village, a few miles inland from Paramot, and the two communities maintain close relations. Paramot received red ochre in small lumps at the rate of one per clay pot, and large lumps of the order of fifty pounds for a pig; the Siassi Islanders obtained the red ochre at much the same rates of exchange from Paramot.[4] In other respects the five trading communities were independent, with equal access to the opportunities of overseas exchange, even though their itineraries and ports-of-call were not identical.

This picture of intra-Siassi trade has altered considerably since early times. Paramot has given up long-distance voyaging and the manufacture of ocean going canoes. Canoe making is in the hands of the Aramots and Mandoks, who sail much less than they used to, while at the same time they now manufacture Tami-style bowls (since about 1930; it is my impression that Aramot emphasizes canoe making while Mandok relies more on the carving of bowls). Most of the canoes made at Aramot and Mandok are sold to Tuam and Malai at the rate of six, rather than three, pigs per canoe. Others are disposed of in New Britain. In 1952, Mr. T. White, a Patrol Officer, recorded that the Aramot craftsmen had recently completed twenty sailing canoes. Nine of these were sold to Malai, three to Kabip, and one went to Kambalap (these two Kaimanga villages undertake voyages of their own to Tolokiwa and Sakar Islands and to Kalingi). The remaining seven were sailed to Tuam where White (1952) observed the ensuing transactions. Five of the canoes were sold for three to five pigs each. The eighteen canoes sold up to that point brought payments totaling about seventy pigs, approximately half of which would be given to the Umboi people who supplied the timber. As already mentioned, the Aramots and Mandoks customarily sell all the canoes that they make, so that for their own overseas voyages they must hire vessels from either Tuam or

[4] The fact that a ball of red ochre (about three inches in diameter) is equivalent to a clay pot within the Kovai area, between Paramot and Tarawe, Paramot and Siassi, and Siassi and Sio-Gitua, presents something of a mystery. It is partly resolved by the fact that the Siassis break down a large lump, purchased for a pig, into small pieces that can be exchanged for two dozen or more pots at Sio and Gitua. In New Britain the pots bring two or three pigs. Secondly, the variation in the size of the pots offers opportunities for gain. In terms of modern cash prices, a large pot is about four times more valuable than a small one.

Malai. A payment of one pound and a wood bowl for the use of a canoe is typical, but the amount of the rental fee depends on the relationship of lessee and owner.

An additional aspect of interdependence stems from the fact that most of the current voyaging to the mainland for clay pots is done by Malai and Tuam, while Mandok and Aramot are now the source of supply for wooden bowls. This gives rise to internal trade in bowls and pots, both of which are essential for long-distance trade and local exchange on Umboi Island.

THE SIASSIS' OVERSEAS RELATIONS

Tami Islands

Before the curtailment of Tami voyaging (see Chap. IX), the Tami and Siassi Islanders exchanged visits for purposes of trade. Independently, the Siassis traded with the villagers of the Finschhafen Coast opposite Tami, while the Tamis undertook voyages to Umboi Island, and Arawe and Möwehafen in southern New Britain. The relations between these two groups of seafarers were critical for their respective overseas trading interests. The Siassis depended on Tami for the carved wooden bowls, then a Tami monopoly, and also clay pots manufactured on the south coast of the Huon Gulf. From the Siassis, Tami received boars' tusks—the principal valuable employed by them in bridewealth—and obsidian, which, from their position at the northeast corner of the Huon Gulf, they distributed to the many coastal villages of the gulf. Occasionally, the two groups sold each other sailing canoes. Dogs brought by the Siassis were exchanged for pigs at Tami, and the Siassis also brought red ochre and canoe rope (creepers used for canoe lashings). In recent transactions reported by Mandok informants, Siassi dogs, canoe rope, and cash were exchanged for bowls, pots, and pigs.

According to Mandok informants, the Tami Islanders were permitted to use Mutumala Island (owned by Mandok) as a temporary base for trading in the archipelago. The main reason for camping for a period on Mutumala was to build canoes with materials close at hand on Umboi. While engaged in canoe making, the Tamis also fished, carved bowls, and traded with the Umboi villagers.

When voyaging by the Tamis declined, contacts were maintained, as they still are, by the Siassis. April, at the end of the Northwest Monsoon, is generally the month for travel to the Tami Group, the return trip being made on the first winds of the Southeast season.

The Tami and Siassi traders are similar in many ways (even in physique, for their conspicuous muscularity is a product of lives spent as canoemen). Both groups had local monopolies or near-monopolies on coconut production, and exchanged coconuts, pandanus mats, and fish for taro in their respective local trade spheres. Their great sailing canoes are identical in design (though superior workmanship is evident in the Tami product). Finally, both groups of traders serve as middlemen for a variety of products which they themselves do not manufacture.

Finschhafen Coast

The small coastal villages from the Yabim area in the southeast corner of the Huon Peninsula to Cape King William in the north are regular ports-of-call for the Siassis during the time of the year (usually April) when they travel to the Tami Islands. They visit such villages as Simbang, Ago, Kanome, Bongu, Rakona, and Kamilaua. Siassi cargoes consist of dogs, boars' tusks, pandanus mats, and betelnut. Dogs and tusks are exchanged for pigs and dogs' teeth, while mats and betelnut pay for tobacco, net bags, taro, and bananas.

A Tuam party sailing in three canoes visited the Finschhafen Coast in late 1963. One of the canoes, with six crewmen, carried a cargo of five dogs (from New Britain), thirty mats, a large quantity of betelnut transported in two copra bags, three smaller rice sacks and ten leaf baskets, and one large packet of lime. This cargo was fully disposed of in return for a pig, tobacco, net bags, taro, Singapore taro, sweet potatoes, and cash. One of the dogs was exchanged for the pig, while the remaining four were sold for cash. Some of this money was used to buy tobacco. The trip lasted about a week.

Trading between Finschhafen Coast people and the Siassis is briefly described by Neuhauss (1911, III, 315) and has since been cited by Hoyt (1926, p. 134) as an instance of "silent trade." In the original account it is pointed out that people familiar with the Siassis and Siassi speech were permitted to mount the canoes and select their gifts, i.e., they could discuss transactions. For the rest, trading was "silent" to about the same degree as our own transactions in a supermarket, and for the same reasons. Haggling is eliminated, and there is nothing to say. Prices are set in the supermarket, so are rates of exchange in native trading, and furthermore, if dissatisfaction should arise in either case, the parties often respond by holding back their respective goods (or money) and refusing to trade (see the descriptions of Sio markets in Chap. V, and of Umboi markets, below).

Sio-Gitua-Sialum

Siassi trading at these three large pottery centers has already been noted. The Siassis bring dogs, canoes (to Sio), wooden bowls, boars' tusks, strings and necklaces of disc beads, *tambu* shell, white cowrie shells, mats, obsidian, red ochre, coconuts, sago, and *Canarium* almonds. They receive in return pots, pigs, dogs' teeth, woven net bags, bows and arrows, and bark cloth. Boars' tusks are exchanged for dogs'-teeth ornaments and pigs; pigs are also received for disc-bead necklaces. Mats, red ochre, obsidian, sago, and coconuts are used to purchase pots, two to four coconuts, one mat, or one ball of red ochre being equated with a medium-sized cooking pot. According to Sio informants, a dozen pots or a pig were given for large blocks of obsidian (the size of coconuts).

In modern trading, obsidian, sago, coconuts, *tambu* shell, eggshell cowries, and bark cloth have been eliminated.

The Sios are canoe builders, and with materials being at hand, visiting Siassis occasionally received help from them in repairing damaged canoes, e.g., replacement of lashings, outrigger booms and floats, masts and rigging.

The Rai Coast

The Malais, Mandoks, and Paramots represented Siassi on the Rai Coast, while Tuam did not venture past Sio. In post-European times Malai and Mandok canoes have touched at points along the entire length of the Rai Coast en route to Madang.

Goods brought by the Siassis—boars' tusks, red ochre, and mats—are exchanged for dogs' teeth, pigs, bows and arrows, "Madang" pots, and black paint (from the region of Malalomai on the central Rai Coast).

A typical itinerary for the Malai Islanders today might run as follows: crossing the Strait in November, initial stops are made at Gitua and Sio, followed by brief visits to such Rai Coast villages as Singorokai, Malasanga, Roinji, Malalomai, Bonga, Yara, and perhaps beyond. They then return along the coast to Sio or Gitua and wait there for the first winds of the Northwest Monsoon to carry them back home. Duration: one to two months, not unusually long for overseas voyages.

ARCHIPELAGO

New Britain

Among the Siassis' most important trade relations are those with a group of coastal villages collectively known as Kalingi, located on the northwestern tip of New Britain, and with several island villages of the picturesque Arawe Islands lying off New Britain's southwest coast. Occasionally, the

Siassis visit beach villages along the one hundred or more miles of coastline between Kalingi and the Arawe Islands, and though the latter form the customary termini on the north and south shores respectively, the Siassis sometimes venture beyond Arawe to Möwehafen and beyond Kalingi on the north coast to the Barriai and Kombe villages and even to Talasea. The Kombe manufacture the shell-disc beads that the Siassis exchange for pigs in such mainland communities as Sio. Both the Barriai and Kombe served as intermediaries for obsidian coming from Talasea, while the Siassis formerly exchanged mainland pots for obsidian with the Kalingi.

Kalingi

These villages form an important market for Tami-Siassi bowls and clay pots. They also buy a limited number of canoes. In return, Kalingi is a chief supplier of pigs and dogs, as well as the only source of disc beads and obsidian. In providing the Siassis with vegetable food, Kalingi is second in importance to Umboi Island. Formerly, coconuts, which were a rarity on the coast of western New Britain, were exchanged there for food, while bowls and pots were reserved for transactions involving pigs, dogs, obsidian, and strings of shell beads. Nowadays, pots are traded for food.

In a recent Tuam voyage to New Britain, five traders who presented for exchange four wooden bowls, ten pots, eight rolls of pandanus leaf strips, and one dogs'-teeth ornament, received payments of three dogs, a pig, three packets of tobacco, sixteen baskets of food, and five plaited armlets. The transactions of the five traders are outlined in Table 4.

Part of the demand for pots in Kalingi stems from the fact that Kalingi trades them to the adjacent Barriai people, among whom pots are highly valued wealth-objects. According to Friederici, whose New Britain studies focused on the Barriai, the customary brideprice is five strings of shell money, three or four pots, and several spears (1912, p. 88).

TABLE 4

TRANSACTIONS OF FIVE TUAM
TRADERS IN NEW BRITAIN (1963)

Item	Siassi Gifts					
	A	B	C	D	E	Total
Wooden bowls	2		1		1	4
Pots	3	3		2	2	10
Pandanus roll	5	3				8
Dogs'-teeth ornament			1			1
	Return Gifts					
Dogs	1	1			1	3
Pigs			1			1
Pkts. tobacco	2		1			3
Baskets taro	3	4				7
Sweet potato (baskets)			5	4		9
Armlets	5					5

Arawe Islands

These island communities, principally Pilelo, Paligmete, and Kapitumete, are also important outlets for bowls, pots, dogs' teeth, and canoes, and secondarily, mats, red ochre, Rai Coast black pigment, and goldlip shells. As at Kalingi, the Siassis seek and receive mainly pigs and dogs.

Goldlip shells are not regarded as wealth goods by the Siassis themselves, who cut them into spoons for home use.[5] The shells were collected on the Siassi reefs and, cleaned and polished, sometimes cut into large breast pendants, they were traded for pigs in Arawe at the rate of two large shells for one pig.

The Arawe Islanders themselves are prominent sea traders along New Britain's south coast, and they forward Siassi imports to various points further east. At Möwehafen, about forty miles east of Arawe, Todd mentions wooden bowls,

[5] Many Siassis have served in the Native Constabulary and find goldlip shells useful if they draw duty in the Highlands. A Sio man who served as a policeman in the Highlands bragged that he once had a half-dozen concubines whose services had been purchased with assorted seashells.

round cane baskets,[6] and dogs' teeth as coming from Siassi via the Arawe Islands. He also lists goldlip shells and red and black pigments, some of which stem from Siassi (1934, pp. 198–200).

To carry on their own trading activities, the Arawe people import Siassi-built canoes. The canoes made by the Arawe people themselves, long dugouts without wash strakes, are not very serviceable for traders who range as far as they apparently do. Except for Malai and Tuam, Arawe probably receives more of the large sailing canoes built on Mandok and Aramot than any other locality. In one of a number of transactions reported by Mandok informants, Arawe bought seven canoes, representing an outlay of two dozen pigs.

Arop, Tolokiwa, and Sakar Islands

While probably the largest part of the pigs and dogs received in trade by the Siassis comes from New Britain (most of the dogs are forwarded to the mainland for pigs or to Umboi for taro), Arop, Tolokiwa, and Sakar Islands are subsidiary sources. Of these, Arop is the most important, though it is farthest away. The bounteousness of Arop with respect to domestic, and especially semiwild, animals is legendary.[7] Pigs are so plentiful there, say the Siassis, that if a pig is shot in the bush it is first examined to see if it is fat

---

[6] According to Todd (1934, p. 199) these baskets are made in western New Britain. Round, flat-bottomed cane baskets of very sturdy construction and three to four feet in diameter are used throughout the Kovai area of Umboi Island in food exchanges, as they are in Möwehafen. Thus, the Siassis may have transported the baskets to Arawe from Umboi, rather than from some point in west New Britain. There is no trade in baskets now.

[7] A Sio story explains Arop's bounty of pigs, dogs, and wild fowl: Once a long-haired man came to Arop, and the islanders wanted to kill him. A big-man of Arop intervened, saved the long-haired man's life, and later helped him to build a canoe—a *sangingi* of the Gitua type. Before the man left Arop in his crude canoe, he warned the big-man of impending disaster and advised him to flee with his family. The big-man complied by going to nearby Crown Island. Soon after, the Arop volcano erupted and wiped out the community. The big-man later returned to Arop with his family to found a new community, and ever since then the island has been overrun with animals.

enough to be worthy of eating. If not, the hunters look for another and fatter one. The Sios say that Arop visitors to Sio customarily complain about not having enough meat to eat and are always anxious to return home for this reason. Arop has additional importance as the chief source of finely made hand drums, which command payments of one to two pounds today.

Typical transactions between Siassi and Arop and Tolokiwa are the exchange of wooden bowls for pigs or dogs. These islanders also occasionally purchase Siassi canoes. In the only reported transaction I have for Sakar Island, two Mandok men first exchanged pots for taro at Kabip, and then traded the taro for two dogs on Sakar.

THE GEOGRAPHIC PATTERN
OF SIASSI VOYAGING

Sailing biographies elicited by Sahlins from twenty-three Mandok men elucidate the geographic pattern of Mandok trading voyages (Table 5). Unfortunately, similar information is not available to supplement the statements of informants of the other island groups. Certain major differences and similarities, however, may be inferred. In general, Mandok and Aramot have curtailed long-distance sailing in favor of canoe and bowl manufacture combined with shorter voyages, leaving long-distance trade, particularly with the mainland, to the Tuams and Malais. Long trips are still undertaken, however, either in newly completed canoes before they are sold or more usually in vessels hired from Tuam or Malai owners. The Tuam and Malai Islanders, then, are currently the most active sailors, and my impression is that Malai voyaging is the more far-ranging.

According to the information provided by the sailing biographies, Mandok traders visit New Britain twice as often as the mainland (see Table 5, below). Prevailing weather patterns as well as the nature of the commodities exchanged at various points, rather than distance alone, determine the varying frequencies of voyages. For example,

TABLE 5
NUMBER OF TIMES LOCALITIES VISITED
FOR TRADE BY TWENTY-THREE MANDOK MEN

Locality	Number of times*	Approx. distance from Mandok Island†
New Britain		
Kalingi	84	35
Barriai	8	56
Talasea	1	200
South coast and		
Arawe Islands	51	75
Total	144	
Islands		
Arop	10	64
Sakar	7	33
Tolokiwa	14	50
Total	31	
Mainland (of New Guinea)		
Finschhafen Coast	37	32–56
Tami Islands	14	58
Sio	4	46
Gitua	10	37
Sialum	4	34
Rai Coast	4	50–100
Total	73	
Western Strait		
Madang	1	160
Karkar Island	1	162
Total	2	

* Strictly speaking, these numbers refer not to voyages but to the number of times the informants described visits to the particular localities listed. In some cases these men were fellow voyagers and hence are describing the same trips. Most of the voyages were made since 1945.

† In miles.

from Tuam Island, Kalingi in New Britain is about forty miles away, while Sio and Sialum on the mainland are forty-seven and thirty-two miles, respectively. The Tuams acquire pots at Sio, Gitua, and Sialum, which may be taken away in sufficiently large quantities at a time to make only one or two trips per year necessary. It will also be recalled that the *kunai* coast on which the pot makers live does not produce exchangeable surpluses of food. In Kalingi, on the other hand, the Siassis regularly receive taro and sweet potato for pots and bowls (and coconuts formerly). Prevailing winds and currents also play a part in determining the greater frequency of trips to New Britain. The Tuams may cross to Umboi, work their way up the east coast of the island, and then wait for favorable breezes to take them speedily across the fifteen miles of water between Umboi and the New Britain Coast. Crossing the Vitiaz Strait to the mainland is more limited seasonally. In fair weather a crossing is possible at almost any time during the Southeast season; the problem, however, is getting back. Hence, voyages are restricted to the change of seasons—e.g., November-December —when southeasterly and northwesterly winds may alternate in quick succession.

SEQUENCES OF TRANSACTIONS—THE PROFITS OF OVERSEAS TRADE

Overseas trade is rewarding for the Siassis. The profits of trade can be appreciated not only in absolute terms, in the frequent surpluses of pigs and taro provided by the operations of overseas and local exchange, but in the returns of specific types of exchanges or transactional sequences.

The inputs of labor necessary to sustain trade—in canoe building, net making, fishing, sailing, and even dancing (see the next section)—may seem to be high, not to mention the risks inherent in voyaging. Nevertheless, there are long periods of inactivity when weather conditions prohibit sailing, and also the considerable amounts of time the Siassis annually devote to visiting in host communities. The Siassi trader spends much of his life sitting, smoking or chewing betel, and chatting amiably with his fellows at home or abroad. While there are some data to indicate the average amounts of labor (in man-hours or man-days) necessary to produce the various products entering trade, I have no statistics to show whether on the whole the average Siassi householder performs more or less man-days of labor per year than his counterpart among the village horticulturists. The varied nature of Siassi activities makes comparisons difficult. The Siassi housewife, certainly, is not overworked: she sews pandanus mats, collects shellfish, cooks, and tends her children. If it is not more work, life for men in Siassi is more complex, dangerous, and exciting than among the horticulturists.

Figure 4. Overseas Transactions in Pigs, Dogs, Bowls, and Pots

		SIASSI EXPORTS			
		PIGS	DOGS	BOWLS	POTS
SIASSI IMPORTS	PIGS		New Guinea mainland	New Britain, mainland, Arop	New Britain, Arop
	DOGS			New Britain, Arop	New Britain, Arop
	BOWLS		Tami Islands		Mandok and Aramot bowls for Malai and Tuam pots
	POTS		Sio, Gitua, Rai Coast, Tami Islands	Sio, Gitua, Rai Coast	

There are a number of characteristic transactions or sequences of transactions, involving one or more voyages, by which the returns of trade are realized in the desired forms. The over-all result of these sequences is to maintain a centripetal flow of pigs focused on the Siassi Islands. While other kinds of goods reach Siassi only to pass on to other points, the bulk of imported pigs have reached their final destination. Some are converted into taro on Umboi Island, and a few may be reinvested in trade, but most are consumed (Malai and Tuam must export pigs as payment for canoes; Aramot and Mandok pay pigs for canoe timber). Some of the transactional sequences by which pigs are acquired may be outlined as follows:

Pots-bowls-dogs-pigs form a series of ascending values, difficult to calibrate precisely because of the differing sizes and qualities of the items themselves, and because of local variation in value. By taking advantage of these variations, the Siassis are able to convert items of least value—pots—into the objects of greatest value—pigs. Thus, the exchange of pots and bowls for pigs in New Britain, or for dogs, which are exchanged for pigs on the mainland, are standard transactions.

(a) 10 pots (or less) or 1 large bowl $\longrightarrow$ pig *or* dog $\longrightarrow$ pig
(New Britain) (mainland)

There are four items in the series, and therefore sixteen possible kinds of simple transactions. The exchanges of pigs for pigs, pots for pots, and so on, occur only internally—within the communities. Transactions involving the export of pigs to acquire dogs, pots, or bowls would occur rarely, if at all. The transactions that do occur are shown in Figure 4.

Pig producing sequences of transactions that involve other kinds of goods may be outlined as follows:

(b) 2 boars' $\longrightarrow$ 3 bowls $\longrightarrow$ 2 pigs (+ 3–4 years = 2 pigs
tusks   + 4 tusks)
(Tami Is.)   (New Britain)

At Tami a boars'-tusk pendant is converted into three or more bowls, which are exchanged for two pigs in New Britain. These are consumed after they have produced two sets of tusks, with which exchange may be initiated again, this time for twice the amount of bowls and pigs, and so on. The same kind of transaction, only with pots, could also occur. (That it is less likely to occur now is indicated by the statement of a Sio man: "They offer the rubbish of the pig they have eaten and want big pay. We are finished with that. If they want to bring a pig they can get big pay.")

As interesting as this transactional sequence appears, it was probably not too important. Assuming that male pigs are acquired, it takes at least three or four years to produce recurved tusks, during which time the pigs must be fed vegetable food, which is in short supply in Siassi. A large bowl or a dozen or two pots, while enough to buy a young boar, could never command a boar bearing curved tusks.

(c) boars' tusks $\longrightarrow$ dogs'-teeth headband $\longrightarrow$ 1 dog $\longrightarrow$ 1 pig
    (mainland)   (New Britain)   (mainland)

(d) 1 pig $\longrightarrow$ 5–10 pkts. of sago $\longrightarrow$ 50–100 pots $\longrightarrow$ 5–10 pigs
    (Umboi)   (Sio-Gitua)   (New Britain)

(e) 1 pig $\longrightarrow$ 50 pounds red ochre $\longrightarrow$ 50 pots $\longrightarrow$ 5 pigs
    (Tarawe)   (Sio-Gitua)   (New Britain)

(f) 10 mats $\longrightarrow$ 1 pig
    (mainland)

(g) 10 mats $\longrightarrow$ 10 pots $\longrightarrow$ 1 pig
    (Sio-Gitua)   (New Britain)

(h) 6–12 $\longrightarrow$ 3 pots $\longrightarrow$ 1 block $\longrightarrow$ 10 pots $\longrightarrow$ 1 pig
    coconuts   obsidian
    (Sio-Gitua) (Kalingi)   (Sio)   (New Britain)

(i) 20–40 coconuts $\longrightarrow$ 10 pots $\longrightarrow$ 1 dog $\longrightarrow$ 1 pig
    (Sio-Gitua)   (New Britain)   (mainland)

The stupendous gains made in these transactions (d, e, h, i) are readily apparent. It is also apparent that quite apart from whatever uses are made of pots by the various groups who secure them in trade—as wealth-objects or only as cooking vessels—they play an especially critical role in overseas exchange. Pots are the link between the high-value series of pot-bowl-dog-pig and low-value items such as sago, mats, coconuts, obsidian, and red ochre.

As already noted, cooking pots are distributed from three widely separated locations on the mainland. No pottery is manufactured in the archipelago, and people there who receive pots via the Siassis (and earlier the Tamis) previously were not even aware that clay pots are man-made products. Rather, they were regarded as exotic products of the sea. Whether the nonpottery people originated this belief is uncertain. The Siassis, however, elaborated and helped to sustain such beliefs, as everyone has since learned. Their story was that pots are the shells of deep-water mussels. The Sios make a speciality of diving for these mussels and, after eating the flesh, sell the empty "shells" to the Siassis. The deception, if it added to their value, was justified by the vital part that pots have in overseas trade.

The rate of ten pots for one pig, which appears in the transactions above, is conservative and probably an overestimate for the early days. It is based on statements that normally two baskets of pots—two of the long coconut leaf baskets containing four to six assorted pots—are equivalent to a pig in New Britain. Even today, however, only two large vessels, especially of the more valuable "Madang" type, are equivalent to a piglet.

The profits associated with the transactional sequences vary, as do the number of voyages and the distances traversed in carrying them out. This variation is summarized in Table 6.

TABLE 6

NUMBER OF VOYAGES IN
CERTAIN TRANSACTIONS

Transactions	Returns	No. of Voyages	Total Distance*
b	2 pigs + 4 tusks	2	200–275
c	1 pig	3	280–350
d	5–10 pigs	3	200–300
e	5 pigs	3	230–320
f	1 pig	1	65–200
g	1 pig	2	180–270
h	1 pig	4	360–450
i	1 pig	3	280–370

* Air miles from Tuam Island, round-trip.

Now one may ask, for example, why are the Siassi traders led to undertake two overseas voyages in order to convert mats into pigs, as in (g) (ten mats → ten pots → one pig), when mats can be exchanged directly for pigs on the mainland (f)? The answer to this question exposes an important underlying condition of overseas trade.

The Siassis are out for pigs. Dogs, pots, bowls, boars' tusks, dogs'-teeth valuables, strings of shell beads—things valued highly by the people of the Vitiaz Strait—are to the Siassis of instrumental value in attaining this objective. Pigs, however, are the supremely valued object in all of these societies. Their tusks are as good as gold, their mandibles are hung as trophies in the clubhouse, breastplates of dogs' teeth are styled "tongues of pigs." Pigs buy wives, they satisfy important social obligations and needs, and they are the *sine qua non* of any important festive occasion or ritual event. Local pig production is geared to the needs of local ceremonial cycles. Transactions in pigs are not initiated without substantial cause, and they are not carried through easily. No community of the Vitiaz Strait specialized in the production of pigs for sale. Even today the mere offer of five to ten pounds, the price of a grown pig, does not insure a purchase. A village may have a hundred pigs on hand, but their owners are bound by previous social commitments, and even unborn litters may be so committed. It is easier to obtain a pig in downtown New York or Chicago than in a New Guinea village.

The Siassis are not horticulturists and therefore do not breed pigs. Their ceremonial cycle depends on the output of other communities. The tactics of Siassi trade are designed to tap these pig supplies, the production and distribution of which are enmeshed in local social relations and ritual requirements. Therefore, they employ a variety of techniques and maintain many "trade roads" along which they supply the goods most valued in particular locales in order to pry loose, so to speak, a quantity of pigs. In addition, the Siassis have inserted themselves into local ceremonial events, serving as guest or hired performers on precisely those occasions when local pig supplies are assembled, displayed, and distributed. Even so they are not always successful, for Mandok sailing biographies recount a number of instances in which voyagers for pigs reached their destination and found none available. On such occasions the traders continue to other points, accept other goods, or return empty-handed to wait for another time.

The reason for carrying on a variety of transactions which vary substantially in their returns is now clear. Because of the difficulties to be overcome in obtaining pigs, any transactional sequence that produces pigs is considered well worth the effort.

SIASSI DANCERS

The Siassi Islanders are famed as dancers. "Die Siassi-Inseln sind für Neu-Guinea die Hochschule der Tanzkunst," wrote Neuhauss (1911, I, 73). They share some of their dancing complexes or *singsings*—dances, songs, and distinctive regalia—with mainland peoples, such as the Sios, and other complexes, such as the *singsing* known as *tumbuan,* with New Britain. Dances are sometimes sold, either *in toto* or as elements which can be incorporated in an existing dance complex of the purchasing group. Thus, an extremely popular dramatic performance involving mimicry of the behavior of dogs which has been incorporated in a Sio dance is said to have been acquired from Arop Island. Recently the Sios were invited by an influential man of Wewak village (in the Sepik District; a woman from this village is married at Sio) to come to his village at Christmas time, 1965, to perform and teach the villagers one of the Sio dances. Besides a round of feasts, the host intended to bear the considerable expense of ship passage for the Sio party traveling to Wewak.

Apart from the recent borrowing or purchase of dances, the Siassis or other groups do not manufacture or create new dances in order to sell them. Rather, the Siassis are frequently called upon to perform old favorites by the communities with which they trade. A local big-man planning a festival may invite a group of Siassis to perform the main dance of his festival. The dancers are rewarded with gifts of food and pigs, and normal trading transactions occur at the same time. Even when trade rather than an invitation to dance is the reason for a Siassi visit, it would be a rare occasion if a *singsing* were not held. For the most part, therefore, the exchanges of overseas trade take place in a festive atmosphere.

Through their performances as dancers, the Siassi traders participate in the ceremonial life of host communities, and there is evidence suggesting the diffusion of Siassi ceremonial forms and paraphernalia following upon this practice. The social anthropologist Todd, who studied the islanders of Möwehafen in southern New Britain, concluded that a circumcision ritual practiced there had been borrowed from Siassi. The general practice of the Möwehafen Islanders is to introduce children (boys and girls) of high rank to the men's clubhouse during infancy. The ceremony involved reciting the various structural parts of the clubhouse, and is concluded with a presentation of gifts and the killing of a pig. Todd's own account continues:

Circumcision is general amongst these people, and in the ordinary course of affairs any old woman may perform the operation a short time after the child's birth, but for the sons of headmen or of other important people the operation is sometimes postponed until they are much older, and is then carried out with an elaborate ceremonial. This is not, I believe, native to Möwehafen, but belongs to the culture of the more western parts of the coast, and has very probably been acquired from Siassi [Todd, 1934, p. 203].

The ethnographer adds:

The bullroarer, though known, is not used in Möwehafen, and it is my belief that its use in the west at Arawe is largely "empirical." According to the statements of several informants, however, it plays a large part in the ritual life of the Siassi natives, and furthermore, I was told that it had been borrowed from them by the Arawe people —a result of their contact through trading voyages [*ibid.*, p. 203, n. 16].

The Arawe Islands are the eastern terminus for regular Siassi voyaging to southern New Britain, Siassi imports normally being forwarded to such places as Möwehafen by the Arawe traders. At times, however, the Siassis did visit Möwehafen. In 1909, when the Hamburg Expedition visited Bugi, one of the islands off Möwehafen, there was a celebration in progress. The anthropologist Reche recorded that "On the beach of the island lay numerous canoes of guests who had come to the celebration; guests had appeared from . . . the Arawe Islands and from Siassi" (1954, p. 51). According to the same author, the purpose of the festival was the circumcision of a chief's son. In his diary, the artist Vogel-Hamburg described the Siassi and Arawe dancers as they were donning their costumes for the *singsing*, which was almost certainly the popular Siassi dance named *sia*, the dance of the white cockatoo (Vogel-Hamburg, 1911, pp. 150–57).

The diffusion of Siassi ceremonial forms, whether limited to Möwehafen or on a more extensive scale (where, for example, did the Sios learn *sia?*) would tend to reinforce the demand for Siassi services as performers. Much of the time, visiting Siassi traders are accorded hospitality gratis. At other times, as it were, they sing for their supper.

UMBOI ISLAND—THE LOCAL TRADE SPHERE

The account of Siassi trading given thus far is not complete, for the overseas system hinges upon local economic relations with nearby Umboi Island. From Umboi via trade come great cedar logs that are used to fashion the hulls and planks of the sailing canoes. The several thousand taro producers of Umboi provide the islanders with supplies of their staple for daily and ceremonial needs, and they constitute the principal market for Siassi imports, such as wooden bowls and pottery. Umboi also provides the fiber for the

Siassi fish nets; tobacco and betelnut; and red ochre, exchanged by the Siassis overseas, comes from the central part of the Kovai area of eastern Umboi—the villages of Tarawe and Obangai.

Geographic Pattern of Siassi-Umboi Relations

Siassi imports find their way to all of the Umboi villages, just as products received by the Siassis come from all parts of Umboi. Siassi relations with some of the Umboi villages, however, are more intensive than with others. The fundamentals of trade have not altered during the past half-century. There have been marked changes, however, in the pattern of the spread of Siassi exchange links on Umboi. These changes may be grouped in three stages or periods:

1. *Aboriginal Period.* The most intensive relations were with the Kaimanga villages of Yangla and Gauru. These communities were (and still are) located near the downstream portions of two rivers with outlets at the southern tip of Umboi Island, opposite Mandok and Aramot. The Siassi canoes were able to move up these rivers to trading sites near the villages. Trading was conducted from the moored canoes. At this time the bulk of imported taro and canoe timber came from these villages.

On the western side of Umboi, relations with the Kovai were mediated by Sampanan, a Kovai beach village, and the coastal Paramots, who at this time were overseas traders. The interior Kovai were despised and feared by the Siassis, and in turn the "wild men" avoided contact with the islanders.

Direct trade with the Kovai side of Umboi was thus limited to two outlets, Sampanan in the south and the Paramot-Tarawe route to the sea farther north. Siassi imports were spread by internal exchange. For example, Tarawe village transmitted wooden bowls, pots, pigs, and dogs to villages to the north—Arot, Gasam, Mararamu, Oropot—for such goods as betelnut, rope for making pig hunting nets, finished hunting nets, and bamboo suitable for making combs and sewing sago-leaf roofing.

In 1888, Ritter Island,[8] lying in Dampier Strait, which separates Umboi from New Britain, exploded in a volcanic eruption that sent a tidal wave crashing against the north-eastern shores of Umboi Island. A village on the northwest tip of Umboi, since resettled and named Mantagen, was wiped out. The survivors of the wave at Kabip and Kamba-lap, with whom the Siassis had direct relations, moved in-land, but later their villages were re-established on or near the coast. As devastating as this tidal wave was, on Umboi and also the opposite New Britain shore, there was only a temporary disruption of trading.

2. *Ca. 1900–45.* Eastern New Guinea was a part of the German Empire from 1884 until 1914, when Australia assumed control. It was not until the first and second decades of the present century that a measure of administrative control was established over Siassi-Umboi. Pacification led to a spread of direct trade relations to include all of the villages of Umboi.

Mandok established close ties with the southern Kovai village of Gomlongon, and a few Kovai women moved to Mandok in marriage.[9] Other Kovai villages as well sought access to the sea in order to establish beach market sites and direct trading with the Siassis.

3. *1945-Present.* In the early years of World War II, as the great Pacific war was developing around them, the Aramots and Kaimanga people had a war of their own. The immediate cause of the conflict was the poaching of Yanglan sago by the islanders, as it had been in the past. Trading was suspended, but at that point the Japanese and a greater conflict came to Siassi-Umboi. After World War II, as dam-

---

[8] Ritter Island was about 2,600 feet high before the eruption; now it rises to only 350 feet (AGS, 1943, p. 65). The island was in eruption when Dampier passed by it in 1700.

[9] The Mandoks date the development of close relations with Gomlongon to German times (1884–1914); middle-aged Gomlongon informants specify the same time—the generation of their grandfathers.

age claims were being computed and paid in New Guinea, the Siassis made their own reparations in the form of a pig, a large bowl, and strings of shell beads, and trade between Kaimanga and Siassi was reopened.

Trade with the southern Kaimanga area, however, soon suffered a more permanent setback. Taro harvests failed, as they have continued to do up to the present time. Whether the cause is parasites or exhaustion of soil fertility is not clear. Among the people concerned, the continued failure of the taro plantings is attributed to Siassi sorcery, and the Yanglans recently employed a Kalingi garden magician to cleanse the soil of magical infection.

Yangla and Gauru still supply the Siassis with yams, sweet potatoes, and bananas, but while these foods satisfy dietary needs, they do not meet Siassi ceremonial requirements. Consequently, in the postwar period there has been a major shift in trade relations from the Kaimanga to the Kovai taro producers. The exchange of pots, pigs, dogs, bowls, and fish for taro is carried on most intensively with the southern Kovai villages of Tarawe, Gomlongon, Opai, and Sampanan.

To summarize these changes briefly, in early times the Siassi Islanders had direct relations with the Kaimanga villages and were connected with the large Kovai region through exchange at two coastal outlets, Sampanan and Paramot. With pacification, direct relations developed with all the communities of Umboi Island. Finally, the failure of taro production among the Kaimanga led to a shift in trade relations from the eastern to the western, or Kovai, side of the island.

It may be that 1964 marks a fourth stage in Siassi-Umboi trade. In that year the government established a weekly market at Barang in the central part of the Kovai area. In time the Barang market may lead to another major restructuring of trade relations, but such possibilities are better discussed in the later chapter devoted to change in the trade system as a whole.

LOCAL TRADING

We may distinguish three aspects of local trading from the Siassi point of view: (1) the exchange of fish for taro for daily subsistence needs; (2) the exchange of pots, pigs, bowls, and dogs for large lots of taro for ceremonial needs; and (3) the provision of fiber and timber to maintain Siassi capital equipment—fish nets and canoes.

Trade in Timber

The Aramot and Mandok canoe makers depend on the Kaimanga and Kovai villagers to cut and drag to the beach large logs suitable for hulls and planks. The Umboi villagers plant "canoe trees," which are regarded as a highly valuable resource. The labor involved in cutting and transporting logs two to three feet in diameter and sixty or more feet long is enormous, and for this reason big-men, who can call up the workers of a village and provide the necessary feasts, are usually in charge. The Siassis take delivery at the beach. The log may be roughly shaped at the ends, after which a crude outrigger attachment is fitted on and the whole assembly is poled along the coast. Alternatively, the log is towed by a canoe. The log must be transported, fashioned into a hull, and the hull cured for six months to a year. When the canoe is finally completed and exchanged for pigs on Malai, Tuam, Arawe, or elsewhere, the Umboi lumberjacks are paid. The traditional payment for a sailing canoe is three pigs. It seems, however, that often this is merely the basic part of the payment. The three pigs are said to pay for the two prows and the mid-section of the canoe. According to Tolo-kiwan informants, a piglet or dog was also given for the outrigger; and it appears that such goods as dogs' teeth, boars' tusks, pots, and dogs were often provided in addition to the three pigs. In any case, the timber cutters' share of the payment consisted of one large pig.

The fish nets of the Siassis are made from bark fiber which is supplied only by the Kaimanga people. Approximately one hundred rolls of bark strips are required to make the twine for an average fish net. This amount is equivalent to a pig. According to Mandok informants, most of their bark material is acquired from Kambalap.

Trade in Taro

In the traditional markets, which were held two or three times per week, the Siassis exchanged smoked or fresh fish and shellfish for taro. Before village coconut plantations were established by the Umboi Islanders, coconuts were also exchanged at the rate of four nuts (one "rope") for a basket of taro. A third item was the pandanus mat, worth a basket or leaf packet of taro. Markets are held less frequently than in the past, and, as we will see in Chapter IX, rates of exchange have altered in favor of the taro growers.

Today, as in the past, definite units are employed in the exchange of large lots of taro for pots, pigs, bowls, and dogs, and also coconuts. The Siassis, Kaimanga, and Kovai count taro in multiples of five up to one hundred taro, which form a "load" (N-M *lod*), and beyond that in loads or units of one hundred. In Siassi the unit of five is *dir;* in Kovai the word for one also means "a one" of five taro. Thus:

munogon	= one	= one unit of 5 taro	= *dir ez*
lale	= two	= one unit of 10 taro	= *dir ru*
alve	= three	= one unit of 15 taro	= *dir tol*
ile	= four	= one unit of 20 taro	= *dir pang*
ponon	= five	= one unit of 25 taro	= *dir lim*

In Kovai a "load" is termed *ai munogon* (*ai* = "man," "twenty"), while in Siassi it is *dir tamot* (*tamot* = "man"). Pots, pigs, dogs, and bowls are counted singly, but coconuts may also be made up in loads consisting of twenty "ropes" (eighty nuts). There is also a tendency to refer to two bowls as "one." By the traders' account, this usage stems from the fact that two bowls are cut from a single segment of a log which is split down the center.

Rates of exchange work out as follows:

1 load of taro (100)	= 1 piglet
	1 wooden bowl
	1 "Madang" pot
	1 dog
	1 load (80) coconuts
2 loads of taro (200)	= 1 six-month-old pig
	1 hunting dog
5 loads of taro (500)	= 1 large pig
10 loads of taro (1,000) or more	= 1 large boar with curved tusks

More or less the same rates are given everywhere, but it is important to observe that informants qualify their statements in one crucial respect: the rates that obtain in a given transaction depend on the social relationship of the parties to the exchange. Thus, the Kovai say (in Neo-Melanesian) that rates of exchange vary according to whether the island partner is a *pren nating* (acquaintance), a *pren tru* (good friend), or *bisnis* (a relative).

Petty transactions in fish and taro and the large-scale transactions involving wealth-objects occur in the same places and often simultaneously. The description of a market held on the southwest coast of Umboi between Gomlongon and Mandok Island (in July, 1964) will illustrate the two aspects of local trade.

The meeting was prearranged. On the morning of the scheduled market, and all the day before, a procession of women transported taro to the beach, a ninety-minute walk from Gomlongon. The appointed spot was the beach site belonging to Opai village, rather than Gomlongon's beach further along the coast. One Siassi canoe appeared just before noon. This canoe, with five crewmen, was nosed into the sand, and the exchange of fish and taro began immediately. On board this canoe there was an Aramot Islander carrying a large wooden bowl, a small pot, and a dog. This man later left the beach for the interior with his goods, though the pot was sold on the beach for tobacco.

A second canoe arrived a half hour later and pulled up alongside the first one. Here again exchange commenced immediately. A crowd of chattering Kovai women waded into the water, placed several taros on the platform of the canoe, and eagerly held up their hands for several small fish in return. Each woman made a half-dozen or more dashes from her taro basket on the beach to the canoe, and the exchange was completed in less than fifteen minutes.

In these exchanges there was hardly any discussion of the transactions themselves, though the women chattered and yelled incessantly. Two or three Siassi men squatted silently toward the rear of the canoe platforms doling out handfuls of fish each time several taro were placed before them. In both cases, a Gomlongon man mounted the canoe platform, overlooked the exchange, and occasionally relayed instructions to the women. There was no haggling as such. A few times women were told to bring more taro, and the men tried to hurry the proceedings (the women were already running). Fish was exchanged first, then shellfish which had been removed from the shell. Each canoe ultimately received a half-dozen small baskets of taro for an equal number of baskets of fish and shellfish. Some of the shellfish was left over and was taken back home by the Mandoks. One packet of lime was also traded for tobacco.

The main purpose of this meeting was not to exchange fish for taro, but to deliver large lots of taro in return for promised pigs. While the initial exchange of fish and taro was going on, large leaf packets of taro, weighing twenty-five to forty pounds each, were being piled up in groups of five and ten on the beach. Thirty of these packets, totaling about one-half ton of taro, were loaded on the canoes by some of the men, while others discussed the transactions and decided upon future meetings. The entire proceeding lasted about an hour, and the canoes departed immediately.

Normally, the large-scale transactions are organized in

this way. The taro, one or two "loads" at a time, is given first, with the promised pigs, bowls, dogs, or pots being delivered at some later meeting. The Aramot Islander mentioned above brought his goods in advance, and in return for the bowl, pot, and dog he was seeking tobacco, cash, or some combination of the two.

The Umboi villagers dislike the credit aspect of these transactions, and they are fully aware that the islanders often promise goods to several Umboi trade-friends at once, thus creating obligations which they cannot possibly meet within a reasonable period of time. My suggestion to Kovai villagers that they threaten to cut off the supply of taro was hardly greeted with applause as an original or workable solution to the problem. If the taro is not given, the precious pots and bowls which are necessary for bridewealth and payments to affines are unobtainable.

Occasionally, by prior agreement between trade-friends, an Umboi villager plants a plot of taro for an island friend. Terms are not decided beforehand. When the plot is ready to be harvested, the gardener indicates what type of payment—pigs, dogs, pots, or bowls—he wants. Corresponding to this practice is the belief in Sio that "our pots are worth whole gardens on Umboi."

TRADE AND KINSHIP

In local exchange of fish for taro, it is advantageous to deal with kinsmen. After all, how could a Kovai woman be niggardly with her taro when exchanging with a brother, and would not he in turn reserve the best fish for her? The Kovai traders say that good friends receive better terms in the large-scale transactions involving pigs, pots, bowls, dogs, and taro, but in these transactions can a kinsman also expect favored treatment? It appears that often he cannot, that in fact it is more advantageous and convenient to deal with trade-friends than with relatives.

The transactions which occurred at the market on Opai beach illustrate the kind of difficulties that arise in dealings among kin. The two Mandok canoes brought men representing two men's houses, Simban and Tavopu. The men from Simban and Tavopu who dealt with trade-friends received two or more loads of taro on the promise to return pigs in the future. On the other hand, two young brothers of Simban, whose mother is from Gomlongon, came away with only half of the taro they wanted, and, in addition, they were subjected to humiliation in the process. Addressing them, a Gomlongon man delivered a lengthy harangue on the morality of trading obligations. This stemmed from an earlier transaction in which the Gomlongon man had turned over to them a load of taro on their pledge to pay a dog which thus far had not been forthcoming. By way of explanation for my benefit, the man said: "I must be angry with them now, but later I will give them the taro they want. These men are half-castes, but supposing their mother were not from Gomlongon, I would give them nothing." On the contrary, it seems that balking is less likely to occur in exchange between trade-friends, and certainly nonrelatives would not submit to the kind of treatment that the two "half-castes" received.[10]

Trade-friendship depends on the two parties meeting their obligations, on a special performance of duty. Kinship relations, on the other hand, are composed of varied obligations and interests, and default in trade specifically does not sever the ties. One can take advantage of kinsmen and get away with it. Trading with relatives, therefore, may be burdensome for either side. The islander may extend his credit indefinitely. On the opposite side, a bush relative may withhold his taro, or ask for bowls and pots as a kinship due. It is good to have kinsmen in faraway places, but it is better to have good trade-friends.

[10] A few Gomlongon women have married at Mandok, but island women are not sent in marriage to the Kovai area. Marriage between Umboi men and Siassi women is by no means prohibited, but it is likely that if such marriages should occur, residence would be in the islands.

VII

The Economics of Status and Group Relations in Siassi and Kovai Society

BEYOND THE OPERATIONS and movements of trade itself is the consumption or use of the various commodities acquired in exchange. The economics of consumption does not form a proper part of the studies of economists concerned with our own society, presumably because the rules governing distribution within the household and family spheres, the consuming units, differ radically from the rules characterizing the market sphere, the main subject of formal economics. Consumption cannot be taken for granted and ignored when we come to study the unfamiliar societies of northeastern New Guinea. The demand for goods provided by trade stems from certain institutions, and values and motives which are an integral part of these institutions; without a consideration of these, the trade system is not intelligible.

The Kovai and Kaimanga villagers of Umboi Island epitomize their relations with the Siassi Islanders in the statement: "We are their parents, we give them food." In their view and that of the Siassis, dependence is mutual, for the latter say of the Umboi villagers: "They originate from us." That is to say, the Siassis provide wooden bowls and clay pots, which are the principal wealth-objects of bridewealth and payments associated with relations established by marriage among the Umboi people, who are thus enabled to produce legitimate offspring in sanctioned unions.

The significance of the Umboi contribution to Siassi life is more than dietary. Some of the pigs coming into Siassi from all directions are diverted to Umboi Island in return for large quantities of taro. This taro, by the canoe load, is destined for special, not ordinary consumption. Under the direction of men who derive their social standing from such activities, the taro is combined with locally produced coconuts in taro puddings, which, together with pigs, are distributed ceremoniously to the men's house groups of the community. Whatever goods may pass through Siassi hands, the returns of trade are counted in taro and pigs, and ultimately in social status. A man who succeeds in trading thereby succeeds in the continuing round of intergroup feasting characterizing life in Siassi. Those who are pre-eminently successful earn the title of *maron*, a man with a name, a leader or big-man. (The Sio cognate *maro* means "great one.") Long-distance trade is thus intimately bound up with local politics; overseas trading expeditions are a part of political strategy.

First, I wish to describe the activities in which the Siassi *maron* is the central figure; this will be followed by a discussion of the marriage payments and affinal exchanges that make up such a large part of traditional life among the Kovai.

THE SIASSI BIG-MAN SYSTEM

Georg Bamler, the first European missionary to work among the Siassi Islanders, was an accomplished linguist and ethnographic observer. In Bamler's view, the big-man system ought to be abandoned, both for practical reasons and because the major features of the system were incompatible with the acceptance of Christianity. The elaborate dances, he said, led to adulterous behavior, quarrels, and fighting, while the large-scale distributions were wasteful and resulted in food shortage and even famine. Though written in a frankly critical and disparaging tone, Bamler's brief published extract (in Chinnery, n.d., pp. 42–45) offers pertinent observations on the economics of status in Siassi society:

> In Siassi, a dancing festival is the necessary part of introduction of a child into the clan; so it forms a definite part of social life. It is incumbent upon a father in Siassi, as a point of honor, to arrange several dancing festivals for each of his children. The more elaborate each festival is, the greater will be the respect paid to the child by the community. Without such festivals, a child has no social status. In considering their obligations towards a person, people say "We have eaten his or her pig", and the liberties and rights allowed to a child are in proportion to the pigs sacrificed by their parents . . . the children whose parents were unable to contribute many pigs may be wronged with impunity, for they are of no importance. The bringing up of young children in Siassi is therefore a very expensive process . . . [p. 43].
>
> A dancing feast . . . gives rise to enormous expense. It requires about 1 ton of taro, thousands of coconuts for the taro puddings, several pigs, betel nuts, tobacco, etc. . . . [p. 44].

The emphasis on the status of the children honored by the feasts is somewhat misplaced; the primary consideration is the status of the adult participants, the child's father or a bigman. In common with many other societies, in Siassi the life cycle has been elaborated and linked with politics in such a way that there are numerous occasions—minor and major rites of passage—on which ceremonial distributions must be provided. This is the principal field of activity for the trader-*maron*, who provides not only for his own children, but sometimes for the ceremonies of others' children. The occasions which call for distributions, particularly the killing of one or more pigs, are the following:

1. At birth, midwives are given a feast.

2. Cutting of a child's ear lobes (generally a ceremonial distribution for the first child only).

3. Donning of a son's first bark loincloth, or a daughter's grass skirt (first child).

4. Initiation into the men's house. A pig for each novitiate is required.

5. A son's first overseas voyage. A pig acquired abroad is distributed to those who greet the youngster on his return.

6. Marriage feasts.

7. Funerary feasts.

While most life-crisis ceremonies are family and kindred affairs, these groups are overshadowed by the men's house (*rumi*), which is the principal unit in large-scale distributions of taro and pigs. The food and pork is distributed by a men's house, led by its *maron,* to the other men's houses of the community. (Tuam, for example, has eight men's houses, Mandok has seven.)

The returns of Siassi trading—taro puddings and pigs— are distributed as part of a competitive potlatching system in which exchange partners, termed *atam,* are the central figures. Lesser men might have *atam,* but for the most part this status is limited to big-men and the other influential senior males of the men's house groups. A big-man's exchange partners are, appropriately, big-men of other house groups. The rites of passage described above provide occasions for competitive distributions involving *atams,* but distributions are made on other occasions as well. Bamler describes this system as follows:

To perpetuate dancing feasts the old people of Siassi invented a custom known as *atam.* There is no appropriate expression for this word in the European language; as near a translation as is possible is the word recompense. Every *pater familias* has a recompenser; he himself is the recompenser of his own recompenser, and the honor, as well as the burden of this office is hereditary. The dancing feasts are prepared as follows:

A native, Aibale, desires to give a feast in honour of his little son, Salum. With the assistance of his neighbors, he prepares all the food necessary; but instead of distributing it himself he sends for his *atam,* Aiwige. Aiwige distributes the food among the gathering of people, and, in doing so, takes over the strict duty in time to come (perhaps after several years) of recompensing his friend and neighbor, Aibale. When the time comes he must return the same number of pigs—and of the same size and condition—the same number of dishes of taro pudding, betelnuts, tobacco, etc., otherwise he will be regarded with contempt by the people. For the food distributed in the name of Aibale, Aiwige is thus indebted and is bound by the custom of recompense. In case of his death before the obligation is fulfilled, the duty falls to his son, and so on, ad infinitum [Chinnery, n.d., p. 44].

While further intensive enthnography must supply the details of Siassi political organization, the main outlines of the big-man system and its relationship to trade are clear. Political motives, arising out of the drive to build a name and win prestige in a context of individual and intergroup competition, form the mainspring of Siassi voyaging and trading. The profits of trade are consumables; they are not reinvested in future enterprise.[1] The prestige won through community-wide distribution of pigs and taro is soon dissipated if it is not supported by additional demonstrations of economic prowess. For the voyager who has set his course for a *maron*-ship, there is no respite from voyaging and trading.

AIBUNG OF MANDOK

If the position of Siassi big-men is founded upon the returns of overseas trade, then the number of voyages a man has undertaken and the number of his overseas "trade roads" (social connections) should provide indices of his social standing in the community. Aibung, a man about forty-five years old, is Mandok's most influential man. His thirty-four voyages outnumber those of other men his age by two to one, and his "trade roads" radiate to the principal overseas

---

[1] Some pigs are used to buy sago and red ochre, which move in overseas trade. The Malai and Tuam Islanders have to give up a large number of pigs to sustain their trading fleets. Nevertheless, the emphasis on consumption is revealed in the statements of Mandok informants that in the old days the Siassis were traders and consumers of pigs, but did not engage in breeding as they do today. Young pigs, easier to manage on long voyages, were raised for slaughter, but mature pigs were slaughtered indiscriminately, females not being preserved for breeding purposes.

communities of the mainland and archipelago. These social links have been formed by intermarriage, migration, and adoption. For example, Aibung's "trade road" to the Arawe Islands was established as follows: His great-great-grand-father, of Kapitumete (Arawe), married and resided at Kalingi. When this man died, his widow remarried and moved to Aramot, taking her son and daughter with her. The daughter, Aibung's father's mother, later married at Mandok. The genealogical links defining Aibung's various "trade roads" are listed below:

Mainland

Tami Islands	Own mother, adopted by Ego's grand-father.
Rakona	Father's father, adopted and raised at Mandok; provides subsidiary roads to other mainland communities, such as Sio.

Archipelago

Kalingi	Mother's great-grandfather (MoFaFaFa) of Ongaia village, Kalingi. Ego's daughter currently married at Kalingi.
Arawe	Father's great-grandfather (FaMoFaFa) of Kapitumete, Arawe.
Sakar	Current connection is the daughter of a Gauru man who lived in Mandok with Ego's FaFa.

Umboi-Siassi

Gauru	Brother of Gauru man above.
Kabip	Current friend is the son of a man "taken care of" by Ego's MoFa.
Tuam	Tami kinsman of Ego's mother residing on Tuam.
Malai	Mother's mother.

It is apparent that in the quest for status, certain social factors confer advantages. Thus, a first-born son has some advantage over his younger brothers, as does a man whose father has numerous trade roads. Aibung is the first of six brothers, and his kindred is scattered from New Guinea to New Britain—his mother was born in the Tami Islands, his father's father at Rakona, his father's mother in Kalingi. Nevertheless, it seems probable that such factors are outweighed by personal qualities of ambition and industry. Aibung certainly has these, as well as far-flung genealogical connections. My firm impression, based on repeated discussion of these matters with people from Siassi and Sio, is that where there is the will to trade, so to speak, distant social links or trade roads will not be found wanting (see Chap. VIII).

KOVAI BRIDEWEALTH
AND AFFINAL EXCHANGE

The Kovai village is composed of a number of local patrilineages interrelated by kinship and marriage. The lineage or *ulum* is a named, exogamous, and land owning group. Each *ulum* owns scattered blocs of land, usually including beach tracts, a men's clubhouse (also termed *ulum*), and groups of sacred stones located in or near present and former village sites. The *ulum* takes its name from the small bloc of village land on which its clubhouse is located (or was located on a previous village site). The lineage has a depth of four to six decedent generations (there are kin terms from the fifth ascending generation).

The southern Kovai village of Gomlongon, with a population of three hundred, including about seventy adult men, is composed of ten lineages. Genealogical information for five of these shows that male members (excluding small boys) number six for the smallest and fifteen for the largest group, the *ulum* of the leading man (*us*) of the community. Some groups include one or more small affiliated segments. In such cases the group's men's house is said to have "two doors." Informants also related that an *ulum* that grows large (and is probably near the point of fission) is apt to have a clubhouse with two doors. Accounts of past lineage segmentation mention the abduction of a girl within the *ulum* as the precipitating event. By its nature, of course, this act signifies the completion of a gradual process of fission. The *ulum* splits, one group founds a new clubhouse, and the segments reorder their relations as independent lineages, which may now exchange wives.

The Kovai practice both the junior levirate and sororate. In instances where there is no younger brother or lineage mate for a widow to marry, it is considered appropriate for her to wed a father's sister's son of her deceased husband, i.e., a son of a woman of her husband's lineage. In the sororate a deceased wife's older sister is prohibited, for she is termed *luamin,* "mother-in-law." Kinship terminology is generational. There is, however, an optional (and reciprocal) term, *ŋasin,* for mother's brother and sister's son.

The *ulum* receives wives from other groups in the village or from without, and it functions as a unit in the collection of bridewealth payments.[2] Each lineage thus has a proprietary interest in wealth-objects—principally pots and bowls —which are given and received in affinal exchanges, and an interest as well in maintaining the trade connections with Siassi, through whom these goods are obtained. A census revealed that a group of three brothers in Gomlongon owned twenty-six pots and twenty carved bowls, including Madang, Sio, and Huon Gulf pots, and both Tami and Siassi bowls. (It is probable that the current household stocks of pots are smallest at Sio, where they are manufactured, larger in Siassi, the distribution point for the archipelago, and largest of all in the interior villages of Umboi Island.)

Payments and exchanges associated with marriage begin at betrothal and continue until the marriage is dissolved by death. That the system of payments is considered to be

[2] Bridewealth among the Kovai is said to constitute payment for the children that a woman produces for the lineage. In the case of barren women, their work as gardeners and in pig raising, as well as their services in cooking for their husbands' men's house, are emphasized.

burdensome is reflected in the statement of Kovai villagers that "We never finish paying for our wives." There are five main marriage payments or exchanges. Girls are betrothed in adolescence. In a ceremony, the intended groom's father decorates the girl with strings of *tambu* shell or disc beads and turtle-shell bracelets (all Siassi imports) and sends a gift consisting of a bowl or pot to the girl's father. The second payment is for "showing the ladder (of the house)" to the bride-to-be, who at this time resides with her future parents-in-law for a period extending up to a month. When she returns home, a small number of bowls or pots are exchanged for taro and other food with her relatives.

The principal transfer of wealth occurs when the bride takes up residence with her husband. Pigs, dogs, bowls, and pots—ranked in that order—are given for taro in a cere-monious competitive exchange involving a large part of the community as participants and perhaps visitors from other villages as well. The main parties to the exchange are the lineages of the bride and groom, but cognatic kin on both sides are also involved. Men who are sons of women of the groom's lineage, since they are entitled to receive widows of this lineage in the levirate, contribute to the payments and receive part of the gifts from the bride's side of the ex-change. The exchange itself takes place in the center of the village. The bride's group displays a dozen to three dozen large baskets of taro and other foods. Presented to the groom's side, each basket of taro must be reciprocated with a bowl or pot. In addition, pigs and dogs are given specifi-cally to the father of the bride.

The exchange is competitive. If every basket of taro is not matched by the return of a bowl or pot (in any case, the taro must be paid for later on when pots or bowls become available), the bride's side is said to "win" the exchange. If, on the other hand, the groom's side succeeds in providing the equivalent of the taro in bowls and pots, they win. (A recent exchange observed by Rev. James Klein of the Aus-tralian Lutheran Mission was the occasion for a large gather-

ing. Once the proceedings were under way, excitement ran
to a fever pitch. A quarrel that developed over one man's
attempt to participate on both sides of the exchange exploded into fighting and was broken up by Klein himself.)

A fourth payment is made at the birth of the first child.
The mother's classificatory fathers, the men of her lineage,
surround the house during childbirth. Their presence is said
to prevent excessive bleeding and to ward off sorcery directed at the mother or infant. The husband gives bowls and
pots to the men of his wife's lineage for this service. A fifth
and final payment of bowls and pots is given to a woman's
brothers or the nearest surviving kin at her death. Besides
these five transfers, however, there are many additional
transactions. A sister is supposed to help her brothers by
giving them taro, and taro so received is reciprocated by
payment of pots and bowls to the sister's husband.

Nowadays the transfer of bridewealth seldom takes the
form of the traditional public exchanges. The bowls and
pots, and often cash too, are turned over to the bride's
relatives without much ceremony. The Lutheran Mission
has attempted to abolish bridewealth, and failing that, has
suggested an upper limit of five to ten pounds in bridewealth
payments. The Umboi villagers continue to pay for their
wives, even if not according to the old forms. Cash is
increasingly accepted in place of traditional wealth-objects.
Tarawe informants claim, however, that just as there have
been no marriages without bridewealth as yet, no bridewealth payments are composed entirely of money. Rather,
one or two *pus* (five to ten pounds) are frequently added to
the payment of bowls and pots. A Yangla man reported that
he provided twenty-five pounds, ten bowls, and ten pots for
each of his two son's recent marriages.

FURTHER CHANGES

Both the marriage exchanges of the Umboi villagers and
the inter-*atam* exchanges of the Siassis are the principal
fields for competition and rivalry, for the building of status.

In the case of both institutions, rivalrous elements have been largely eliminated in recent times. Younger Kovai men say of large-scale distributions: "We fight over food, and this is no good." They have accepted the missionaries' view that competitive feasting is unchristian and immoral, or has immoral consequences. "There is only one big-man, and his name is God."

Among the Siassis there has been a shift away from the competitive *atam* relationship to an exchange relation termed *baliŋ waro*. A man's *baliŋ waro* might be his mother's brother, and while this exchange partnership calls for the distribution of taro puddings and pigs, it is noncompetitive. Certain evils, say the Siassis, were associated with the rivalrous potlatching carried on by *atam* partners. The pressing demands of exchange obligations led to sharp practice and frequent defaulting in trade with the Umboi villagers, who in turn sought redress by resorting to sorcery. In any case, status rivalry has been eliminated by the absorption of *atam* functions in the noncompetitive *baliŋ waro* relationship.

VIII

The Social Basis of Trade

THE ETIQUETTE governing incessant casual and impersonal encounters of persons who are strangers is taken for granted in complex urban societies. No such etiquette exists in primitive societies. Regularly, however, there are "border mechanisms" which create paths for interaction across tribal boundaries under conditions of peace and personal security. Among such mechanisms, trade-partnerships have been described often in the ethnographic record. In outlining the nature of this institution in general terms, Sahlins also aptly portrays the dynamics of trade-friendship as it is found in the societies of the Vitiaz Strait:

Trade-partnerships, often developed along lines of classificatory or affinal kinship, particularly incapsulate external economic transactions in solidary social relations. Status relations essentially internal are projected across community and tribal boundaries. The reciprocity then may lean over backward, in the direction not of *wabuwabu* [Dobuan sharp practice] but something to the generalized side. Phrased as gift-giving, the presentation admits of delay in reciprocation: a direct return may indeed be unseemly. Hospitality, on another occasion returned in kind, accompanies the formal exchange of trade goods. For a host to give stuff over and above the worth of things brought by his partner is not unusual: it both befits the relation so to treat one's partner while he is traveling and stores up credits. On a wider view, this measure of imbalance sustains the trade partnership, compelling as it does another meeting [1965, p. 155].

It may be best to describe the general features of trade-friendship before examining the social basis of these relationships in greater depth. While much of the discussion refers specifically to Sio, it is generally applicable to the neighboring societies of the Vitiaz Strait.

In an analytical sense, trade-friendships are special-purpose relationships. In reality, however, they present the multifaceted or "functionally diffuse" character of social relations within the community. There is no special ideology that sets apart trade relations from social relations in general. Rather, the conduct of trade-friends is an expression of the social ethic of kinship; it partakes of the qualities of such relationships as father and son, siblings, and mother's brother and sister's son.

There is no special term to distinguish trade-friends—they are termed simply "friend" (Sio *mete*, Komba *buku*). They may be referred to and addressed by kin terms, but normally personal names are used.

Trade-friends visit each other by prearrangement, or they may simply "drop in" unexpectedly. The purpose of some of these visits may be largely social, though social visiting always provides an opportunity for exchange and to arrange future transactions. People are sometimes invited to attend marriage feasts, funerals, and other ceremonies in which their trade-friends are principals. Trade-friends arrange markets or meetings for exchange between their respective communities, and they frequently act as representatives for others who do not meet for exchange. (In fact, people sometimes keep planned trade journeys a secret in order not to be burdened with the business of kinsmen and neighbors.)

Several explicit rules govern the conduct of trade-friends: (1) One acts as host and protector of a visiting trade-friend, and as intermediary if exchanges are conducted with other members of the host's community; (2) it is a serious offense to steal or to attempt to lure away another person's trade-friend. In the old days, a man would attempt to kill an errant trade-friend as well as his new partner; (3) one is obliged to accept graciously a gift given initially or as a return gift; (4) one may make requests for specific goods in advance, or between the time an initial gift is given and a return made. In requesting specific gifts, there is seldom any bargaining, though reciprocity is implied. A man phrases his request as a need; he does not make it explicitly conditional on the gift he may have promised or already handed over. In a sense, gift and countergift, which never change hands simultaneously, are viewed as unconnected acts.

(Trade transactions are not terminologically distinguished by the Sios from ordinary dealings among kinsfolk. The transactions are described with the words *-lua* and *-kai*, "give" and "receive"; *-palua*, "to exchange," does not refer to economic transactions. Two workers, jointly engaged in a task, who exchange tools, or men who exchange bits of newspaper, tobacco, or betelnut *sipalua*, "they exchange"; *-ko* is translated as "buy," and refers to purchases at trade stores [e.g., *iko rais*, "he buys rice"] and to transactions of bridewealth. Time did not permit investigation of the economic terminology of the Siassis.)

Trade-friendships are inherited patrilineally, and sons are normally introduced to their opposites at an early age. Exchange links households, and though male household heads are the principal parties in exchange, their wives or other family members, men or women, carry on the relationships in the event of their death. Children sometimes live for extended periods with families of their parents' trade-friends. Sios have lived in various communities on the Rai Coast and in the outer islands, but only rarely in the mountains. Mountain children, on the other hand, often live for a time at Sio, and several Komba and one Selepet child were living with Sio families in 1964. It is through such visits as youngsters that many people have learned the languages of their trade-friends, but facilitating future trade dealings is not offered as the reason for extended visits.[1] It would be unthinkable to exchange children solely for this purpose, as Neuhauss reports (1911, I, 366).

People meet their obligations to trade-friends because it is to their social and material advantage to do so. In recent years, however, Administration officers sitting as magistrates have occasionally adjudicated disputes arising out of trade and have enforced the payment of debts. The Siassi traders are particularly notorious for defaulting, or for allowing themselves extended credit, and over the years patrol officers in Siassi have dealt with many cases in which Umboi Islanders were seeking to recover debts. Siassi trade contacts and Siassi indebtedness, however, are spread over a wide area, which makes collecting debts by this means extremely difficult. Thus, if creditor and debtor are located in different patrol circuits or jurisdictions, as they often are, it is unlikely that a magistrate will take any action. A Sio man who had given a dogs'-teeth headband to a Siassi friend in return for the promise of a pair of boars' tusks threatened after two years to bring the matter to court. At the same time, he knew that there would be little chance of getting magistrate, defendant, and plaintiff together.

To my knowledge, there is no shame associated with defaulting in trade. Future material interests enforce payment—plainly, good trade-friends are valuable things to have, and people with reputations for being responsible and generous traders are much in demand. One Komba man who is esteemed for his generosity complained that some Sio friends were being intentionally impolite to him. He was very offended: "They want me to visit them, but I am only one man. What do they want me to do, cut off my arms and legs and distribute them around?"

---

[1] Nowadays, children from the interior are sent to Sio to attend school. One older lad, whose father had died, was dispatched to live with his Sio "mother's brother" because of wrangling among his relatives over who was to have responsibility for the boy's upbringing. Some middle-aged informants said that as young men they had spent extended periods at Sio simply on holiday.

There appears to be a considerable amount of dissatisfaction arising out of trade, which is especially noticeable in dealings between Sios and inland friends. This is due in large part to the attempts of some younger Komba and Selepet traders to exact higher payments of cash and trade goods for food and especially tobacco. Even so, dissatisfaction is usually expressed in private grumbling rather than openly. A Komba man complained to me about the small cash payment he received at Sio for tobacco, but when I asked him why he did not complain to his trade-friend, he said: "What he gives to me is up to him. If he wants to give me more he will do so" (cf. rule 3 above). Older men, in general, are content with conventional patterns of exchange —what was good enough for their ancestors is good enough for them.

THE SIO CONCEPT OF KINSHIP

As trade relations are modeled on those of kinship, Sio notions of kinship help to illuminate the nature of trade-friendships.

Sios do not divide their social world into rigid categories of kin and nonkin, friends and enemies. All Sios are kinsmen. The non-Sio world is divided into four groups of people, whose general locations correspond to the cardinal directions: (1) *kumboi* are the mountain people in the south; (2) the *kaboi* are the islanders to the north; (3) *labuna*, the coast dwellers to the west; and (4) *lapoto*, the coastal people to the east. Of these terms, incidentally, only *kumboi* (like its Neo-Melanesian equivalent *bushkanaka*) has a derogatory meaning; a *kumboi* is a rude, unwashed bumpkin.

Often Sios speak of "our bush people" (*maka sema kumboi*), which may convey the patronizing attitude of the coast dwellers toward the bush people and the dominance the coast exerts over the interior. On the other hand, the phrase expresses the interdependence and exclusiveness of relations between particular coastal people and their hinterland. This is expressed in the modern intertribal milieu of the town native quarter or the native laborers' compound. In labor compounds throughout the area, Kombas, Selepets, and Timbes are known as *bush bilong Sio,* or simply as Sio,[2] and when the lines are drawn for conflict, the Sios and their bush brothers combine against the "Sepiks," "Chimbus," or whoever the opponent may be.

The four categories of non-Sios are not thought of as strangers and enemies, but mainly as friends and kinsmen. Aboriginally, *kumboi, kaboi, labuna,* and *lapoto* inhabited the known Sio world. Beyond that were only *nia tamɔta* (literally, place men), "strangers," or, more generally, "unknown beings."[3]

Sios refuse to generalize as to whether they have closer relations with one or another of these groups. As they are quick to point out, individual cases differ—some people have close relations with people of one sector, some with others. (The actual distribution of out-marriages is shown in Table 7, below.)

Interestingly, the four terms are applied within Sio to indicate the predominant ties an individual has with one sector or the other. Thus, depending on one's antecedents and outside relations, Sios are apt to be called *kumboi* or *kaboi.* In joking contexts, the appellation of one of these terms is taken as a mild and humorous insult, which, because of the myriad external ties, can usually be reciprocated on the spot. The Sios' ideology emphasizes their mixed origins and the intermixture that has continued since early times. The Tami and Siassi Islanders express the same views.

The Sio concept of kinship is a flexible one. As in many other New Guinea societies, the notion of descent is not

---

[2] Sio was formerly a main point of embarkation for bushmen leaving home to work as contract laborers. According to Peter Worsley, a patrol officer (personal communication, 1964), the Wain and Naba peoples south of the Sarawaged Range refer to the Komba, Selepet, and Timbe on the opposite side of the range as "Sios."

[3] In mission writings, *nia tamɔta* is used as a synonym for "God" in the sense of First Cause.

strongly developed, and intragenerational ties are emphasized at the expense of cross-generational links. The word for kinship is *se*, also meaning blood. Kinsmen are *se tetu* (one blood). Opposed to kinsmen in the close sense are *se toŋge* (other kin, nonkin) or *mete* (friend). Nonkin are not *ipso facto* strangers or enemies.

Although *se toŋge* means other kin or nonkin, among the people who are referred to as *se toŋge* there are many who are counted as kinsmen. Sio is a small, largely endogamous society, and Firth's observations on Tikopia (population 1,323) fit Sio as well: "Tikopia is too small a community for kinship ties to be entirely lost. . . . Here there are no strangers; there are merely peripheral kinsfolk" (1963, p. 245). In Basakalo village, informants speak of most people as kin (though the genealogical relationships may not be known precisely), the non-Sios are referred to as affines, while a few people are described simply as friends.

There are, of course, degrees of kinship, and these are broadly delimited by genealogical propinquity. People descended from a common pair of great-grandparents (*neŋgusoko*) are close relatives (*se laiti*), too close to marry. Distant relatives are *se maliwai*, less distant kin *se maliwai masa* (kin far somewhat). Usually, however, it is impossible to specify the degree of kinship in these terms by genealogical reckoning alone. Additional potent factors—cooperation, comembership in men's house groups, neighborhood, age-mateship, the sharing of food—often supersede genealogical relationships. Except within a very restricted genealogical sphere (e.g., close agnates), genealogical distance is an unreliable predictor of social distance. For example, one Sio elder proposed this test of social distance, which illustrates the significance of cooperation: "When we ask people for help and they do not come, and when we don't help them, we are no longer *se tetu*. Our children may marry." If closely related persons are obliged to cooperate, it is also true that people who do cooperate are close kin.

FOOD AND KINSHIP

The Sios have very definite ideas about the relationship of food and social relationships. Kinsfolk should and do share food in good times and in bad, and those who forsake their kin during lean periods are "bad people" (*tamɔta s'kamau*). In the opinion of older men—if this is not merely the inevitable assessment of youth by the aged under changing conditions—young married women engage in much less day-to-day sharing than older women. Their explanation is that the young girls today have not learned or taken to heart the proper modes of behavior.

The failure to share food in prescribed ways may lead to more direct action than name calling and ridicule. It was mentioned earlier that when wild pigs are killed in the gardening areas, it is customary to slaughter and share out the pig to all gardeners in the vicinity, whether they took part in the kill or not. On one occasion Urai had charge of distributing such a pig, and perhaps through a simple oversight, he neglected to give a portion to Boto, a classificatory brother who had been gardening nearby. Subsequently, Boto reciprocated in kind. At a later distribution of the same type, in which both men were to be included, Boto made off with Urai's portion in addition to his own. Still later, Boto had charge of a distribution, and he purposely excluded Urai. Afterward Boto publicly taunted Urai in the village, saying that if he had any complaints about his theft and subsequent breach of etiquette, he had no one to blame but himself. Not everyone, of course, would seek redress in this manner.

The giving and sharing of food act powerfully not only to sustain but to create social relationships. This may be illustrated by examining a case involving Sio customs of adoption and exogamy in connection with underlying ideas concerning the social significance of food.

Adoption is frequent in Sio, and it assumes many forms or degrees. Men without male heirs—even bachelors—seek to adopt sons, typically a sister's child. Also, men whose sisters have married and reside away from Sio often adopt one of their children. People without children have a right to ask for and expect to receive a child from siblings. Sometimes adoption is quite formal, as when payments are made by the adoptive parents to the child's parents. Since adoption often takes place between closely related siblings, the payment actually goes to the unrelated spouse (e.g., a sister's husband), and is deemed compensation for the effort expended in previously caring for and sustaining the child. Once the payment is made, the child refers to his original parents as father's sister (*nuŋgutawpi*) and mother's brother (*nuŋguwawa*). In other cases adoption is informal and involves no payment. Through the death, absence, or incompetence of a mother, the responsibility for a child may come to be shared by two households, that of the child's father and that of his father's sister or mother's brother. The child is not fully adopted but is said to be "halfway" between two sets of parents.

In 1963 such a case of "halfway" adoption became the subject of extended debate. A young man who had lived for many years with his father's brother and his wife eloped with the daughter of his adoptive mother's sister. By adoption the couple had common maternal grandparents and the union was considered to be incestuous. On several occasions, heated debates arose among the relatives on both sides, and one of these led to fisticuffs. The anger of the girl's relatives was directed particularly at the young man's adoptive father. In the course of one exchange, this man, in a rather transparent play for sympathy, attempted to set fire to his new house, only to be restrained by a neutral villager. The situation soon cooled to the point where a majority of people were willing to assent to the marriage. It was allowed to stand, though the young man soon departed to work aboard a ship. Compensation was paid to his father's brother, who had been struck and knocked to the ground in a fight, in addition to being subjected to a great deal of verbal abuse, and a peace making feast was provided by the bride's older brother.

On one side of the argument it was pointed out that the young man had not been fully or formally adopted as an infant. But for those who remained opposed to the marriage as being "too close," there was the inalterable fact that the young man's adoptive mother had regularly provided him with food, and therefore she was his own mother (*nana*), whatever one wished to say about the ambiguous status of the man vis-à-vis his two fathers. To many people, this position was borne out when several months later the adoptive mother, a woman about fifty-five years old, suddenly died. Her death was regarded as supernaturally inflicted punishment for the incestuous behavior of her junior kin.

To be sure, other factors—previous grievances as well as the personalities of the disputants—contributed to the conflict over the marriage. But though the giving of food is one of the most important expressions of kinship reciprocity, this case shows that it has greater significance. One might say that it is a principle of organization: the provision of food creates social bonds.

Of those factors of performance which modify or supersede genealogical relationships, creating intimate bonds out of distant ones, food sharing seems to be especially potent. Any two persons—even if one of them is non-Sio—are styled *senda tetu*, "one blood," if they habitually share food. People who are distantly related become more closely aligned for various reasons and in various capacities, as gardening associates, simply as friends, or perhaps one man becomes the political protégé of the other. In any case, the sharing of food cements such ties.

The sharing of pig feasts within the men's house has the same effect, and a man who allies himself with a new men's house signifies his break with the old group by sending a pig of which he does not partake. This pays for the pork he has eaten in the past, and it is considered to dissolve the social bond with his former group.[4] Regardless of genealogical relationship, people who regularly share food consider themselves to be too closely related to permit marriage among their descendants—children and grandchildren.

The implications of Sio notions of the relationships of food sharing and kinship for trade relations are obvious. The provision of hospitality accompanies all dealings between trade-friends. In addition to cooked vegetable food provided to visitors and their families, male trade-friends formerly were the guests of the men's houses of their Sio partners, and they shared in the group's consumption of pigs. Also, the guests of particular men's houses, visiting trade-friends from the interior, Siassi, or elsewhere, could act as contributors or recipients in inter-*mbawnza* distributions, thus strengthening their ties as affiliated members of Sio men's houses. (Among the Kuma of the New Guinea Highlands "The term for 'trading partner' is . . . 'I together I-eat' [*Na te nont*]" [Reay, 1959, pp. 106–7]. The Mailu Islanders of Papua refer to trade-friends as *isigoina*, "food relative" [Saville, 1926, pp. 50, 162].)

PETTY TRANSACTIONS

Trade-friends are apt to engage in transactions that cannot be regarded either as a part of exchange proper or of hospitality. The objects that change hands, often variants of items available at home, include bamboo combs, betelnut mortars, hand drums, lime gourds and spatulas, woven net bags, baskets, new varieties of food plants, and minor ornaments of all kinds.

[4] Sio informants say that the giving of a pig is the correct procedure when people change *mbawnza* membership, but at the same time it is stated categorically that such changes in membership are not possible. Frequently, a man may help to sponsor the feasting activities of his mother's brother's men's house, but he retains membership in his father's *mbawnza* and lineage. One man, still living, did change membership. When this man married, his father-in-law, an influential man with no grown sons, and who had been ailing for some time, asked the man to live with him and help supervise his affairs. A pig was sent to the husband's old group.

The economic significance of the transactions by which such goods circulate seems slight compared with their social meaning. When they are exchanged in a certain way, these goods form the small change of social relations between trade-friends, new friends as well as old established ones. Bamboo combs, betel mortars, and lime gourds are particularly appropriate as gifts between trade-friends because they are personal goods, closely identified with the person, and perhaps manufactured by him and bearing his own distinctive designs. Or take this example: A mainlander exchanges his own soiled and partly worn net bag for his island friend's woven straw basket. This is hardly equivalency in the material sense—a *bilum* takes weeks to make and may last for years, a straw pouch takes an hour or two to make and wears out quickly. Socially, however, it is an appropriate transaction. The trade system does not exist for these kinds of transactions, but it continues to exist partly because of them.

THE KULAMBI MYTH

Most trade-friendships take the form of kin relations. Trade is conceived to be founded on kinship, though in reality kin-like bonds develop partly as a consequence of socially conducive exchanges. Not unexpectedly, the widely ramified kin relations of the Sios find support in myth, if not also in genealogy. One of the best preserved Sio stories relates the historic relations of Sio with various communities of the Vitiaz Strait region to an ancient migration issuing from the Sio homeland. In legend, Sio history has a depth of seven to eight generations. It begins with a group of people who may be called the canoe ancestors. The canoe ancestors came from the west to settle the Sio Coast (the Sio spirit home lies to the east). The names of the principal colonists, the places where they first landed, and the villages they founded are well-known. There were four early settlements, and among the Komba and Selepet peoples of the interior, Sio as a whole is known by the name Tambali, one of the "ancient" villages.

In Chapter V, I described the legend of the canoe ancestors, and the settlement of Sio Island by their descendants. Contemporaneous with the canoe ancestors, the Kulambi, a "tribe" or group of related communities, occupied the extensive *kunai* plain and the slope of the coastal range south of Sio. This area is now dotted with Sio yam gardens. The names of the Kulambi villages—Guvang, Lopo, Sambana, Kambanunggu, and Kwata—and their approximate locations have been preserved. Some elder Sios profess to know words and phrases of the Kulambi language, which is said to have been different from both Sio and Komba. One aged man claimed that as a youth he had seen old house posts still standing on the Kulambi village sites. Others disclaimed this, but said they had seen giant clam shells (used as pig feeding dishes) and other signs of human habitation.

Kulambi fought and intermarried with Sio, and it was through a strategic marriage that Sio acquired its vast *kunai* land. Sungolo of Kulambi was given in marriage to Rumane, the son of Pasa, one of the cofounders of Sio Island. Sungolo's kinsmen attended a marriage feast at Sio, and when they were about to leave, they were presented with a large pig. Impressed by this extra act of generosity, the Kulambis plucked a bunch of *kunai* grass and, symbolically handing it over to the Sios, declared: "Sungolo and her husband and all their descendants may burn the *kunai* and they will eat plenty of pigs." Today the right to initiate the annual burning of the *kunai* and the pig drives associated with it belongs to a lineal descendant of Rumane and Sungolo, and, in theory, Sios who are not of Kulambi descent may not initiate gardening on former Kulambi lands. Once when the Lambutina people were lax in clearing the government track that runs across the *kunai* plain, their headman declared: "Very well, Latoa can give you a pig." By this he meant, of course, the return of Sungolo's pig, which would thereby cancel Lambutina's rights and responsibilities in the *kunai*.

It was not long after this strategic marriage that the

Kulambi people disappeared as an organized entity. The cause was internecine warfare, which, according to the story, erupted simultaneously in or spread to all the constituent villages. In one village a jealous husband touched off the fighting, while in another two brothers bent on revenge for the death of their parents by sorcery were the immediate cause. The survivors of the strife migrated in small groups to distant areas—to Sio, to Komba and Selepet and other inland portions of the Huon Peninsula, to the Rai Coast, and even to the Siassi Islands. Their diaspora laid the foundations of a dispersed "tribe"—all people of Kulambi descent—and of the concept of Kulambi kinship which operates today as an important basis of trade-friendship.

The Kulambi myth is not known over as wide an area as that covered by the presumed migrations of the Kulambi people. Besides the Sios, the lower Komba and Selepet villagers are familiar with the story, but they usually refer to Sio elders as the authorities on the Kulambi migration and genealogy. Upper Komba and Selepet people who knew the story said they had heard it recently from Sios or people living nearer the coast. At the same time, Sio informants claim to have found further evidence of the Kulambi migrations in traditional stories of other peoples of the Vitiaz Strait. Finding common strands, and especially common ancestors, in local legends appears to be a favorite pastime among hosts and visitors from distant areas. Such mythological concordance has an obvious social function, especially when people are first becoming acquainted or when they are renewing old relationships.

In theory, descent from Kulambi ancestors distinguishes individual and group hunting and cultivation rights within the Sio domain. In practice, any attempt to apply the events of the myth to internal affairs produces only confusion. The conclusion follows that the Kulambi story is not a "mythic charter" for Sio society, but rather for the trade system viewed from Sio. The Sios, together with the four groups of people constituting the non-Sio world of the Vitiaz Strait, make up a supertribe founded upon the Kulambi disaspora.

KOMBA-SELEPET MYTHS

While relatively few mountaineers are familiar with the Kulambi myth—it is not their story—the Sios are not alone in emphasizing historic ties with other areas. From various observation points in the upper Kwama Valley, and looking northward down the river's deep canyon, one may catch a glimpse of the sea. In the early morning mists, Umboi Island, a massive and jagged chunk of land, gives the appearance of being suspended in the sky. In local legend Umboi, or "big Siassi," is the *Urheimat* of the Komba and Selepet peoples.

There are numerous local versions and variations, but one abbreviated account of a legend recorded at Gilang can be taken as representative:

The ancestors lived somewhere in Siassi. A big fight developed over the gathering of sago leaves for house thatch, and as a result some people migrated to the Mainland coast, arriving at a place called Kanziriba (near Sialum). Later on a man named Pupunda went to Gitua where he lived by collecting wild foods, and then to Manot (near Sio). Then he traveled inland, which at that time was forested and rich in game. (Pupunda was a solitary pathbreaker in the style of Daniel Boone.) First he went to Sambori, then to Dolongo, Kepume, Umbiaman (Gilang), Tinggarumdo, and finally to Iloko. Having reached Iloko, Pupunda realized that he was an old man and that he could go no further. His relatives and friends followed the road of his explorations of the country and built villages and made gardens at each site. His descendants settled the Timbe, Selepet, and Komba country.

Thus, the ancestors of the hinterland peoples sojourned on the coast, at Sio, Gitua, and so on. It is perhaps significant that in most versions of Komba-Selepet settlement, Sambori, located near the confluence of the Kwama and its two tributaries, the Puleng and Pumene, is described as an important staging point for the exploration and settlement of the virgin mountain country. A number of informants from the upper Selepet, upper Komba, and Puleng Komba claimed ties with Sambori based on intermarriage, clanship, or migration. As noted in Chapter V, Sambori is one of the most important links—aboriginally and in modern times—between Sio and the hinterland. Most trade routes to the coast lead to, or rather converge at, Sambori.

The Komba and Selepet regard themselves as one people. Traditional accounts gathered at Indum village, for example, relate that two brothers searching for new hunting grounds wandered into the upper Pumene Valley, where they then parted company. The younger brother crossed the Kwama River and founded the Komba tribes, while his older brother became the ancestral founder of the Selepet people. Geography, ties of clanship and kinship, and differences in language are viewed as the decisive criteria dividing these related peoples into smaller groups. Cultural traits, on the other hand, unite the Komba and Selepet with such coastal groups as the Sios. To paraphrase informants' statements succinctly: "The Sios use bows and arrows and cut their ear lobes like we do. In common with us they were not cannibals. We have one way of life." The Sios, by contrast, hold cultural differences, particularly elements associated with the sea and watercraft, to be significant, while at the same time they emphasize the historic social ties with the interior peoples stemming from the Kulambi migration.

INTERMARRIAGE

Not all Sio trade-friends are Kulambi kinsmen. Especially with regard to coastal and island friends, genealogical relationships are often traceable. Sio tends toward endogamy—less than 10 per cent of marriages are out-marriages—and marriage within Sio is preferred. Exogamy never entails the exchange of women, though it is felt to be proper for a daughter of a Sio woman who has married away to return to Sio to marry and live (thus women are returned in alternate generations, sometimes as children who are adopted by their mother's brother). In discussing out-marriage, Sio men usually emphasize the disadvantages of having a non-Sio mate, rather than the advantage of establishing new relationships for exchange. Marriages with distant or neighboring communities are not arranged in order to establish trade relations, and only a small percentage of trade could be classed as exchange between affines. A single marriage between communities produces in time many more kin relationships than will ever be activated for trading purposes. It is not felt that intercommunity ties must be renewed or multiplied by the repeated exchange of women.

Thirty-six cases of out-marriage taken from genealogies, or which are currently in force, are distributed among the four groups into which the non-Sio world is divided as follows:

TABLE 7
SIO OUT-MARRIAGE

	Kumboi (Interior)	Kaboi Arop Siassi	Lapoto East Coast	Labuna Rai Coast
Sio wife	0	8	4	10
Sio husband	5	6	1	2
Total	5	14	5	12 = 36

Sio women are sent in marriage only to coastal or island localities. It is believed that they could not endure the hard life of the highlands. A number of Sio women have married on the Rai Coast, but few Rai Coast women have returned in marriage to Sio. Men say that Rai Coast women are undesirable, not for physical but for economic reasons. Rai Coast women do not make pottery. They are unfamiliar with the triangular framed handnets used in fishing at Sio, which are thought to be superior to the small oval nets in use on the Rai Coast. Thirdly, since Rai Coast women are accustomed to gardening in rain forest, it is believed that they would be lazy and inefficient gardeners if forced to work in the exposed savanna at Sio. Thus, in the view of the Sio male, a

Rai Coast wife presents a triple threat to the establishment of a viable domestic unit.

Because of past intermarriage, migration, and the Kulambi diaspora, Sio people feel that any individual has numerous potential kinsmen, and hence trade-friends. On one occasion a man who told me he had no trade-friends was upbraided by his companion: "That is what you say, but if you straightened out your ancestors you would find plenty of them."

THE ETHIC OF TRADE

Trade-friendships are modeled on kinship. Relations between siblings, father and son, and mother's brother and sister's son provide the appropriate models. Not only are trade-friends described as kinsmen, their conduct in exchange is guided ideally by the social ethic of kinship—the ethic of generosity and mutual aid.

The economic obligations of kin within the community are expressed in many ways, in the daily give-and-take evident within the domestic and kin group spheres, as well as in public and ceremonial transactions and presentations. Trade resembles the day-to-day activity of kinship, and trading transactions go on constantly and rather inconspicuously. Trade, after all, is mainly an activity of the household. It is therefore a part of private rather than public affairs.

The formal presentations of the inter-*mbawnza* feast are balanced, recorded (by means of knotted cords), and are a matter of public record. The number of yams or the size of the pigs may be discussed long after the pigs and yams have been consumed. This is not so with the movement of goods in trade. Like the constant give-and-take of daily life, keeping accounts is contrary to the spirit of giving, contrary to the social ethic of kinship on which trade is based. With regard to local trade, people are generally reluctant to discuss transactions except in general terms. The rather explosive reaction of one man to insistent questioning about precisely how much food he had received in a recent exchange seems to epitomize the dominant attitude toward trade: "How should I know? I didn't count them. I didn't weigh them. That's not our fashion!"

In overseas trade also the professed ideals of the social ethic, and also that characteristic nonchalance or disregard for the gift on the part of the giver noted often in primitive societies, are evident. My Sio companions were critical of the rates of exchange provided by Siassi informants because, as they said, "Lots of times we give them pigs and pots for nothing."

More than any other group, the Siassis are dependent on trade for their livelihood. Corresponding to their dependence on and preoccupation with trading are their reputations as wily and sagacious traders, as tellers of tall tales, as brazen liars, cheats, and thieves. It would be off the mark, however, to compare the Siassi with the stereotype of the Yankee trader. Typically, the Siassi trader is a genial con-man—a "man belong grease true." He is the practicing exponent of what is known in current American parlance as the "soft sell," but in a Melanesian setting.

As already mentioned, the visits of the Siassis are normally the occasion for festivities—sometimes they are explicitly invited to come as performers—and it is in this festive milieu (a milieu of heightened sociability) that transactions take place. Their reputations as storytellers and retailers of gossip are also significant, for this forms part of the entertainment function. In exchange and in the preliminaries to exchange the emphasis is personal. The Siassi seeks to create compassion for himself, to "sell himself" rather than his wares. Further, he is armed with trading magic, which endows his speech with the power to engender boundless generosity in his trade-friend. His nonmagical techniques, at least, are effective. As one Sio man told me, "When I hear that those Siassis have arrived I am angry. But after they are here a while I feel good about it." Thus do the Siassis annually make their way, as freeloaders, storytellers, and the most amiable of traders.

The Siassi Islanders are not dominated by a commercial ethic, as superficial observation might make it appear. Rather, they operate wholly within the social ethic, successfully exploiting it to the fullest. If in his tactics the Siassi trader resembles any social type found in capitalist society, it is not, certainly, the entrepreneur, but the gypsy—a marginal capitalist at best.

IX

Change: Expansion and Decline

THE CULTURES of the Vitiaz Strait region of northeastern
New Guinea are highly acculturated. In the coastal and
island areas, European influence was felt soon after the
German annexation of New Guinea in 1884. Missionization
began at the same time, although there had been an abortive
attempt to establish a mission on Umboi Island in the
middle of the nineteenth century (see Reina, 1858; Souter,
1963, p. 23). As a part of the far-reaching changes in native
life instigated by colonial rule and the Christian missions,
indigenous warfare, initiation ceremonies, much of magical
knowledge and practice, and major features of social organization, such as clans and men's ceremonial houses,[1] now
exist largely as "memory culture." Amidst the cultural

[1] The clubhouses themselves have been preserved in many communities,
in the Kovai villages of Umboi, the Siassi Islands, the Komba and Selepet
villages, and elsewhere. They might still be in existence at Sio, too, were
it not for the relocation of the community on the mainland brought about
by the war. Generally, the clubhouses are indistinguishable from ordinary
dwellings. This and the fact that they are referred to in Neo-Melanesian as
haus boi and not *haus tambaran* (ancestral spirit house) reflects the dis-
appearance of the ceremonial functions of the old men's house organization.
Young boys sleep in the clubhouses, and they serve as social centers where
men spend their leisure, engage in crafts, or hold meetings.

shambles created by the encroachment of European culture, the trade system, by a seeming miracle, survives. Indeed, during much of the period from 1884 to 1964, while other institutions and customs were passing out of existence one by one, native trade seems to have flourished.

Part of the explanation of this record of persistence, but only a small part, is that the agents of change—colonial officers and missionaries—who sought to modify or eradicate so many aspects of indigenous culture, naturally viewed trade favorably, as something to be encouraged. Of course, many economic and cultural practices functionally related to trade came under attack. Competitive feasting, for example, was considered to be wasteful, not to mention its association with intergroup rivalry, sexual licentiousness, and pagan religion.[2] The intercommunity exchange of fish for taro, and the like, however, could not be viewed as anything but beneficial to native welfare. At times government officers have advised the suspension of or have imposed bans on overseas sailing, or sailing between particular points, such prohibitions usually being provoked by a tragedy at sea.[3] The traders, however, have generally ignored the bans, and there have not been other repressive measures aimed specifically at trading.

The larger explanation of the persistence of the trade system lies in the adaptability it has exhibited in the face of external pressures. In adjusting to these pressures, trading has not only survived with modification, in some respects it has expanded. The manifold interconnections of trading

[2] For example, Rev. Georg Bamler, the first missionary in Siassi, objected strongly to feasting and dancing because, as he said, such festivities lead to flirtations and seductions, quarrels and fighting, food shortage and famine. See the section entitled "Dancing," pp. 42–45, contained in Chinnery's report (n.d.).

[3] On many occasions along the north coast of New Guinea, European ships have gone to the rescue of shipwrecked native traders. In July, 1964, off the west coast of Umboi Island, a disabled Siassi canoe, both sails of which had been blown away, was pursued and taken in tow by the ship on which M. D. Sahlins and I were passengers.

with other institutions mean that as these institutions give way, the trade system must eventually collapse. It is also true that the complexity of the cultural matrix, of which trade is an element, confers a kind of staying power, so long as trade itself is not directly attacked, and changes affecting the whole work themselves out gradually.

The main concern here is the other side of the culture contact situation, for the adaptations undergone by the trade system have depended largely on the specific nature of the alien cultural influences brought to bear upon it. One can show—and this may be taken as the main theme of this chapter—that the major factors impinging on native trade have tended to have a two-edged effect. Wage labor, the introduction of European goods, cash cropping, and missionization have led to a decline of the trade system, their influence playing directly on some aspect of trading itself or indirectly on closely related aspects of culture. There is also a positive side, for in other respects these same factors have contributed to the maintenance or expansion of trading, sometimes along nontraditional lines.

It is evident from the foregoing chapters that anything contributing to the decline of kinship organization, traditional crafts, bridewealth payments, indigenous polity, ceremonial life, and navigation implies negative consequences for the trade system. Indeed, the destructive acculturation of these features of cultural organization has imperiled the trade system to the degree that one may predict its final demise within a decade, if not sooner.

There are signs of imminent collapse on all sides. In 1963, with the aid of the Administration, the Malai and Tuam Islanders, for whom trade is still an urgent necessity, acquired land on Umboi Island. They have become part-time farmers on a much larger scale than ever before, in addition to being sailors and traders. The great canoes now ply back and forth between the newly planted mainland gardens and settlements and the old island villages. Some day the islanders may take up permanent residence on Umboi. That day is apt to come when the elaborate wooden bowls and clay pots are no longer regarded as essential forms of wealth among the Umboi villagers and others. For their part, the Kovai villagers are certain of one thing—while they still strive to accumulate these wealth-objects of old, their children will not perpetuate the social system in which the bowls and pots play an indispensable role, and from which they derive their value.

In the local trading spheres, trade between coast and interior is dwindling in the wake of the development of differently based cash economies—copra on the coast, coffee in the highlands. Newly emergent economic subregions overlie and overshadow the old subregions of the trade system, and economic interdependence is being transformed into self-sufficiency combined with autonomous dependence on the world market. If Sio suffers famine in the future, it will be due not to drought or failure of the yam crop, but to a depression of copra prices.

Another recent development in the Siassi-Umboi area indicates that in the future local trading will be organized along new lines. Early in 1964 the government officer in charge of a newly established patrol post—Siassi's first government station—started a weekly native market at the nearby village of Barang. The market is centrally located in the most densely populated Kovai region, but people from all parts of the Siassi-Umboi area visit the market. The staple food of the Kovai, taro, is the principal item sold, but a variety of other foods and craft goods are offered for sale. Transactions are in cash, most items being sold in one shilling lots. The popularity of the Barang market, especially among the inland people, is probably symptomatic of dissatisfaction with traditional forms of exchange.

Although at present the trade system maintains a precarious existence, the effects of European contact have been spread over at least eighty years, from the 1880's on, and during that period the trade system has not merely suffered simple breakdown, it has also been adaptively modified within the terms set by the ambient conditions. If the main trend has been downward, in the direction of ultimate decay, adaptive and compensatory changes have also preserved the system. Crippled in one area, trade finds new life in another. In common with many primitive institutions en route to oblivion under the impact of European culture, the trade system will not have gone out without a struggle.

The ensuing discussion of modifications of the trade system during the postcontact period is organized in terms of the major determinants of change, such as pacification, wage labor, and the influx of European goods. It should be pointed out that locally the response to such determinants has varied in part according to the particular role a community has within the trading network. A high degree of awareness of the array of new economic opportunities and alternatives, which in many cases compete with traditional economic pursuits, may be assumed. At the same time, the perception of the relationships of new opportunities and old-time activities is shaped by the way in which a participating society is structured for trade as well as its vantage point within the contemporary money economy. These perceptions help to explain variations in local responses to changing conditions, and to pinpoint those communities where resistance to change is most apt to continue.

Among the Siassis, the opposition of the various economic alternatives, those presented by trade on the one hand, and by wage labor and cash cropping on the other, is explicitly recognized and discussed. There is the road of the ancestors and the new road of the Europeans, and for the Siassis at least the choice of one precludes the other. Increasingly threatened by rapidly changing circumstances, native trade is the cause for policy discussion and decision on the household, kin group, and community levels. As crises develop—the increasing rate of male absenteeism in Siassi is a case in point (see below)—community pressures are mobilized in the interest of preserving the trade-based economy.

For the Sios and other groups for whom trade is not such a

vital phase of life, there appears to be much less explicit antagonism between the demands and alternatives associated with trade and other economic activities. Trade is largely a household affair, and in this context the different sources of subsistence and wealth—wage labor, gardening, gifts from kinsmen, cash cropping, and trade—contribute in complementary ways to household income and economic well-being, and are viewed as such. For the Umboi Islanders, the significant alternatives are posed not as the question of whether to discontinue trading in favor of other economic activities, but whether to preserve the system of bridewealth payments and affinal exchange on which much of the trade —for them and others—hinges.

This leads to a second point, namely, that the relationship of local trade on one side, and the overseas trade in wealth-objects on the other, is viewed in different ways in the various areas. As far as the Sios are concerned, they are separable phenomena, each to be judged according to its respective merits. Local trade is worth maintaining, while the value of overseas trade is highly questionable; the Sios can now afford to substitute cash for those overseas imports traditionally used in trading with the hinterland. For the Umboi villagers, too, local trade, particularly the issue of rates of exchange for the trade in taro and fish, is distinguished from the large-scale transactions through which they import pots and bowls. To the Siassis, on the other hand, local and overseas trade are highly interdependent— anything threatening one field of activity thereby threatens the other.

In trading activity there emerges the conflict and tension between traditional practices, ideals, and attitudes, and those imposed by or growing out of contact with European culture that are characteristic of all major phases of life in modern New Guinea societies. On the whole, however, the organization and conduct of native trade continues to express traditional practices and ideas rather than European-derived ones. Such a generalization, of course, must take into account the kind of local variations in economic position and attitude just described.

INTENSIVE CONTACT
WITH GOVERNMENT AND MISSION

In 1884–85, when Finsch conducted his cursory ethnographic investigations in the Vitiaz Strait from the decks of the steamer *Samoa*, there were three active groups of overseas traders—the Bilibili, Siassi, and Tami Islanders. Finsch was among the first Europeans to encounter the Bilibilis—one of their great canoes laden with pots pulled up to the *Samoa* to offer its cargo for sale—and he was impressed by their boldness and enterprise (Finsch, 1914, p. 273). He was also one of the last observers to view their traditional way of life as an ongoing affair. For after two to three decades of European contact, only the Siassis remained active in overseas trade.

The uncertainties which exist with regard to the precise roles of the two island trading groups at the extremities of the Strait—Tami in the southeast and Bilibili in the far west —as well as the relations of Tami, Bilibili, and Siassi to each other, were mentioned in Chapter II. The geography and nature of European contact show, at least, why the ethnographic picture is apt to remain incomplete. Even though the available information on the early period of contact does not permit a detailed reconstruction of the events that precipitated the curtailment of Tami and Bilibili trading activities, the main outlines of the story are apparent. The major causes are to be found in the Tami case in their direct and intensive relations with the newly founded Christian mission in Finschhafen, while the Bilibilis were caught up in a ruthless and expansive land grab on the part of German colonists in the Madang area. In any case, the results were disastrous for both groups from the point of view of indigenous trade, and had similar influences operated in the central Vitiaz Strait—the Siassi sphere—the trade system would have ceased to exist a half-century ago.

New Guinea became a German colony in 1884, the powers of administration initially resting with the chartered New Guinea Kompagnie with its mainland base of operations at Finschhafen. The Neuendettelsau Lutheran Mission, whose missionaries were to be responsible for christianizing most of the native societies of the Vitiaz Strait, founded their first station at Finschhafen (the village of Simbang) at the same time.[4] In 1892 the Kompagnie headquarters were moved to Stephansort in Astrolabe Bay, and later to Friedrich Wilhelmshafen (Madang).[5] Thus, the focus of administration and colonization on the mainland shifted from Finschhafen to the western end of the Strait, from the Tami sphere in the southeast to the sphere of the Bilibili Islanders in the west. Finschhafen remained, however, the base of operations for the mission.

Rev. John Flierl, the leader of the first group of Lutheran missionaries at Finschhafen, provides a valuable account of the early history of Tami in his memoirs (Flierl, 1927). The German missionaries soon learned of the trade system, and in casting about for a location for a second mission station, they decided upon the nearby Tami Islands. The possibility of utilizing the existing channels of communication provided by the trade system was an important consideration underlying this decision. In explaining the move to found a station among the Tami Islanders, Flierl writes:

> They were, as it were, the Phoenicians of all the coast as far as the Huon Gulf to the west and as far as the Siassi Islands and the large island of Rook [Umboi] to the north.
> Being born traders, friendly, polite, and adaptable they frequently came to Finschhafen to sell their carved work to the white people, and also came to see us missionaries at Simbang. They invited us to

---

[4] The Kompagnie's first New Guinea party arrived at Finschhafen on Nov. 5, 1885 (Souter, 1963, p. 71). The mission station was founded at Simbang in 1886.

[5] Administrative responsibility for the colony reverted to the Imperial government in 1899. The capital was transferred from Friedrich Wilhelmshafen to Herbertshohe (Rabaul) in New Britain. See Souter, 1963, pp. 75, 110.

their islands and when they noticed that we liked it there, they asked us to build a house like the one in Simbang and come to stay.

We knew well enough that their friendliness was business policy. That was natural and not really objectionable. We pursued a missionary policy in the enterprise; we believed that if these people could be won for the Gospel, they would as traders in a large region, carry it to many other tribes . . . [pp. 27–28].

The Tami Mission was founded in November of 1899, and soon after, often with the help of Tami assistants and evangelists, posts were established on the shores of the Huon Gulf and to the north—at Sialum in 1907, Sio in 1911, and Umboi Island in 1911, the latter post being established by Georg Bamler, one of the two original missionaries to Tami, and a Tami coworker.[6] Flierl gives this appraisal of the policy based on the decision to concentrate early missionary efforts on Tami:

If you ask whether the hopes which we placed in the founding of the island station of Tami have been fulfilled, we can confidently answer: Yes, they have been fulfilled. Within a period of about fifteen years the island population has been christianized. Native evangelists from Tami have gone to the Siassi Islands and to the island of Rook [Umboi], and the influence of the Tami Christians together with that of the Jabem congregations on the coast has made way for the Gospel among all the tribes living about the Huon Gulf [*ibid.*, p. 30].

It definitely appears, then, that Christianity spread quickly, in part because it moved along the pre-established channels of the trade system.[7] The Tami Islanders were

[6] A complete chronology of Lutheran Mission history in the Vitiaz region is contained in Frerichs, 1957. Bamler was killed by a falling tree in 1928 and was buried near the Umboi village of Yangla.

[7] The success of the mission policy, however, was not unmarred by setbacks, and though many native groups proved to have a "kindly yielding disposition" (as Flierl wrote of the Sios), some were hostile. For example, on Umboi Island "the Papuan tribe in 1913 robbed and cruelly murdered the two brothers Weber and their Melanesian laborer, who were about to start a plantation there" (Flierl, 1927, p. 67). According to local accounts these murders were committed by the Kovai people of Gomlongon village, and according to the same accounts, their crime was punished by a swift and devastating reprisal. A company of German officers and native con-

directly involved at many points in this process. Tami assistants and the sailing canoes provided logistic support for the
mission, ferrying supplies in the Finschhafen area and transporting the missionaries themselves for purposes of further
exploration (*ibid.*, pp. 29, 62). Tami evangelists went
farther afield, helping to establish and run new posts. As this
involvement deepened, the likelihood that the Tamis would
be able to maintain their trading and manufacturing activities decreased sharply.

There are no statistics to document the extent to which
the Tami Islanders were engaged in the new activities associated with the coming of the Europeans. Involvement in
these activities surely increased steadily from 1899 on. Apart
from the substantial number of islanders devoting their time
to evangelical service or working in other capacities for the
mission, it is likely that still others were employed as boat
crewmen, in the native constabulary, and as plantation
workers. In 1913 the two-masted, seventy-foot motor
schooner *Bavaria,* built in Rabaul, began service for the
Lutheran Mission. A published photograph entitled "Crew
of the 'Bavaria'" (Flierl, 1927, p. 74) shows fifteen native
crewmen. It is likely that some, if not all, of the young men
shown in the photograph are Tami Islanders.

At the time the Tami Mission was founded in 1899, the
population of the two island communities was two hundred
or a little more. In time, the withdrawal of several dozen
young men from a community of this size would seriously
impair the ability of the Tamis to continue overseas sailing

---

stables from Madang, using the Mandok Islanders to lure the Gomlongon
people down to the coast for a market, surprised and ambushed them when
they appeared, killing large numbers of men, women, and children. The
events of the murders and subsequent massacre have been woven into a
myth according to which all the Gomlongon people were annihilated with
the exception of a young boy and girl. They were spared and instructed
by the German officer-in-charge to return and repopulate their village.
The Gomlongon villagers have perhaps had the last word in this story of
hostility, killing, and reprisal: recently a large number of them were converted to Roman Catholicism, and thus once more they are an impediment
to the Lutheran Mission in Siassi.

and trading and craft activities—principally the carving of wooden bowls—on which their trading position depended. Before 1930 the Tamis were the sole manufacturers of the large and elaborately carved bowls that were their main export. Then the supply apparently began to fail, and although their manufacture was not discontinued—they are still being made today—it evidently declined to the point where the Siassis could no longer rely on the Tami carvers for an adequate supply. Probably fewer carvers were practicing their craft, and many young men absent from home were not serving their apprenticeships as carvers. In any case, the bowls were vital to the Siassi trading interests in the archipelago, and by about 1930, if not before,[8] the canoe makers of Mandok and Aramot began manufacturing imitations of the Tami-style bowls, as they continue to do today.[9]

THE BILIBILI ISLANDERS

At the time of European contact, Bilibili Island in Astrolabe Bay was inhabited by a group of traders and pot makers numbering 200 to 250 persons (Finsch, 1888a, p. 81). Their sailing canoes were built in the Tami-Siassi style and were described as the finest in the western Strait. Finsch called

[8] But not much before. The government anthropologist Chinnery visited Siassi in 1926, and although he describes the trade in bowls with Tami, he does not mention bowl carving by Mandoks and Aramots (Chinnery, n.d.).

[9] The historical reconstruction presented here and in Chapter IV is provisional and rests on the direct testimony of Siassi informants regarding their adoption of bowl carving from Tami and their "theft" of Tami designs. Their accounts are matter-of-fact and strictly nonmythological in character. The testimony is supported by (1) the negative evidence of Chinnery (n.d.), who did not observe the manufacture of bowls at Mandok and Aramot in 1926, and (2) the fact that conditions for borrowing were highly favorable, especially in view of the pre-existing skills of the Siassi carvers. Siassi Islanders were often resident for long periods in Tami, while Tami carvers camped in the Siassi Group, where they made bowls for trade on the spot. The fact remains, however, that bowl making may have been a long-established craft in Siassi itself, and that when the supply of the Tami product diminished, Aramot and Mandok craftsmen merely intensified production. If this is what happened, it would not necessarily conflict with informants' statements that they appropriated Tami bowl designs.

the Bilibilis the patricians (*Patrizier*) of Astrolabe Bay and said they maintained their aristocratic dominance by fighting (a suggestion supported, in his opinion, by the war scars borne by so many Bilibili men). Other observers attributed the dominant position of the Bilibilis to their aggressive trading—if not aggression in support of trading—and Krieger states that only the Bilibilis had won the privilege of bypassing coastal middlemen in order to trade directly with mountain villagers of the Hansemann and Ortzen ranges (1899, pp. 223–24). Hagen noted that the Bilibilis know the languages of the communities with which they have economic relations, and that the islanders as a group could serve as informants for most of the languages of the area (1899, p. 218).

The chief export of the Bilibilis was clay pots, but like the Tamis and Siassis, they acted as carriers for a wide variety of products manufactured by other groups. The range of Bilibili sailing, the extent of their trading sphere, is not clear, and there is considerable disagreement among the early German sources on this point. According to Krieger, the Bilibilis regularly traveled to Umboi Island and the Finschhafen area, sailing during the Northwest season and returning by the Southeast Trades. The Umboi Islanders, the Bilibili's "principal friends," accompanied them on the return voyage to spend a season on Bilibili Island, during which time they applied themselves to the manufacture of plaited work. Furthermore, the Tami Islanders sailed to Bilibili in order to trade their products of carved wood and tortoise shell for clay pots (Krieger, 1899, pp. 223–24). Modern Tami informants deny that such voyages were made, and it may be noted that supposed voyages of the Bilibilis from one end of the Strait to the other would cover two to three times the distance normal for Siassi and Tami voyages.

Hagen states that the Tami and Bilibili Islanders maintain separate and sharply bounded trading areas; Bilibili does not visit Tami, and vice versa. Rather, Bilibili trading voyages were confined to the Rai Coast, Karkar Island, and the mainland coast to the north and northwest as far as Hatzfeldthafen (Hagen, 1899). Werner's account suggests that voyages to the north extended only as far as Cape Croisilles (1911, pp. 278–79; cf. Kunze, 1896, p. 194), while Baron Maclay's trip along the Rai Coast by native canoe in 1877 established that Sio, and not Tami or the Finschhafen area, was the eastern limit of regular Bilibili trading voyages on the mainland (1951–54, II, 358–72). If we accept Maclay's report, based on first-hand information, the Rai Coast constituted the area of overlap of the Bilibili and Siassi spheres.[10]

As the Lutheran missionaries foresaw in the case of the Tami Islands, Finsch suggested after a first visit that there would be no more advantageous place than Bilibili to undertake missionization (1888a, p. 85). It was not the mission, however, but events contingent upon the government-supported establishment of European coconut plantations in

---

[10] Maclay's information does not specifically rule out the possibility that the Bilibilis sailed to the Siassi-Umboi area. Even so, he had extensive contact with the Bilibilis, and it seems that he would have learned of such voyages if they occurred.

His trip along the Rai Coast in 1877 definitely showed that Sio was the eastern terminus of Bilibili voyaging on the mainland. Maclay hired two Bilibili canoes, and with two crewmen each, along with his Mohammedan servant, they moved from village to village along the coast. The prior agreement was that they were to go only as far as Sio or Teliat (probably the Bilibili name for Sio; the Sio cape is now known as Teliata Point), but once there, Maclay wanted to move on to Cape King William. The Bilibilis absolutely refused to go farther. He reports his efforts at persuasion in his diary.

> In the evening I had a long meeting with Kain, trying to persuade him to set out further; I promised him one and even two axes, knives, red calico, beads, in a word, countless treasures for him, but he stood on his "no," "impossible," "they'll kill us," "they'll kill us all," "they'll eat us," and so forth. So that's all I could get out of him. I indicated my revolver. Although he asked that I conceal it, he continued to say, "they'll kill us," "Maclay is alone, they are many." I struggled with him in this manner for about two hours, but still I couldn't talk him into it [1951–54, II, Diary, July 8, 1877].

Up until this point in the journey, Maclay was well received, as he said, because of his Bilibili companions. Clearly, Sio was the last port-of-call for the Bilibilis on this coast.

the Madang region that delivered the fatal blows to the Bilibili trading "empire." The curtailment of trading in Bili-bili appears to have occurred more swiftly and decisively than in the Tami Islands.

The amount of land taken over for German plantation enterprise and settlement between 1884 and 1914 never amounted to more than a minute fraction of the land area contained within the German possessions (Rowley, 1958, pp. 89–90). Alienation, however, was concentrated in a few areas, Friedrich Wilhelmshafen and the Madang Coast being one of them. The German Administration controlled land purchases from natives, at least in areas where control could be exercised. The techniques as well as the consequences of alienation, reported by Rowley, will be familiar to students of colonial history:

A common practice in the outlying areas seems to have been to land from the boat, make a rough survey, and in return for payment of trade goods to the natives assumed to be the "owners," to have their leader mark with a cross a written statement of willingness to alienate. The sale was arranged between the purchaser and the government subsequently. Language difficulties, native concepts of land tenure, and a buyer's ability to dominate the natives in the bargain, would make any genuine assessment of the native's attitude very difficult, as it remains today.

Legal safeguards for natives meant little when purchasers made the initial arrangements with them, as they often did, in areas beyond effective government control. Even allowing for the best of intentions and full administrative control, land purchases inevitably provoked resentment, which has continued, for these communities do not concede the right of any of their members to give up land on terms binding for subsequent generations [Rowley, 1958, pp. 88–89].

It was not long before "the land which formerly belonged to the natives of the small islands Ragetta, Siar, Ruo, Bilibili and others, and to those of villages on the mainland, . . . [was] . . . cut up into plantations owned and managed by whites" (Flierl, 1927, pp. 113–14). Inasmuch as each new bloc of land put under cultivation by Europeans meant that

a certain number of native laborers was diverted from traditional pursuits to copra production, land alienation had a
doubly disruptive effect on indigenous economic life, consequences which such people as the Bilibili traders must
have quite fully appreciated. According to Flierl, the resentment that soon developed among the native peoples over the
question of land was a major impediment to missionization.
Because they had been cheated out of their lands, "a deep-
seated dissaffection spread among the natives, a bitterness,
intense and lasting, . . . And where the soul is filled with
hate and enmity, the heart is closed to the Gospel . . ."
(*ibid.*, pp. 114–15).

More revealing is that growing resentment led to native
conspiracies aimed at annihilating the German settlers of the
Madang area. Lawrence (1964a) has recently summarized
the events of the Madang Revolt of July, 1904, and the
circumstances surrounding a purported conspiracy in 1912.
Plans for the 1904 revolt, which were agreed upon at a
meeting of the Yam, Bilibili, and Jabob people on Bilibili
Island, called for the island peoples to cross over to the
mainland, rush the police barracks, seize the rifles, and thus
armed, kill the whites. The Bilibili and Jabob Islanders,
however, later defected, and at the last moment the plot was
betrayed. The police restored order, and in the aftermath,
"Nine ringleaders were executed, and the remainder of those
involved (including the people of Yabob [Jabob] and Bilbil
[Bilibili] because of their initial complicity) were forced to
leave their island homes and settle on the mainland, where
they could be watched more closely" (*ibid.*, p. 69).

Continued native hostility, expressed in passive resistance,
characterized the period following the abortive uprising.
Then, in 1912, the District Officer in Madang was alerted to
the possibility that another conspiracy was brewing. Con-
clusive evidence of a renewed plot was not forthcoming, but
after a summary trial, he exiled most of the Bilibili, Jabob,
and Yam people to the Rai Coast, and sent those suspected
of being ringleaders to New Britain (the exiles were allowed

to return home in 1914 when the Australian Military Administration took over the colony) (*ibid.*, pp. 72, 233).

Available information does not allow us to measure the decline of Bilibili trading prior to their forced move to the mainland in 1904 and their subsequent exile. Nevertheless, the rate and extent of land alienation on the Madang Coast (locations and areas of plantations shown in Lawrence's [1964a] Map V, p. 38, and Tables I and II, p. 39), the character of native resistance to white colonization, and the disruptive resettlement of the Bilibili community itself, leave no doubts about the fatal outcome for the trading role of the Bilibili Islanders and the indigenous patterns of trade.

As in the case of the famous Tami bowls, however, the fine red pottery continues to be made by the Bilibilis and the Jabob villagers, and it is extensively marketed for cash in the Madang area today. Through Siassi voyages to Madang or the Rai Coast, and the purchases of returning laborers and visitors to Madang, the pots continue to play a role in the trade system.

Far from administrative and mission centers, the Siassi Islanders were not touched by the events that so drastically affected the Tamis and Bilibilis. They remained, as they remain today, the overseas traders of the Vitiaz Strait.

PACIFICATION AND THE WIDENING
OF TRADING CONTACTS

The cessation of warfare had far-reaching effects on native trade. Peace and security of travel made possible the establishment of more remote contacts within the local trading spheres. The spread of trade relations between Siassis and Umboi villagers to include all the communities of Umboi has already been described. For the Siassis also, pacification eliminated the hazards faced by traders who spent a large part of their working lives among alien communities. Aside from the risks associated with a forced landing at a locality where the party lacked friends, the security that the Siassis could expect to enjoy must have varied even among the regular ports-of-call, depending on the social ties linking hosts and visitors, possible grievances developing out of exchange, and other specific events as well. As one Malai elder told me, "The Sios are kinsmen of ours, and we always slept well there. In the Rai Coast villages half the men slept while the rest stood guard." This, of course, is one man's view; Sio may not have been considered to be without danger by others.

In the Sio-Komba trading sphere, pacification led to the formation of trade-friendships between upper Komba-Selepet villagers and Sio. It appears that the first visits to the coast by the distant mountaineers, the *kumboi kalawe* as the Sios call them, were made under the aegis of the mission. The Sios enjoy mimicking the fear these bushmen had of the sea, some of them running away when they first witnessed the action of waves and surf. They recall, too, their own fear of the grimy, evil little men with their net head coverings stuck through with magically charged darts. A dart stuck in the ground covered by a man's shadow induced debilitating disease and death.

Not many years after the founding of the mission station near Sio in 1911, some of the first Sio converts were visiting mountain villages to spread the Gospel. The first step toward conversion? Removal of the net head covering that concealed the death dealing darts. And it was not long before inlanders from the remote interior were visiting Sio for purposes of trade.

Pacification proceeded at different rates in different areas, but probably by about 1930 warfare and raiding had ceased in all but the more remote parts of the interior. Certainly the Sios had acquired many new trade-friends by then. The expansion of direct contacts between coast and interior to include the upper Komba and Selepet regions and the populous Timbe region as well, leapfrogged the villages of the coastal range, which had formerly acted as the exclusive intermediaries for coastal and overseas imports coming from Sio. Travel routes were also altered, because traders could now move without fear along the best rather than merely the safest routes. Formerly, each village tended to have its own route to the sea. Nimbako traders, for example, who now may cut through Komba territory on the way to Sio, formerly stayed west of the Kwama River in order to avoid contact with hostile communities.

The simple, direct, and informal manner in which new trade-friendships were initiated is revealed in accounts such as these:

One day when I was still a little boy, a group of Timbes, carrying *bilums* of food, came to Sio. I don't think they had come here before. They sat down on the beach opposite the island. I saw one woman with an enormous bag of sweet potatoes. I went up to her and took her by the arm. When we got across to the village, a Sio woman tried to take her away from me. I said I wanted to take the bush woman to my mother's house. She was a good woman and let us go. We ate the potatoes and my mother gave her pots. She became one of our friends.

One day I saw this bushman walking along the road. I could tell from the way he acted that he didn't have any friends here. I took him by the hand and led him to my house. We have been good friends ever since.[11]

It is appropriate to mention the spread of Neo-Melanesian in connection with pacification, since the two are intimately related historically speaking. Indeed, the connection is made by New Guineans when they observe that enemies became friends with the arrival of the mission and the spread of Neo-Melanesian. The role of a lingua franca in establishing amicable relations, for trade and other purposes, is obvious. The question arises, though, of the means of communication

---

[11] The taking of visitors by the hand or arm, which tends to recur in these accounts, is probably not significant in any symbolic sense. Many new trade-friends from among the *kumboi kalawe* were acquired before the war when Sio village was located on the island. The island is connected to the mainland by a sandy path across a reef several hundred yards long. The water is shallow enough at low tide to permit crossings on foot, but to people who feared the water as the bush people did, crossing was a harrowing experience, and they were actually led by the hand, sometimes half carried across. Visitors who had as yet no Sio trade-friends did not—had no right to—cross to the island village on their own.

among trade-friends during pre-European times. Informants give two answers to this question. First, there were always a few men, as there are now, who knew the languages of particular alien communities. Secondly, Sio informants say that communication was also based on a pidgin form of the Siassi language (*tok Siassi haphap*), a trade lingo with a Siassi vocabulary which was useful not only in meetings with the Siassis themselves, but with other island and coastal peoples.[12]

Pidgin Siassi, if it did exist widely as a consequence and adjunct of the trade system, was not spoken by the inland peoples. Today, and probably in the past, each group of hinterland people learns something of the language of their coastal trade-friends. Many Komba and Selepet men have an extensive word and phrase knowledge of Sio, and a few I encountered speak Sio fluently (alas, of my grammatical slips it was said that I was speaking Sio like a Komba). On the other side, the Sios have very limited knowledge of Komba or Selepet vocabularies, and I obtained positive proof of fluency in Komba in the case of only one Sio man.

THE DIVISION OF LABOR

The regional division of labor underlying the trade system remains intact. The various craft skills entailed in the production of articles of exchange have been preserved. Canoes, pots, wooden bowls, shell and teeth valuables, bows and arrows, mats, and net bags are manufactured as they were in the past, except that, where appropriate, steel implements are employed. Of highly valued wealth-objects, only the turtle-shell bracelets appear not to be made at the present time. Older people bear the main burden of craft production; relatively few young men, but a larger number of young women, are proficient in traditional handicrafts.

12 In the *hiri* trade of Papua "the Motu and the various Gulf tribes visited by them make use of a common trading dialect which is in some measure distinct from the very widely divergent languages of either . . ." (Barton, 1910, p. 96). Barton provides a short vocabulary of the trading dialect—the *"lakatoi* language"—on p. 119.

While the practice of some crafts is less localized than in the past, the limited diffusion that has occurred has not impaired trade. On the contrary, the adoption of bowl carving by Mandok and Aramot and of pot making at Sialum has helped to preserve the trade system. The manufacture of sewn pandanus mats, an important article of exchange for the Siassis and Tamis, has diffused to the Kovai villagers of Umboi, Sio, and elsewhere. The Sios, however, sew few of their own mats, and the bulk of the mats currently in use are Siassi products. To a limited extent the weaving of net bags, a mainland speciality, has spread to the archipelago. A few Umboi women who now make net bags learned the craft while they were patients in mainland hospitals. The Umboi carrying device for women, a sling of bark ropes, is still more widely used than net bags.

MIGRATION FOR LABOR

Migration for wage labor has been one of the main avenues for the acculturation of indigenous New Guinea cultures. The removal of large numbers of people—removal in a physical, and ultimately in a moral, sense as well—from the distinctive social systems with which the characteristic operations and values of the trade network are intimately linked, has had a largely negative or destructive influence on that network. Migration for labor, in feeding the development of a territory-wide society—from the point of view of native participation, a culturally impoverished or "deculturated" subsociety of New Guinea workboys—has had a leveling effect, eradicating or making irrelevant the regional distribution of resources, skills, needs, and opportunities out of which the trade system has been created. Being a New Guinean is in some ways more than, but in a multitude of ways less than, being a Siassi, Sio, Tami, or Komba.

The significance of migration for wage labor may be judged partly by the increasing postwar rates of male absenteeism shown in Figure 5. The right-hand bars of the graph

Figure 5. Migration for Wage Labor

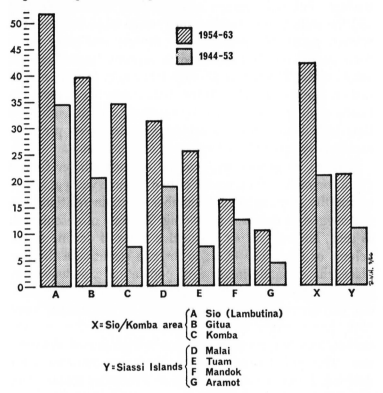

(X, Y) show that on the average, the percentage of men annually leaving the villages of the Sio-Komba area of the mainland is double the percentage of migrants from the Siassi Group. The rate of absenteeism of Sio for the period 1954–63 is three times that of Mandok and nearly five times greater than the Aramot rate. Indeed, the low absenteeism of Mandok and Aramot is a measure of their steadfast conservatism and their continuing economic commitment to canoe building, the carving of wooden bowls, and trading. The increasing migration of laborers from Malai and Tuam —in 1963 absenteeism climbed to 52.4 per cent and 47.6 per cent,[13] respectively, rates comparable to those of Sio—is not necessarily indicative of a corresponding decline in overseas trading. With only meager earnings from copra production and the collection of trochus shell, wage labor becomes the primary means of acquiring cash, *laplaps,* and other European goods, which have become essential ingredients of native trade. The profits of wage labor help to fund and to sustain trading activity. What better way to maintain a family trading concern than by sending a son to work for a time in Rabaul? (Such considerations, however, probably explain only a part of the increase in absenteeism.)

Even so, in general the removal of each laborer from a given community for a period of two or three years at a time means the suspension of a number of trade relationships, and suggests a decrease in trading. The rate of absenteeism as such, however, is not a sensitive index of decline in the volume or frequency of trade for two reasons. In the first place, the dramatic increase of population experienced by many communities tends to offset the effects of migration. Sio, for example, in nearly doubling its population since 1910, has a larger resident population now than a half-century ago, in spite of the extremely high rate of absenteeism. The populations of the Siassi communities have doubled, in one case trebled, since European contact (see Chap. II, n. 4). In the second place, migration affects primarily young, unmarried men who, if they stayed at home, would still be associated with older kinsmen in trade rather than independent traders. Later, when these men return (and most men aged forty or forty-five come home for good), they may activate or form trade-friendships on their own.

If migration for labor has been a main avenue for acquir-

[13] Absenteeism is usually computed as the percentage of "able-bodied" males (between ages sixteen and forty-five). The figures given here are the percentage of all adult men sixteen and above who are absent. Often in traditional economic pursuits men over forty-five are the most able.

ing knowledge of European culture and economic practices, it has also provided the opportunity to learn more about the indigenous economic system. To a degree, the trade system has suffered decline as knowledge of that system increased.

Formerly, the Siassis alone were in a position to view the trade system as a whole, or rather their perspective was the central or essential one. They knew the sources of all articles of exchange entering the trade, the labor inputs associated with the various products, the difficulties and dangers to be expected in securing particular items, and the local and temporal variations of supply and demand. More than any other group they were in a position to fix the terms of trade, partly, it appears, by a calculated misrepresentation of actual conditions. To whatever extent the Siassi position depended upon their superior knowledge and also the withholding of such knowledge, to that extent their position has been undermined by the expanded horizons now vouchsafed to all the peoples of the Strait. Traveling and working in all parts of the area, and far beyond, others have discovered the trade system, so to speak, and have perceived the Siassi role in it with new awareness. No one believes any longer, for example, that clay pots are a kind of giant clam shell secured by the skill and daring of Sio divers. The effects of the expansion of knowledge have been a reappraisal of the old-time Siassi tactics and a reluctance to comply with the former terms of exchange, based as they were on ignorance shaped by exaggerations and falsehoods. One man expressed the newer view in succinct, albeit crude, terms: "Nowadays we say bullshit to all of that."

Migration for wage labor has had largely negative effects, but the phrase covers a complex of factors, types of events, and experiences, some of which have contributed in a positive way to sustain or extend the trade system. Like pacification, the system of wage labor created new and favorable conditions for human social contacts and communication.

Beginning before the turn of the century, young men from different parts of the Vitiaz Strait, including men from communities that had never had direct dealings, were thrown together as workmates in centers such as Rabaul and Madang, on ships, and on isolated plantations. Understandably, friendships were formed, especially along lines of cultural and linguistic affinity and the established network of intercommunity relations—among Siassis, Arop Islanders, Sios, Rai Coast villagers, and so on. In some cases the labor compounds brought together young men whose parents or relatives were already related as trade-friends. In many cases enduring friendships and subsequent trade-friendships developed out of workboy camaraderie.

The status of age-mate, structurally significant in connection with the men's house organization of these societies, provides the appropriate social model for such relationships. In addition, there developed bonds focused on the status of native foreman or *bosboi,* an older more experienced man in charge of a line (*lain*) of younger workers. In a general way, the *bosboi* resembles the traditional big-man, though his specific roles are dictated by the conditions peculiar to the labor system. The *bosboi* is the protector and spokesman of the group, his *lain,* in dealings with local villagers; he organizes his men for fights with other ethnically distinct *lains,* or he stops such fights; he is in a position to dispense favors (e.g., he may overlook pilfering, laxity on the job); he is usually in charge of distributing rations, as well as other goods locally appropriated and some times misappropriated;[14] and in occupying the key intermediary position in the chain of command extending downward from European employers and managers, he has powerful sanctions at his disposal. There are many examples but no proper statistics to show how many trade-friendships currently described as senior-junior sibling relationships stem from an earlier *bosboi-wokboi* relation.

---

[14] Aside from pilfering of local livestock and garden produce, and from plantation stores, laborers sometimes stole their employer's copra, which they sold for trade goods or cash to local traders (Rowley, 1958, p. 185).

INTRODUCTION OF EUROPEAN GOODS

The introduction of European manufactured goods has affected native trade in a number of important ways. Such goods as cloth (*laplaps*), knives, nails, bottle glass,[15] and various trinkets began circulating in traditional trading channels at an early date. European goods competed with and have tended to replace indigenous equivalents. The effects of the influx of European goods, however, have not been simply additive or substitutive. The new goods were not equally accessible to all communities at the same time. The coastal and island peoples were first drawn into the European orbit as wage laborers and targets for missionization, and were therefore the first to enjoy a steady source of supply of European goods. At Sio, for example, many men had worked as indentured laborers by 1910 (Flierl, 1927, p. 67), and in 1911 a German missionary began a twenty-year residence there, thus providing a local market for native goods and services. The greater access to European goods possessed by the coastal groups initially reinforced their dominant or advantageous trading position with respect to the interior, their role as middlemen for overseas imports. Elder Sios recall the time when knives and plane irons were scarce and were in constant circulation within the community. (Maclay's visit brought a few knives and axes to Sio in 1877.) It was not long, however, before steel knives, like obsidian flakes previously, were being sent inland in return for pigs. Sio continued to enjoy an advantage in the exchange of European goods for indigenous hinterland products until after World War II. The prewar period was indeed the *gud taim*, when a pig now worth five pounds could be had for a few shillings, and a span of dogs' teeth for a cheap bush knife.

---

15 When the New Guinea Kompagnie moved its headquarters from Finschhafen to Stephansort in 1892, it left behind a large graveyard of malaria victims and middens of beer, wine, and champagne bottles. These rich deposits of glass must have been nearly fatal for trade in obsidian in this area.

After eighty years of contact, the extent to which indigenous products have maintained their value, the continued demand for such products side-by-side with a lively demand for European manufactured goods may seem surprising. In part, this is accounted for by extremely low purchasing power. At the same time, however, European goods are not always and necessarily regarded as being superior to native equivalents. New Guineans have become discerning customers. They recognize the shoddiness of many of the goods they can afford to buy, and perhaps they are close to realizing that because of their low incomes New Guinea is more a dumping ground than a proper market for European goods (unlike more "sophisticated" peoples in other parts of the Pacific, these people own no sewing machines, bicycles, and radios; shotguns and pressure lamps are the most expensive items usually purchased).

The value of native-produced goods depends in large part on maintaining the culturally valued uses to which they are put, and these include social as well as technical-utilitarian uses. The universal abandonment of brideprice institutions, for example, would alter the "demand schedule" considerably. In providing an alternative to involvement in the cash economy, the exchange of traditional goods remains especially attractive to certain classes of people. Men who for reasons of age, inclination, or village responsibilities decline to work for Europeans, usually have low and uncertain money incomes.[16] Local specialties—pots, bows and arrows, mats, tobacco, taro, and so on—can be converted

[16] It appears that among the Komba and Selepet, young returning laborers often turn over most or all of the proceeds of their labor, in the forms of purchased goods and cash, to senior kinsmen. This is not true at Sio. There is, however, a constant flow of gifts from absentees to their senior kin at home (there are no facilities for sending remittances by mail). In return for such gifts home kinsmen often plant garden plots for an absentee relative. The plot is known by the name of the absentee. Even though he may have given no indication of his intention of returning in time for the harvesting, the plot is there just in case. If he does return it is handed over to him and provides the planting stock necessary to become re-established as a gardener.

directly or indirectly into other traditional goods, European manufactured goods, or cash.

Some native goods have been phased out completely by European equivalents. Tools of stone, shell, and obsidian, of course, have been completely replaced, at least as far as trade is concerned.[17] The shell and teeth valuables seem to have been devalued to a minor extent, and though cash is a substitute for the ornaments in many traditional payments, they continue to be symbolic of status and are prized as family heirlooms.

It will be useful to consider briefly the circumstances surrounding the substitution or nonsubstitution of native by European goods, for herein lies one set of clues to the persistence and modification of the trade system.

Earthenware Pots

In spite of the widespread use of metal cookware, there remains a lively demand for clay cooking pots. At the Komba village of Balup, for example, a census revealed an average of four to five pots per household, exclusive of an unknown number of vessels stored in garden shelters and pig houses. Since Balup is a principal point for the forwarding of pots to the interior, the number of pots there is normally larger than in more remote villages; and for the same reason, the number of pots on hand is apt to fluctuate considerably. In the upper Komba village of Gilang, which formed trade-friendships with Sio in early post-European times, but which has not maintained direct relations in recent years, half of forty households canvassed had one or more pots. Many of these were very old, some were said to have been acquired before the war, and most were still regularly used. On the coast a pot is considered to have a probable life span of about two years if it is used continuously. They last longer in

17 At Sio, trochus shells are used to bore holes in coconut water bottles and shell scrapers are also used occasionally, for example, in teasing the bark used in canoe caulking (a woman's task, men do the caulking). Stone sago beaters were used until after World War II, when they were replaced by six-inch lengths of steel pipe mounted on wood elbow hafts.

the highlands, however, because of the great care with which they are handled and stored. Even broken pottery is not thrown away, and pots with cracked or broken bottoms were traditionally converted into food steamers. (The bottom is carefully knocked out, and banana leaves are tied securely over the original mouth of the vessel. Inverted, the pot is placed on the ground, and fire is built up around it. Peeled tubers and a small quantity of water are added through the hole in the bottom, which is then covered with leaves to hold in the steam.)

The clay pot has been retained side by side with metal cookware, not because people cannot afford to buy enough of the latter, but because of the pot's superior heating characteristics. The cheap, lightweight metal pans in use, as any housewife knows, cook rapidly and unevenly—food prepared in pots, people say, is better cooked and tastes better. New foods such as rice and flour require metalware, while the preparation of traditional foods such as sago-coconut puddings requires a clay vessel. In the vicinity of Kainantu, Eastern Highlands, Watson reports that

Although to some extent tins have come to replace clay jars for boiling, particularly where portability is a factor, the clay jar is still preferred by most individuals for boiling because of the alleged superior flavor of the food cooked in it and the greater ease of mashing the food with a stick [1955, p. 125].

In the Vitiaz Strait portability is also a factor. The Sios, for example, usually use the lighter metalware rather than pots for cooking in distant gardening areas. Among the Komba and Selepet, on the other hand, who have gardening shelters or "pig houses"—proper dwellings—clay pots can be stored in or near the gardens, and cooking utensils need not be carried from the village house.

An equally if not more compelling reason for the continued high level of the demand for pots is their role as wealth-objects in the communities of Umboi Island and New Britain. In a single house in the Kovai village of Gomlongon were stored thirty-five "Sio" and "Madang" pots, owned principally by three brothers. At the time, only two pots were being used for cooking, the rest being held in reserve for payments to affines. It is evident from the previous discussion that the elimination of pottery from the "demand schedule" would be a crippling blow to native trading.

Wooden Bowls

Some of the reasons adduced for the maintenance of trade in pottery also explain the continued importance of carved wooden bowls. Enamel wash basins are used universally in the preparation and serving of food in the same way that bowls are, and, as a result, the Rai Coast–style bowls appear to be much less widely traded now than in the past. European imports, however, cannot compete with the large Tami-Siassi bowls. Because of their size, weight, and shape they are far more suited for the preparation of taro puddings than enamel basins. Bowls are more highly valued and more widely used in brideprice than pots.

Bows and Arrows

Formerly the chief weapon of war on the mainland, the bow is now used in hunting and to some extent in fishing. The only European equivalent available to natives, the twelve-gauge shotgun, is expensive (twenty-five pounds in 1963–64), and the supply is limited by law to one gun per fifty natives, though people are under the impression that licenses are allocated on a one gun per village basis. In addition to their great expense and the regulated supply (only three Sio men own shotguns), the shotgun's range is not much greater than a bow unless solid ball cartridges are employed.

Tobacco

People seem to prefer locally grown leaf tobacco to commercial tobaccos. Village trade stores usually stock leaf tobacco, and it is much cheaper than stick or twist tobacco.

Net Bags

To some extent airline bags, canvas haversacks, and large women's purses have replaced or are used in addition to the small men's *bilum*. As yet there is no substitute for the large woven net bags in which women carry food, water containers, and infants, or which they wear hanging empty as an item of apparel.

Bark Cloth

Laplaps and trousers have taken the place of bark cloth, except for the costumes of festival dancers and of a few diehard conservatives.

Red Ochre

To a considerable extent, commercial paints have replaced red ochre and other indigenous earth pigments and vegetable dyes. According to the Tarawe villagers, who supply the red ochre, the former trade has dwindled to almost nothing in recent years. Nevertheless, the Sios, so lacking in conservatism in other respects, insist on using Siassi "red paint" for the painted designs that adorn the wash strakes of their canoes.

Pandanus Mats

Purchased grass mats, wool blankets, camp stretchers, and homemade beds, though widely used, have merely been added to and have not replaced pandanus mats.

Canoes

Because of the expensiveness of European built boats, there is no replacement for the ocean going canoes. At the same time, an expansion of traditional trading would probably occur if small motor vessels were somehow made available to the principal trading groups. Currently, a half-dozen cargo vessels plying the waters of the Vitiaz Strait play a role in native trade. These ships enable people other than

Siassi Islanders to travel to remote parts of the Strait for purposes of exchange at all times of the year. Paying customers as well as hitchhikers are allowed to carry a considerable amount of cargo, which is stowed on deck. Often traders who do not wish to travel themselves can induce crewmen, who may be kinsmen or friends, to act as supercargo and see to the delivery of goods.[18]

RATES OF EXCHANGE

New Guinea, in common with the rest of the world, has experienced postwar inflation. As a part of this process, the prices of native produced and traded goods in the Vitiaz Strait have increased over prewar and premonetary levels. Unlike general inflation in the cash sector of the economy, however, which is felt by all classes of consumers, the changing terms of native trade have had decidedly unequal effects on the various groups of native traders and phases of trade. In general, the balance of exchange has shifted to the

[18] The ships that regularly serve the interests of native traders are:

1. M.V. *Vitiaz.* Operated by the Finschhafen Marketing and Development Society, a native cooperative. Former Tami Island skipper recently succeeded by a Sio man. A Siassi crew. Home port: Finschhafen. Regularly calls at coastal villages between Finschhafen and Wasu, the Siassi and Umboi Islands.

2. M.V. *Sirius.* Privately owned cargo vessel based in Madang. Sails between Madang and Lae, and may call at Sio, Wasu, and other points. European skipper, Sio boatswain, and crew of Sios and Arop Islanders.

3. M.V. *Beringa.* Owned and operated by Ted Foad, an Australian trader. Based in Finschhafen, regularly calls at coastal villages as far west as Roinji on the Rai Coast, Arop, and Siassi Islands. Chief crewman a Tami Islander.

4. M.V. *Umboi.* Operated by the Australian Lutheran Mission in Siassi. Travels between Siassi and Lae. Former Sio skipper succeeded by a Siassi.

5. M.V. *Karapo.* A small vessel operated by the Australian Lutheran Mission in Siassi. Local travel in the Siassi-Umboi area. Skippered by an Umboi Islander.

6. M.V. *Kauri.* Operated by NAMASU, a Lutheran-backed cooperative. Calls at many coastal and island villages of the Strait. Skipper from Sialum.

7. M.V. *Simbang.* Modern, well-equipped flagship of the NAMASU fleet. European skipper, crew includes a Sio man. Travels on a regular schedule supplying Lutheran Mission stations between Madang and Lae.

advantage of the inland groups at the expense of the island and coastal peoples. The people themselves attribute the increasing prices of inland products to the new awareness of the bush people, who previously "did not know the value of things." As inland living standards—measured by the consumption of European goods—have risen, approaching the standard in the coastal areas, the inlanders have increasingly demanded higher payments for their principal exports—taro and other foods and tobacco. Specifically, they have attempted to apply as a new standard for local trade the prevailing prices for the same goods in the town markets of Madang, Lae, and Rabaul. More and more inlanders demand cash and European goods and prefer more impersonal and balanced forms of reciprocal exchange. Understandably, such people as the Siassis, Sios, and Gituans complain that prices in the town markets have no relation to the realities of intervillage trade, and demands for cash are considered unreasonable in light of the fact that the cash incomes of villagers are generally low, uncertain, or nonexistent. To an extent, however, the bushmen have been successful in altering the terms of exchange of inland for coastal products in their favor, though much of local trading is still nonmonetary and the prices are not as high as in the native markets of the towns.

The evidence of changes in the rates of exchange comes from informants' testimony and early reports (Chinnery, n.d.), checked at some points by records of individual transactions and observation. In such testimony conflicting statements are to be expected, quite apart from actual local variation. Many more observations are needed, but the fact that rates of exchange are checked on both ends of the coast-inland trade is some guarantee of accuracy. In any case, a general order of magnitude is consistently indicated: the "prices" of inland products have increased at least two to four times over those of prewar or the traditional rates of equivalency. This increase is illustrated in the comparisons for the Gitua and Siassi local trade below:

Gitua-Inland (Exchange at Market)

		Prewar	Postwar
1 coconut	=	4 taro	= 1 taro
1 fish	=	4 taro	= 2 taro
1 pot	=	1 *bilum* taro	= 3–4 taro

Siassi-Umboi

		Prewar	Postwar
4 coconuts	=	1 basket taro (*ca.* 12/basket)	= 4 taro
2 sm. fish	=	5 taro	= 1–2 taro
1 lg. fish	=	10 taro	= 3–4 taro
1 sm. pot	=	2 baskets taro	= 5 taro
1 mat	=	1 basket taro	= 4 taro

There are no comparable figures for Sio because the bulk of trade there is carried on among trade-friends, and in the exchange of pots, fish, and coconuts for taro and sweet potatoes, the latter are measured in the traditionally imprecise manner of the net bag (a fact of which the neighboring Gituans are enviously aware). Nevertheless, the Sios join with the Siassis and Gituans in lamenting particularly the declining value of fish in exchange for taro. The decline is often epitomized in the statement that formerly fish were broken in two, the head paying for one lot of taro, the tail section buying another. According to the new standard, and allowing for differences in the size of both the fish and taro in particular exchanges, equivalency in local markets is on the order of one-for-one. Thus, in a market held between the Kovai villagers of Gomlongon and a group of Mandok Islanders, transactions ran as follows: one large taro = four small fish; one large taro (slightly smaller) = three small fish; two medium taro = three small fish; eight small taro = seven small fish; five taro (two large and three small) = six small fish; four small taro = three small fish. There was no haggling or lengthy appraisal involved in these transactions, the fish and taro being handed over as quickly as possible. In the newly founded Barang market, a medium-sized fish and a large taro are priced alike at one shilling.

The inlanders' knowledge of the native town markets is the basis of their demands for greater returns in local trading. In the Siassi-Umboi area other developments have had the effect of stabilizing if not also determining increased prices. The establishment of the weekly native market at Barang by the local government officer must be mentioned again in this context.[19] The largest group of sellers is made up of Kovai housewives selling taro at the rate of one shilling for one large, two medium, or four to five small taro. Other goods offered for sale include *mami,* sweet potatoes, green beans, onions (scallions), papaya, *Canarium* almonds, taro puddings, *manggit* (a pudding of taro, coconut, and greens), bark rope, red-dyed rattan, tobacco, pork, pandanus mats, clay pots, and fresh and smoked fish. The mats, pots, and fish are brought by the Siassis, although fish also comes from Barim and Mantagen. The market is popular among the Kovai villagers, for whom it is centrally located, and on one of the first Saturdays the market was held, over twelve hundred people assembled. The market is not so popular among the Siassis, for obvious reasons. On one Saturday in mid-July, 1964, three men from Malai were the only Siassis present as sellers. In order to attend the market, the Siassis must travel twenty miles or more by canoe and then walk inland several miles. Once there, they may sell fish (thus far in short supply at the market, fish is sold immediately) for a shilling apiece and buy taro at the same rate. Obviously, it is far more convenient for them to meet with the Kovai villagers at the traditional and less remote market sites and

[19] Irrespective of the government officer's role in founding the market, it is clear that the Umboi people have modeled their practice on the town markets. At Barang, as in the Rabaul market, most items are sold in one shilling lots (not by weight); sellers are mainly women who arrange themselves by village; sellers do not try to undercut their neighbors' prices and they do not bargain with customers (see Epstein, 1961). A Saturday in Rabaul is apt to find over two thousand vendors present at the market, and Epstein estimates that the annual turnover is £ 130,000 (*ibid.,* pp. 10–11).

exchange fish directly for taro. Because of the difficulty of transport for the Siassis and the southern Kovai villagers, the traditional beach sites will continue to be used for exchanges involving large amounts of taro. At the same time, the weekly market at Barang gives every sign that it will continue to be held, and it is probable that in the future, rates of equivalency will be increasingly determined by the prices established in the market. At present the one-to-one equivalency of fish for taro corresponds to the Barang market prices.

The government officer had some role in establishing the initial prices in the Barang market, if not by formal decree, at least in the form of authoritative advice. The government has also had a limited role in regulating the terms of payment in traditional trading. Litigation arising out of default on the part of the Siassis in their dealings with Umboi Islanders provides at least the opportunity for the Administration to assume regulation of rates of exchange. There seems to be, however, little continuity in policy or practice between successive administrative officers, cases are treated as they arise, and no enduring policy or body of rules has been laid down. (If one officer were posted to Siassi for a long period of time, it is likely that he would try to establish some rules, to reduce the load of complaints and litigation if nothing else. With officers coming and going—from Finschhafen and before that from New Britain—people are less likely even to bring complaints to their notice.) There have been, nevertheless, attempts in this direction. Thus, in 1952 a government officer presided over a joint meeting of officials from Mandok, Aramot, and the Kaimanga villages of Yangla, Gauru, and Birik concerned with payments for timber. It was resolved that Umboi people were to supply suitable trees for canoe hulls to the islanders at the rate of one pig per log, and, secondly, that in cases wherein the Umbois cut and transported canoe timber to the coast, the Aramots and Mandoks were to forward half of the payment subsequently received from the Malai or Tuam Islanders for the finished canoe. These resolutions appear to be in line with traditional practice. Government regulation of disputes may help to stabilize trade, and perhaps in the future certain phases of trade will be fully administered, probably by a Local Government Council.

It should be mentioned also in this context that government-fixed prices for the purchase of native foodstuffs have had no effect on rates of exchange in native trade. A considerable amount of taro and sweet potato is regularly bought at the low price of one to three pence a pound to provision laborers at government stations. The terms of trade in food remain more favorable in traditional exchange. The cash value of pots, fish, or coconuts received for a *bilum* or part-*bilum* of taro equals or exceeds the value of the same *bilum* on the government scales. It is not this fact so much, but the wants and needs of food sellers, that are important. These continue to include the traditional coastal products.

With regard to overseas trade, change in the rates of exchange means alterations in the terms of trade faced by the Siassi traders in their relations with the various communities that are their regular ports-of-call or local suppliers of goods carried in overseas trade. With limited opportunities for local cash cropping, and committed to preserving the trade-based economy, the Siassis have watched the growing prosperity of neighboring communities based on wage labor and copra production. As the money incomes of these communities grow, and as money increasingly finds an accepted role in native trade, the Siassis are forced to keep pace by augmenting their cash resources within and outside of trading. As the trading of particular types of goods declines or is discontinued, money is substituted for the items lost, particularly, one might suppose, when these are the money-like valuables. To illustrate, in Siassi's relations with Tarawe village, seven of eighteen items are seldom traded or have been discontinued, as shown below:

	Currently Traded	Infrequently Traded or Discontinued
Siassi Exports	Pots Bowls Pigs Dogs Mats Fish Lime	Dogs' teeth Disc beads *Tambu* shell Turtle-shell bracelets Net bags Coconuts
Tarawe Exports	Taro Betelnut Tobacco Timber for canoes	Red ochre

The use of cash in trade means an increase in the cost of trade for the Siassis. Given their limited opportunities for copra production and the necessity of restricting absentee wage labor in the interest of continuing trade and trade-related activities, the acquisition of money is more difficult than maintaining supplies of the discontinued or infrequently traded goods. Coconuts, turtle-shell bracelets, and *tambu* shell were produced locally, while disc beads, net bags, and dogs' teeth were acquired overseas. Especially with the decline of the European market for trochus shell, which formerly provided locally earned income in Siassi, the Siassis have no alternative but to release some members of the community for wage labor. Thus, in order to earn the cash they need for trading, they must go outside of trading.

The increase of the money equivalents of some goods has so altered the terms of exchange that trade is no longer worth-while. For example, the Siassis must offer payments of one to two pounds plus *laplaps* for the hand drums made on Arop and Tolokiwa Islands, and it is doubtful that they can often command payments higher than this in other communities, especially since the latter are now in a position to deal directly with Arop for drums. Trade in sago provides another illustration. Formerly, a large packet of sago flour could be purchased on southern Umboi for fish. This in turn could be exchanged for enough pots at Gitua or Sio to pay for a pig in New Britain. The same amount of sago is now apt to cost one pound. Now if a trader has one pound, he is better off trying to purchase a pig outright than buying sago.

Not all changes in rates of exchange have reduced the volume of trade. Payments for sailing canoes, for example, have doubled from three to six pigs. The Umboi villagers who supply canoe timber have probably forced this rise. In any case, while the export of canoes to the mainland and New Britain may have declined, there is no evidence that the number of canoes made and traded within the Siassi Group has decreased. Indeed, canoe production has undoubtedly increased with population. Mandok, for example, would not have needed 50 canoes when its population was only 120.

Pigs, dogs, bowls, pots, and the valuables of teeth and shell form a relatively closed exchange sphere—the critical sphere of overseas exchange. Paradoxically, the money prices of the valuables have increased, with inflation, while total demand has diminished. This is due to the unequal effects of acculturation on different communities and segments of the community. Some people continue to convert cash, traditional goods, and labor into valuables of teeth and shell; others are simply not interested. Some examples from Sio indicate the range of individual variation:

1. One of the most influential men of the community, about sixty years old, the head of a residential cluster and ŋgu. Except for a brief stint as a plantation worker, has been a subsistence gardener most of his life. Spent ten years as an evangelist on the Rai Coast (but lived as a villager and gardener during this time). A canoe builder and craftsman, active in inland trade. A traditionalist. Holds one small breastplate of dog's teeth for an absent son, owns none of his own.

2. Brother (FaBrSo) of 1 above, and second in command

to 1. Age about fifty-five. Most of his life prior to World War II spent away from home as a wage laborer. Active in inland trade. A modernist in some respects, firmly traditionalist in others. Attitude toward ornaments is indicated by his statement to a Siassi who offered for sale a pair of boars' tusks: "You bring the rubbish of the pig you have eaten and want big pay. We are through with that. You bring the pig and you are entitled to a big payment."

3. Son of the *luluai* of Sio (Latoan section). Age about forty-five. Wage worker at various times, but village responsibilities (assistant to his ailing father) kept him home. A modernist. Owns the following valuables: one string of disc (*patawuku*) beads, secured from a New Britain friend in Lae; one pair of boar's tusks, bought in Lae for one pound from a Wain man; one string of dogs' teeth (eighty-nine teeth), a gift from his father.

4. Son of past Paramount *Luluai*, a former teacher, owns two trade stores, at Sio and Wasu Anchorage, Sio's wealthiest entrepreneur. Age about forty. A modernist. This man's hoard of ornaments—boars' tusks, belts, and headbands of dogs' teeth, breastplates and decorated *bilums,* and embroidered *tambu* shell—is worth about two hundred pounds, although it is hard to put a definite price tag on the larger and more elaborate pieces. Informants agree that a hoard of this size could have been owned only by the most influential of big-men.

It is difficult to predict the attitudes toward valuables in individual cases, but there is one common element that tends to maintain the value of the ornaments. All of them—dogs' teeth, boars' tusks, *tambu* shell, and disc beads—are items of personal adornment used by dancing performers. Although money is an acceptable substitute for ornaments in payments of compensation and, together with such goods as Siassi bowls and pigs, in brideprice, it cannot compete in this ceremonial-recreational sphere of life. Many young men enthusiastically participate in dances, and for this reason they are often led to purchase ornaments with cash if they cannot be acquired in more traditional ways. This situation may be compared with that of the Santa Cruz Group, where the traditional red feather money used in bridewealth payments and interisland trade is being driven out by Australian currency. The red feather money cannot be worn, and it is not displayed (Davenport, 1961, p. 65).[20]

TRADE STORES

A large part of the European manufactured goods entering the Vitiaz Strait region is purchased in stores in the towns —Lae, Madang, and Rabaul. In the past local sources of trade goods—the government and mission stations and a few European owned stores—were scarce. Understandably, the location of these outposts, since they provided a limited market for native produce and labor, altered somewhat the aboriginal patterns of travel and communication. In the prewar period, Sio's position as a coastal entrepôt was reinforced by the location of a mission station there (from 1911 to 1938) and by virtue of its all-weather anchorage, which made it a major point of embarkation for migrant laborers leaving the area. A competing source of attraction for hinterland communities was Ulap Mission, twelve miles west of Sio and a few miles inland, founded in the 1920's. Following the war, Ulap station was reoccupied and a government patrol post was established at Wasu Anchorage (since moved inland to Kalalo, adjoining Ulap). The Sio Mission was not re-established, but a European trader based at Finschhafen opened a trade store there. Thus, for a period

[20] In the Central Solomons (San Cristoval, Guadalcanal, Gela, Malaita, Ulawa, and southern Santa Ysabel) the traditional strings of shell money are being driven out by money. This replacement results from: (1) the scarcity of the ornaments themselves—the specialist communities have ceased making them, and formerly European traders and recruiters bought shell strings for use in other areas; and (2) the decline in the number of uses for shell money. Their uses in clubhouse ritual, compensation, and payments to sorcerers and canoe makers have disappeared. Brideprice maintains some demand for the ornaments. All of the various shell ornaments of the Central Solomons are worn—as necklaces, anklets, waistbands, and head ornaments (Belshaw, 1950).

of about four decades, both Sio and the Ulap-Wasu centers attracted hinterland peoples who traveled to the coast or toward the coast (to Ulap) to obtain European manufactured goods.

Within the last five years the situation has been modified by the establishment of a government patrol post at Kabwum in the central part of the hinterland. Both NAMASU (the Lutheran-backed cooperative) and F.M.D.S. (the government-sponsored native cooperative) have established trade stores and buying points for coffee at Kabwum. Although introduced before the war by the mission, coffee growing was of negligible significance until the extension of plantings supervised by agricultural officers since 1960. There is no road for transport of the coffee to the coast, and because of the expense of road building in such rugged terrain, it is unlikely that a vehicular road will be built for many years to come. An airstrip at Kabwum, however, allows coffee to be flown out by aircraft to Wasu Anchorage, and trade goods are taken back on the return trips. While the cash economy based on coffee growing represents only an incipient development thus far, in the future Kabwum will doubtless be the dominant focus of the hinterland economy. Correspondingly, the importance of Sio and other coastal points as suppliers of trade goods will diminish. Already the trading visits to Sio on the part of the upper Komba and Selepet villagers, who first established direct relations with the coast after pacification, have been largely curtailed.

Another development of the last five years is the establishment and rapid proliferation of native trade stores, at Sio and in the hinterland. Some of these stores were established by individual entrepreneurs, but most of them are cooperative enterprises involving a kin group, a group of neighbors, or the village as a whole. As one Sio store manager remarked: "We do business like the Chinese. A group of relatives starts a store and some of them run it while the rest loaf." In 1964 Sio had a dozen trade stores, although two were unlicensed and some others appeared to be nearly defunct. Two stores were community enterprises of the Latoa and Lambutina ŋgu, respectively, while the others were formed by smaller groups of investors or by individuals. Examination of the history of the first Sio trade store, begun in August, 1958, will give an idea of the scale of operations. A young man who was to be the manager and who built the store, together with thirty-three relatives and neighbors, provided the initial capital of £73.6.0 ($164). A second and larger capitalization of £114 ($255) was collected a month later from the same investors and provided for the original purchase of stock worth £100 and operating expenses. The owner-manager's contribution was £8.9.0, about 4.5 per cent of the total. In September, 1963, the retail value of stock on hand was £58.10.0 (the mark-up on many items is 100 per cent). The "Golemata Trade Store," as it is called, has shown a profit for six years, and though it has not paid dividends to investors, it may be judged a success compared with the faltering and short-lived operations of many other trade stores.

The goods sold in these stores typically include food— mainly rice, sugar, tea, biscuits, and tinned meat and fish; soap, toothpaste, shampoo, and talcum powder; native leaf tobacco, stick tobacco, cigarettes, tinned tobacco, matches, and newspaper; clothing, eating and cooking utensils, fish hooks, and kerosene.

Sio tradesmen are fortunate in being situated to receive semiregular deliveries of stock by ship from Lae. Supplying the highland stores, which stock a smaller variety of goods and are constantly subject to shortages, is more difficult. Owners must rely on costly transport by human porterage from Wasu Anchorage and sometimes expensive emergency purchases at the Kabwum stores at retail prices.

With its dozen trade stores, Sio thus remains a more dependable source of a wider variety of European goods than the village stores of the hinterland. However, the more convenient locations of the well-stocked stores at Kabwum and Ulap, together with the fact that these centers have a small but constant demand for garden produce, have relegated Sio to the role of a secondary center. Clearly, the existence of these centers has been detrimental to traditional trading between Sio and its hinterland.

Even so, the terms of trade are more favorable at Sio for the sale of native staples, and while people cannot count on being able to sell their produce at Kabwum and Kalalo, the government stations, it is always accepted at Sio in return for gifts that at least represent part payment. A Komba or Selepet villager traveling to Sio can expect to receive, besides hospitality in the form of food and lodging, either the specific goods he may need at the time, such as clothing, or a gift of cash with which he may buy what he wants at one of the local trade stores. He may also sell coffee for cash at Sio, which is an F.M.D.S. buying point. And of course, as in the past, he may want coconuts, fish, and pots.

CHANGES IN PRODUCTION AND LOCAL TRADE

Since low productivity and particularly seasonal food shortages were principal determinants of coast-inland trade, changes affecting the productivity of subsistence agriculture and the distribution of food supplies through the year have an important bearing on the persistence of trade. At Sio the directions of change in the subsistence economy and their implications for local trading are clear. The principal factors promoting change have been the introduction of steel tools and new crops, an extension of gardening territory, the planting of extensive coconut groves, the development of cash cropping, and the intensification of certain aspects of indigenous horticulture. The net effect of these developments has been a marked increase in the amount of food available to the society, and hence a decreased dependence on trade. Most apparent is a suggested increase in the amount of food produced by each household per annum. But there has probably been an absolute increase in the total food output of the society as well, since rapid population growth has tended to offset the withdrawal of men as wage laborers, keeping the resident population at a level equal to or exceeding the aboriginal level. In addition, increasing female involvement in productive tasks that were formerly reserved for men tends to compensate for the selectivity of male migration.

The increase in food production has been achieved in spite of certain losses in the traditional economy. First, the stimulus to production provided by traditional large-scale ceremonial and competitive distribution of food has been reduced as the politico-ceremonial system has disintegrated. A loss of a more direct kind stems from the suspension of productive net fishing by men, which appears to be part of a gradual process of orientation of the Sio economy toward horticulture and away from the sea. Thirdly, the introduction of steel tools meant the replacement of the male production teams of the digging stick technology by individual hoe cultivators. Probably this is to be counted more of a felt loss than a real one, since steel tools more than compensate for the loss of the teams. Nevertheless, the Sio attitude is clear-cut, and it merits close scrutiny. In their view, the substitution of individual hoe (hoes, spades, crowbars) cultivation for teamwork means that tilling the ground, the heaviest task for grassland farmers, is prosecuted less efficiently and less effectively. The work tends to proceed in fits and starts rather than being completed in a single day as in the past. In the absence of the specified obligations and the stimulation of effort entailed in teamwork, many gardeners tend to postpone this most toilsome task. Finally, hoes, in contrast to team-wielded digging sticks, do not work up the soil to a sufficient depth, and this is said to explain a reduction in the size and quality of yams.

Horticultural production received its first new impetus, chronologically speaking, from the introduction of iron tools. First came plane irons, which were mounted in the traditional elbow-hafts. The adzes were of little significance for gardening compared with the later bush-knives, hoes, spades, and axes. The efficiency conferred by these tools is the primary reason why yam gardens are both larger and more numerous than in the past, and these increases are a large part of the augmentation of the food supply.

An expansion of territory is also important. Arable land in general has never been in short supply, but land suitable for taro cultivation in particular was. Planting of the Sio varieties of taro (*deŋa, aŋgo*), which appear to be tolerant of dry conditions but which are less esteemed than mountain taro (*be*), was restricted to small areas of bush (such as are found along watercourses) and to open tracts near the coast, which are favored with sufficient ground water to allow the crop to survive the dry months. The cessation of warfare in the early twentieth century left the way open for the extension of gardening into more remote areas favorable for taro. Because of its strength of numbers and island position, Sio had little fear of frontal attack. The risk of attack came when the village was dispersed in small groups over the coastal plain. Aboriginally, then, the outer limit of Sio cultivation was defined in part by a line beyond which it was deemed unsafe, where the risk of attack was too great. Pacification has allowed the utilization of areas five or six miles away, where small groups can safely camp for days at a time. The slope of the coastal range, directly south of Sio, and the extensive tract of rain forest to the west of the Kwama River delta, are the chief areas involved. Still, with this added territory, supplies of taro are not considered to be sufficient.

The significance of introduced cultigens has been varied. Such vegetables as corn and beans do not prosper on the coast as they do in the highlands, and although they add variety to the diet, they are grown only in small quantities. The cultivation of both dry rice and peanuts was tried at Sio, but they did not catch on. Of nonindigenous crops, only manioc and pumpkins are grown in large quantities.

The sweet potato, however, is of much greater significance than nonindigenous crops. There has been widespread redistribution of varieties of sweet potato in New Guinea in modern times, and at Sio many, if not most, of the principal varieties planted (as their Neo-Melanesian names indicate) are recent introductions. Returning plantation workers, it appears, have been largely responsible for this redistribution, for plantations regularly maintain sweet potato gardens to help feed their workers. According to informants, sweet potatoes were formerly planted (interplanted with yams) in small quantities. In 1963 and again in 1964, however, large joint gardens of sweet potatoes were made at the beginning of the gardening cycle. The effect of these gardens, representing a total of twenty to thirty acres and production of perhaps more than one hundred tons annually, will be to virtually eliminate seasonal hunger. The records of household consumption given in Chapter V show that the sweet potato already serves to bridge the gap between successive yam harvests. Of the indigenous and nonindigenous crops, only the hardy sweet potato has offered this possibility.

Coconuts were planted at Sio in large numbers, mostly under government supervision, long before there was any opportunity for marketing copra. At first, therefore, the new plantings produced only food and nuts for the inland trade, and for about two decades Sio has had a supply of coconuts far in excess of the requirements for ordinary and ceremonial consumption and exchange. Today a household (conjugal family) uses at least twenty to thirty nuts per month in cooking, exclusive of numerous nuts consumed as refreshment and snacks when traveling and working. Such would not have been the case in the past, when coconut palms were few and when at times all coconuts were tabued in order to insure sufficient quantities for ceremonial distributions. With their present wealth of coconuts, the Sios have an enormous food reserve, which can be tapped at any time of the year.

With cash income from copra sales, the food supply was

made even more secure.[21] Much of the sun-dried copra made by women is sold in small lots and the proceeds used to buy rice and tinned meat at the trade stores for daily household consumption. Men's earnings, if they go to buy food, are used to purchase larger quantities of rice and meat for ceremonial occasions, to feed helpers and workers, or for special foods (usually tea, sugar, and hard biscuits) with which to entertain friends.

Insufficiency of food affecting particular households is less cause for worry than in the past. As always, one can expect aid from kinsmen and, to a lesser extent, from trade-friends. But the first line of defense against shortage appears to be coconut holdings, the possession of which allows the household to be more self-sufficient than formerly. For example, a survey of one man's yam gardens indicated that he had planted much less than the amount normally required. When queried on this point, he explained that there was no reason to worry: "I have plenty of coconuts to eat, and I can sell some copra and buy rice." Rarely in this context do people talk of making up deficiencies by fishing, sago making, or the collection of traditional famine foods, such as wild yams.

In case of serious scarcity affecting the community as a whole, Sio formerly had several alternative courses of action: exploitation of wild foods; reliance on trade-friends and markets; and migration of part of the community (as is recorded in a story of a local famine which occurred in the late nineteenth century). To these traditional alternatives some new ones have been added. People can appeal to town kinsmen for cash and gifts of food, and, of course, they could

21 The M.V. *Vitiaz* owned by the Finschhafen Marketing and Development Society started calling regularly at Sio to pick up copra in 1959. Before that the Sios contributed four thousand pounds in cash savings from copra sales toward the purchase of the *Vitiaz*. A history of F.M.D.S is contained in McSherry (1962).

According to Basil Kidd, Co-operative Officer of F.M.D.S., Sio provides about 25 per cent of the copra currently purchased by the Society; the Siassi-Umboi area provides 50 per cent (personal communication, 1964).

make a direct appeal to the Administration for emergency relief.

Thus, of the traditional means of coping with food shortage, inland trade remains important. But trade, in turn, is far outweighed by the means offered by the cash economy and intensified subsistence production.

THE CASH ECONOMY AND TRADE

Beginning before 1900, the coastal and island peoples of the Vitiaz Strait were presented with the opportunity of participating in and benefiting from the new economy being established by the Europeans. The opportunity came in two forms: by turning over part of their land to coconut production, they could become primary producers of copra, or they could become wage laborers on European plantations. During the prewar period the system of labor recruitment insured that most young men served a term as an indentured laborer at one time or another. Relatively few, however, became copra producers except on a small scale, for it was not European policy to encourage the development of independent native producers who would both compete with European plantations and also make it difficult for these same plantations to satisfy their needs for native labor.[22]

The entrance of the Europeans destroyed the near monopoly on coconut production formerly enjoyed by the island-traders—the Siassis, Bilibilis, and Tamis. As plantation workers people became experienced in the planting and care of trees and the methods of processing copra. Finally, the provision of marketing facilities since World War II has

[22] ". . . the Germans refrained from serious efforts to increase village production, because of possible effects on plantation labour supplies. If more natives worked and earned taxes in the village, the immediate effect would be to reduce the numbers willing to go out to work." While the Australian military administration (1914–1921) "encouraged natives to grow more coconuts as a cash crop, it had in mind the needs of European business, and the main object of concern was copra, and not the native producer. A policy of developing village agriculture to meet the needs of the village would have increased labour problems and have clashed with the labour policy" (Rowley, 1958, pp. 189, 242).

made native copra production more rewarding, while at the same time the number and variety of employments for natives have increased markedly.

Sio, among all the communities of the region, may best illustrate the maximization of both opportunities—wage labor and copra production. The large size of the community —about eight hundred in 1900, close to fifteen hundred in 1964—combined with the abundance of land, are important conditions of Sio's economic success. By 1910 a number of Sio men had worked away as wage laborers (Flierl, 1927, p. 67); by 1933 the majority had done so (Groves, 1934, p. 48); and in 1964 about one third of the population was living and working away from home, mostly in or near the towns of Madang and Lae. Most people leaving Sio initially went to plantations. Nowadays such work is considered demeaning and unprofitable—fit only for bush people—and jobs as policemen, clerks, teachers, storemen, mechanics, boat crewmen, and servants are preferred.

Extensive coconut plantings were made at Sio before World War II, and with the development of marketing facilities in the form of a cooperative-owned ship, the cash benefits of these plantings have been realized increasingly since about 1950.

The comparatively high standard of living at Sio—as measured by the use of purchased foods, European clothing and other goods, and large, well-built houses—is based on cash income from copra sales, but also partly on a cash increment from Sio town labor. Close ties are maintained with town kinsmen, and visiting back and forth goes on continuously. When people visit their relatives in town, they take gifts of such things as pots, sago, yams, pigs, leaf tobacco, and betelnut (items which are expensive or impossible to get in the town markets), and they return home with presents of cash, European clothing, food, tools, and utensils.

On the whole, subsistence production and local trading have not suffered because of involvement in the cash economy (recent development of cash cropping in the highland interior has hurt the trade more). Even with the high rate of absenteeism and the increasing importance of copra, subsistence gardening has expanded. These developments have been possible because of the abundance of land and a large, expanding population. Former gardening land on the coast has been removed from subsistence gardening, but the land under cultivation—gardens and coconuts—remains a small fraction of the arable land available. The large population provides a sufficient labor force to carry on the three main activities of subsistence gardening, copra production, and wage labor.

The relative prosperity of the Sios affects their attitudes toward trade. In particular, they know they are wealthier than the Siassi Islanders, and it is likely that purely social considerations will determine whether or not they remain interested in Siassi trading visits. On the other hand, the benefits of the inland trade decidedly make it worth maintaining.

The general pattern of economic change in other coastal communities is similar to that of Sio, except that, being much smaller, less favorably situated, and for still other reasons, most communities have not been as successful. The degree to which they have remained poor—the small and widely dispersed villages of the Rai Coast and of the south New Britain Coast are cases in point—is a measure of the degree to which they remain committed to trading, and captive to the Siassi traders.

What of the Siassi traders themselves? How have they adjusted to the far-reaching economic and cultural changes precipitated by the Europeans? In retrospect, there may have been several courses open to them. It can be shown, however, that as the actual situation developed, the Siassis had no alternative but to attempt to maintain the traditional economic network and their role in it.

The course of development at Sio—combining subsistence economy with copra production and absentee wage labor—was not feasible for the Siassi Islanders. The former coconut-monopolists had little or no land with which to expand plantings for extensive copra production.[23] The tiny islets and sandbanks of the archipelago were already covered with coconut palms. Secondly, the islanders lacked the manpower necessary to develop a combined economy of the Sio type. Before World War II, each of the island villages had a population of less than three hundred. Unlike Sio, whose traditional economy rested largely on yam cultivation, the Siassis practiced no more than token agriculture. The mainstays of their economy were net fishing and trading—both male activities. Local trading with Umboi was necessary to obtain vegetable food, material for fish nets, and timber for canoes. The long-distance trade was necessary to maintain the local trade. Thus, withdrawal of male labor to the point that any phase of these activities was impaired would bring about the breakdown of the whole. The continuation of the trade was clearly an all-or-nothing proposition, and the Siassis' takeover of the manufacture of wooden bowls when the supply from Tami failed indicates that they clearly perceived this.

One can imagine other courses of development, and the necessity of the course actually followed may be made clear by discussion of such possibilities. Siassi men could have left the islands in large numbers to work as indentured laborers, leaving the people at home—women, children, and elders— to eke out an uncertain existence as fishermen and reef scavengers. The awful consequences of such a move for kinsfolk who remained behind must have been sufficient to prevent its happening. One imagines, too, that Siassi men would have found life as plantation workers much less bearable than agricultural peoples. It is true that many Siassis have spent large parts of their adult lives working

[23] Tuam has about four thousand coconuts, Malai half that number. Aramot and Mandok have only enough for subsistence and trading needs. Four thousand mature coconuts represent about two thousand pounds' worth of copra per annum, or for Tuam, about four pounds (ten dollars) per capita per year. Under plantation conditions, where the trees are properly spaced, four thousand trees might produce twice as much copra.

away from home, but unlike the people of Sio and other New Guinea communities, the Siassis have had a significantly low rate of absenteeism over the last twenty-year period for which records are available, and this during a period of great expansion of the labor market.

There is still another, albeit drastic alternative. The Siassis might have deserted their island homes en masse and settled in the towns—Rabaul, Madang, or Lae. No crisis occurred, however, which could have provoked such a move. As the preceding discussion has shown, the forces of change have acted gradually. In the history of New Guinea, the only communities that have been converted into urban proletarians are those engulfed *in situ* by the growth of the towns. Siar in Madang, Wewak village at Wewak, and Hanuabada at Port Moresby are examples.

Vis-à-vis the peoples of the coasts, the Siassi Islanders have an interest in maintaining traditional economic practices and values. In turn, coastal peoples such as the Sios attempt to maintain the traditional system in their relations with the inland people. Here comes a seeming paradox: The people of the coast and islands, who for the longest time have experienced the most intensive contact with European culture and on that account might be expected to be the most progressive, are rather in many respects the most conservative. For people like the Sios, conservatism is narrowly applied, for they simply want to get the most from both economic worlds. For the Siassis, conservatism is a way of life,[24] forced upon them by their commitment to maintain

---

[24] In the Siassi case there is something of the pseudo-conservatism suggested in Firth's observation that "consciousness of the changes in so many spheres may lead, as in Polynesian societies, to a renewed emphasis on traditional or modified (pseudo-) traditional forms, which are as it were obtruded as evidence of a social solidarity which may in fact be threatened or lost in other fields" (1954, p. 410).

Siassi conservatism is also expressed in their resistance to missionization. Bamler established the first mission post in Siassi (on Umboi Island) in 1911, but during the prewar period the Mandoks refused to become Christians. Since then they have become Catholics, partly because the Catholic Mission shows a greater tolerance of native customs. Approximately half of

an economic system under circumstances which admitted no satisfactory alternatives. The Siassis have worked out this commitment creatively and successfully, and we may hope that when circumstances finally direct them to desert the "road of the ancestors" for that of modern New Guinea, they will be successful once again.

---

the Aramot Islanders are Catholics, while the other half are Lutherans. The Tuams and Malais are Lutherans. Tami Mission workers preceded Bamler to the Siassi Group, and undoubtedly their presence was important in preparing the way for the conversion of the Tuam and Malai Islanders.

X

Conclusion

THE PURPOSE of this chapter is to examine the trade system within the context of Melanesian culture in general and, secondly, to explore some further material consequences of trading which emerge from the previous discussion.

MELANESIAN TRADE: SOME SPECULATIONS

Local cultural and ecological diversity and intertribal trade based on local differences are not confined to Melanesia, but the degree to which local diversity is turned to account and intensified by means of large-scale trading systems seems to be a distinctively Melanesian development. Furthermore, while middlemen or communities which act to some extent as intermediaries in regional exchange are found widely in the tribal world, Melanesian specialists in long-distance trade—such as the Siassi Islanders, the Langa-langans of the Central Solomons (Hogbin, 1939), and the Mailu of Papua (Malinowski, 1915) are practically unique. These groups are set amidst a large number of primitive horticulturists, some of whom are also craft specialists. In their great mobility and their rarity—the fact that a large number of horticulturists are necessary to support the activities of a few traders—the traders resemble the "top carnivore" of the ecologist's food chains (see Odum, 1959, pp. 46–48; the analogy is incomplete since the traders are not predators—indeed, peace is a condition of trade—but the Tugeri raiders of west New Guinea, to cite one example, remind us that predation is a sometime Melanesian alternative to trade; Wirz, 1933; Haddon, 1891).

The distinctiveness of Melanesia with regard to the efflorescence of trading is probably explained in large part by cultural-geographic factors. Historically, certain characteristics of the natural and cultural environments presented to the Austronesian colonists of the Melanesian Island chain favored the development of trade. These characteristics may be outlined as follows:

1. Compact diversity of environment engendered local specialization of production, and compactness, specifically, means that distances by land and sea between major ecologic and productive zones or regions are short. Since all land transport is by human porterage, this is a vital consideration. Short overseas distances mean also that only the most rudimentary kind of navigational technique is required.

The Vitiaz Strait, for example, exhibits most major ecologic types: upland savanna, highland and lowland rain forest, raised coral islands, high volcanic islands, and arid savanna. Barrier reefs, true atolls, and large rivers are lacking. In the area of the Vitiaz Strait investigated, a twenty-four-hour hike and a four-hour trip by sailing canoe are sufficient to cover every major type of geographic zone.

2. Melanesia is a land and sea area, a chain of archipelagoes. The trading systems depend on the Oceanic outrigger canoe, or its variant, the double canoe. These vessels, in their various local forms, represent one of the most effective means of water transport and ocean travel devised until recent centuries. The first Austronesian colonists may have arrived in western Melanesia by 2,500 B.C., if not before (Murdock, 1964, p. 124), and presumably they came by means of outrigger sailing craft similar to those in use today. Thus, the fundamental technological item required for trad-

ing was a part of the earliest Melanesian cultural complex. Clearly, the archipelago environment and the existence of effective watercraft favored the development of overseas trading.

3. Western Melanesia (New Guinea, the Bismarck Archipelago, and the Solomons), where Austronesian settlement occurred first and where trading systems probably developed at any early date, was not an open environment for the settlement of Austronesian speaking colonists. This area had already been occupied for millennia by preagricultural peoples. Up to late Pleistocene times, Australia and New Guinea were joined in a single continent. The most recent radiocarbon dates for the human occupation of Australia are 14,000 to about 17,000 B.C.[1] Of course, these dates imply a similar antiquity for man in New Guinea.

As a linguistic map of western Melanesia shows, Austronesian speaking communities are often located on small islands and along the coasts; in New Guinea they have rarely penetrated inland, and large sections of coastline are occupied by speakers of non-Melanesian languages. Sometimes settlement occurred on island and coastal sites lacking any potential for agriculture. In such cases trading must have been a necessity from the beginning of occupation.

It is probable that migration of Austronesian speakers occurred over a period of several millennia, some migration continuing up until the present; also, Austronesian migration took place according to no simple pattern (to judge from the varied geographic possibilities and the nature of migrations in recent times). The complexities and duration of migration, combined with the fact that the later Austronesian colonists often met head-on with or settled in close proximity to the long-established non-Melanesian societies, probably accounts in part for the mosaic of cultural diversity encountered in Melanesia. It seems likely that this dimen-

---

[1] At the Kenniff Cave site, the earliest date was 14,180 ± 140 B.C., while the Lake Menindee site has produced materials with a date of 16,850 ± 800 B.C. See Mulvaney (1964).

sion of local diversity arising from culture contact, in addition to environmentally based specialization, added to the potential for the development of trade networks.

All the trading systems of Melanesia need not be explained as parallel responses to similar geographic and cultural conditions. Probably the kind of trade networks that are found now in western Melanesia developed there first— perhaps before any colonization of eastern Melanesia had taken place—and colonists who engaged in trading in their homeland sought to establish trading networks in the new areas where they settled. Recent linguistic work (see Grace, 1964) points to New Britain and the adjacent area of northeastern New Guinea as the Austronesian homeland. A large part of this hypothetical center of dispersal is enclosed by the present boundaries of the Vitiaz Strait trading system. Now, traveling back and forth across the Strait, large trading canoes with women and children aboard, and with cargoes of pigs, dogs, pots, taro, yams, and fishing gear, would be well equipped for more extended voyaging. The major clue to migration in the Pacific is not, I think, to be found in Murdock's suggestions that trade was a motive inducing extended oceanic migration (see 1964, pp. 124f.), but rather in the possibility of forced voyages of well-provisioned sailing canoes out of such an area as the Vitiaz Strait. Correspondingly, diffusion by migration may have played a large part in the development of trading systems in some parts of Melanesia, for the establishment of economic relations with local inhabitants would be an expectable adaptation on the part of migrant traders attempting to gain a foothold in a new area.

INTEGRATION OF MELANESIAN
TRADE SYSTEMS

Perhaps the most distinctive feature of Melanesian trading systems is that they exhibit a measure of organic integration —in the absence of any developed or hierarchical political institutions. (The trading network of the Vitiaz Strait, for example, encompasses hundreds of politically autonomous communities.) That special mechanisms of regional integration have developed in Melanesia and not, apparently, elsewhere seems to be related to the greater scale of Melanesian trade, and specifically to the existence of far-ranging sea traders whose activities make large-scale networks possible.

In the Vitiaz Strait, geographic differentiation of production helps to explain the pattern of trading. But even if the trade system owes its existence in part to favorable environmental conditions, its viability as a system rests on cultural elaboration of the division of labor. As a consequence, interdependence is more varied than one might expect on the basis of geography alone.

Durkheim demonstrated at length that the division of labor in society is bound to be heavily freighted with moral sentiment—functional expediency is transformed into moral necessity. Part of the reason for the ideological buttressing of the division of labor is expressed in Durkheim's critique of Spencer's view that the organic integration of modern society rests on exchange and free contract:

In the fact of exchange, the various agents remain outside of each other, and when the business has been completed, each one retires and is left entirely on his own. Consciences are only superficially in contact; they neither penetrate each other, nor do they adhere. If we look further into the matter, we shall see that this total harmony of interests conceals a latent or deferred conflict. For where interest is the only ruling force each individual finds himself in a state of war with every other . . . and any truce in this eternal antagonism would not be of long duration. There is nothing less constant than interest. Today it unites me to you; tomorrow, it will make me your enemy. Such a cause can only give rise to transient relations and passing associations. We now understand how necessary it is to see if this is really the nature of organic solidarity [1960, pp. 203–4].

Durkheim found, of course, that self-interest and free exchange are not the sum and substance of organic solidarity, and went on to show how the state, administrative law, the customary usage associated with the law of contract, and other institutions support and regulate the division of labor. Tribal societies have none of these advanced means of integration. In the case of the Vitiaz Strait trading system, if not in Melanesian trading systems generally, an interlocking network is created by means of several mechanisms: kinship ideology, the use of delayed reciprocal forms of exchange, and special elaborations of the division of labor.

The trade system is a vast interpersonal network. Traders do not maneuver in relation to the demand of an indefinitely large group of buyers or customers, but are restricted to a small number of social contacts. For individual traders the market is expandable only to a limited extent and along lines of kinship—the kindreds of trade-friends. In addition, demand in the immediate sense is phrased as personal need. The obligation to satisfy the wants and needs of trade-friends is matched on other occasions by the obligation to accept whatever trade-friends have to offer.

Much exchange—local and overseas—is of a delayed form. Delayed exchange—which is a significant departure from balanced reciprocity in its pure form—is a measure of sociability and helps to promote sociability in exchange. Most important, the temporary imbalance involved in delayed transactions, as Sahlins has pointed out (1965), helps to sustain social relations of transacting parties in as much as it compels further meetings for exchange.

Certain transactions have the effect of institutionalizing delayed exchange. The movements of ornaments in the Vitiaz Strait are often of this type. A Siassi receives a dogs'-teeth headband in one year from a Sio trade-friend and reciprocates with a boars'-tusk pendant during the following year. *Kula* transactions are typically carried on in the same way.

These exchange patterns have an artificial character in the sense that they are not determined by actual distributions of resources and skills relevant to the production of the objects exchanged. Or to put it in another way, the division of labor appears to be a function of patterns of exchange rather than the reverse. There is, in fact, a distinctively Melanesian class of transactions which appears "curious" and "absolutely unbusinesslike" from the Western point of view. The function of these transactions would seem to be integration (cf. Uberoi, 1962). The circular movement of armshells and necklaces connecting the island communities of the *kula* ring is the best-known example of the class. Apparently, a similar trading ring involving two contrasting types of shell ornaments linked New Caledonia and the Loyalty Islands (Belshaw, 1954, p. 11, n. 8). On a smaller scale, in local trade, the Roro of Papua sell shellfish to the Mekeo, "Who eat the fish, and sell the shells back to the Roro in the form of lime" (Murray, 1912, p. 163). Finally, in the Vitiaz Strait we find that pigs' tusks and dogs move from the archipelago to the mainland, while pigs and dogs' teeth move in the opposite direction. These latter movements have the effect of reinforcing the complementarity—the necessity—of trade between the two sides of the Strait.

One may distinguish two main elements of regional integration. There is first the intercommunity level, a personal network consisting of multiple "dyadic" links. Here participants to exchange are bound by a moral code derived from kinship ideology. On the more macroscopic level of interregional relations, an artificial component superadded to the division of labor creates an interlocking system of exchange.

SOME FURTHER CONSEQUENCES OF TRADE IN THE VITIAZ STRAIT

Having briefly considered the Vitiaz Strait trade system within its broader Melanesian context, I wish to examine in turn the relationship of trading in the Vitiaz Strait to the exploitation of marginal habitats, interregional specialization, and the political organization of economy.

Marginal Environments

The collection of environments making up the Vitiaz Strait region have varying potentials for human-cultural exploitation. The trade system raises the potential of these environments by connecting them one with the other, thus creating cultural ecological niches out of "raw habitats." The productive and cultural potential of some habitats, in particular, is enhanced by their transformation into trade-based ecological niches.

It is possible that some way of life based on fishing, coconuts, and pandanus could sustain small populations in the Siassi Archipelago in the absence of trade—in a kind of Ur-Austronesian existence (see Murdock, 1964, p. 124). Tuam Island, for example, might support fifty people, but not surely five hundred (its present population), under such conditions. As presently organized, however, exploitation of the reefs, sandbanks, and islets of the archipelago requires seaworthy canoes and fish nets. The materials required for the manufacture and maintenance of this equipment are not available locally, so that some type of trade seems necessary. Surely small groups of fishermen could not take what they needed from more well-endowed neighboring areas by force. It appears that life would be precarious at best.

As the central base for far-flung trade, on the other hand, the unpromising archipelago becomes part of a specialized cultural ecological niche with a high material and cultural potential. By means of an elaborate cultural device—outrigger sailing canoes—the Siassis are able to tap the productive capacity of dozens of small-scale societies lying far beyond their own restricted land and sea habitat. If, in a sense, the Siassis have captured these surrounding societies for their own purposes, they themselves are captive to the demands of the politico-ceremonial system which drives them forth to trade.

The *kunai* littoral of the Huon Peninsula, with its aridity, uncertain returns from agriculture, and seasonal shortages, is a second region whose potential is modified and enhanced by its incorporation in a trade-based ecologic niche. The clay pots produced here are not merely the most efficient cooking device available to the peoples of the Strait, they are a primary means of converting low-value into high-value goods in overseas trade. Pots connect the circulation of elite goods and utilities. It seems likely that, in part, the large size of the industrial communities of this coast—from several hundred to over a thousand—is connected with this vital contribution to the overseas trade system.

The rugged coastal range of the mainland is a third habitat of low potential. Human settlement in this zone is sparse—less than 3 per cent of the Komba live here—and, as the history of Balup and Mula shows, settlement is unstable. Reaping the benefits of modern medicine, the populations of other areas are increasing rapidly, while the small communities of the coastal range still seem barely able to hold their own. Some local trading spheres did without intermediary villages in this zone, and with pacification and improved overland tracks, the mountain middlemen have been largely bypassed (see Chap. IX). In the past, however, the opportunities of coast-inland trade added an important cultural dimension to the unpromising habitat of the mountain zone that encouraged and fixed settlement at strategic points within its bounds.

Interregional Specialization

Overseas trade links mainland and archipelago. With respect to a number of productive specialties, the opposite sides of the Vitiaz Strait are complementary: such goods as pots, net bags, bows and arrows, bark cloth, and black pigment move from the mainland to the islands and New Britain. In return come red ochre, pandanus mats, and obsidian. Overseas trade enlarges the territorial scope for interregional specialization. Perhaps it doubles or even triples the rate of production and consumption of the various need serving goods.

Production is wed to exchange by the material demands of social ritual—a Siassi prestige building feast or a Kovai marriage exchange, for example—which directly or indirectly raise the level of regionally specialized production above what might be stimulated by the demands of utilitarian consumption alone. For example, a Siassi feast—let us say that five pigs and five pigs' worth of taro are distributed and consumed—is contingent upon a number of different kinds of prior "production events": ten bowls must be carved by Tami Islanders; *or* one hundred mats are sewn in Siassi while simultaneously about thirty woman-days of labor are expended in the manufacture of one hundred clay pots at Sio; *or* several sailing canoes, representing thousands of man-hours, are assembled and sold; *or* one hundred pounds of obsidian are collected and transported from Talasea to Kalingi and thence to dozens of points in New Guinea; *or* a half-dozen sago palms on southern Umboi Island are felled and processed while one hundred pots are produced on the mainland. If we suppose that feasts of the scale indicated are taking place simultaneously in all the Siassi communities, these estimates are quadrupled: four hundred mats, four hundred pots, four hundred pounds of obsidian, and so on.

Let us suppose that the pigs and taro for the feast are obtained through this transactional sequence:

(a) 1 pig $\longrightarrow$ 10 pkts. sago $\longrightarrow$ 100 pots $\longrightarrow$ 10 pigs
    (Umboi)   (Sio)   (New Britain)
(b) 5 pigs $\longrightarrow$ 1,000 taro
    (Umboi)

The labor requirements for the feast include thirty woman-days[2] at Sio, forty man-days[3] on Umboi, plus a substantial expenditure in growing and transporting one thousand taro, an unknown number of man-days devoted to tending and producing food for ten pigs in New Britain, and, finally, two overseas and two local voyages.

[2] At Sio, the production of five pots consumes one and one-half days. Digging, transporting, cleaning, and kneading of the clay = one-half day; shaping = one-half day; firing = one-half day. It is possible to save time by firing the five pots at once, but depending on the potter's place of residence, the first phase of digging and so forth may take a day. The one and a half days may be spread over a month.

[3] A team of eight men can cut and process a sago palm, producing a large packet of flour, in half a day (= four man-days). Ten packets therefore equals forty man-days.

One outcome of all of this is an expensively won quantum of prestige for the Siassi traders, who organize the feast and who carry out the preliminary trading. The returns of trade —pigs and taro—are partly consumed, dissipated, and even wasted, and in part they are transformed into social structure. The build-up and maintenance of a local cultural organization is thus made an integral part of a self-perpetuating cycle of production, distribution, and consumption on a vast regional scale.

Polity and Economy—Indirect Effects

Through trading we see the production and redistribution of large quantities of wealth-objects. Strings and necklaces of disc beads are distributed from northwestern New Britain, goldlip shells are exported from Siassi to the Arawe Islands, boars' tusks from the archipelago are taken to the mainland while dogs' teeth are returned, imitation boars' tusks are distributed widely from one or more points on the Rai Coast. Together with the ornaments are pigs, dogs, bowls, and pots, things that are highly esteemed quite apart from considerations of utility. Collectively these objects constitute the highest category of wealth—in Sio they are *mbaliŋa ŋalai,* "important wealth." They are important because they form the currency of important social ritual. These rituals assume a variety of concrete local forms: the name building rites of the Siassi *maron,* the similar activities of the Sio *koipu,* the affinal exchanges of the Kovai villagers, payments of bridewealth, compensation or indemnification, payments to sorcerers and assassins who act in support of the authority of big-men.

Leaders or big-men are the focal agents of these social rituals. They act as sponsors and bankers in transactions involving wealth-objects. Their pre-eminent role in determining the circulation of wealth-objects connected with social ritual symbolizes as it helps to create and sustain their political status.

In providing the wealth-objects in the first place, trade

contributes to local politics in the various importing societies, just as pigs and taro form the material basis of politics among the overseas traders. But more than this, if we accept the hypothesis put forth by Sahlins (1960) that the role of tribal leader is the key mechanism promoting community-wide or tribal-level economic activity, then we can specify yet another, albeit indirect, material consequence of trade. Trade, via the political factor, is a stimulus to the community level of local economic life.

The wealth-objects distributed in overseas trade are intimately associated with political status. Their ownership, accumulation, and decisions regarding their display, use in payments, and trade are particularly in the hands of influential men—the Sio *koipu,* the Siassi *maron,* the Kovai *us,* and the like. The principal prestige building activities, however, usually involve the mobilization and distribution of food. In addition to his personal contribution of productive labor and management skills, a leader's performance in large-scale distributions of food depends on the labor of his political supporters. The number of a leader's supporters and the extent of their obligations to him are therefore basic determinants of leadership. It is here that the wealth-objects play a critical role. Gifts of valuables create obligations—claims on labor and services—which can be converted into food and goods for distribution. The bestowal of wealth-objects allows the leader to expand his base of support both by recruiting new supporters and by intensifying the obligations—indebtedness—of existing followers. In this way, pigs, wooden bowls, pots, and ornaments form the "currency of politics."

To assert a relationship between external trade and internal politics leads to the more fundamental issue of the role of local politics. If political status is partly dependent on supplies of wealth-objects secured in trade, then what are the internal effects of leadership—one may ask, politics for what? It is instructive to approach this question from the point of view of one of the earliest theories of primitive

economic life, Bücher's concept of "closed household economy." Granted the obvious empirical defects of Bücher's
"no exchange" thesis, it nevertheless appears incontestable
that in primitive societies generally there is a tendency
toward "closed household economy." Production and distribution do tend to be confined within a narrow sphere,
oriented toward the needs of small-scale units or households,
and based upon the resources and organization available to
such units. Bücher's theory is wrong only if taken literally
rather than as an expression of a tendency or set of prevailing forces. For in all primitive societies there are institutions
which invoke a countertendency, which encourage a spread
of economic relations between households and attempt to
project the economy beyond the selfish interests of the
household.

Among these institutions, as Sahlins' essay on political
power and the economy makes clear, leadership in particular
provides a powerful impetus toward expansion of the economy on a suprahousehold basis. Leaders and their status
achieving activities become the driving mechanism of a
wider economy. In Melanesia the role of leaders is frequently conceived and expressed in economic terms—
leaders are economic managers, and as their personal-politi-
cal influence increases their impact on the economic life of
the community grows accordingly. In the words of a very
successful Sio leader, power to direct economic affairs is
naturally considered to be a part of power in general: "A
leader talks and there is war, he speaks and there is food; he
speaks and canoes are built; he speaks and men die. He is a
king" (Jekei, former Paramount *Luluai*).

To summarize these suggestions: The prestige motive,
expressed in the politico-ceremonial system directed by
Siassi big-men, is the mainspring of the trade system. Overseas trade, in turn, provides the wealth-objects which are the
currency of local politicking abroad—it helps to fund the
political process in its various local manifestations. Political
activities react upon the economies of the importing soci-

eties at the kin-group and community levels, promoting higher levels of performance.

Out of a patchwork of habitats, a babel of tongues, the parochial interests of dozens of minuscule and weakly organized societies, and the anarchy of primitive production organized by households has come an embracing order and organization. In the technologies, knowledge, skills, and social practices, ideas, and motives that make up the elements of the trade system, there is nothing that pertains specifically to the transcendent organization—that is to say, these are all elements that might evolve and exist in purely local settings. But modified, intensified, and related in distinctive ways, they provide the building blocks of a supra-local organization.

The human actors in this organization—viewing it from special and local vantage points—do not recognize its full scope. They have no name for the system, such as *hiri* or *kula*. Trade means a variety of things to the different participants; no central dramatic act stands out, no common strand runs through the whole. For the Siassi traders it means mainly a quest for pigs and all the diverse activities necessary to sustain this quest. For Nimbako villagers it means devoting their slack season to the shaping and carving of palm-wood bows. To the Sios, those extraordinarily hospitable people, it means continuously acting as hosts to their many and ethnically diverse trade-friends. The trade system has no origin, no history or ideology or mythology that corresponds to its full organizational scope.

In recent times, however, more explicit awareness of the trade system has come to the peoples of the Vitiaz Strait. The conditions of this new awareness stem from that world embracing system—Western Society—which, as it engulfs the trade system, now threatens to destroy it.

Appendix I

SIO KIN TERMS

CONSANGUINEAL

timbuŋgu
Grandparent and grandchild. All members of second ascending and second descending generations. Reciprocal. Address: *baba.*

tamɔŋgu
Father, father's brother; MoSiHu. Address: *mama.*

tinɔŋgu
Mother, mother's sister; FaBrWi. Address: *nana.*

nuŋguwawa
Mother's brother; FaSiHu. Address: *yaya.*

nuŋgutawpi
Father's sister; MoBrWi. Address: *api.*

tuwɔŋgu
Senior siblings, parallel and cross-cousins; all members of Ego's generation older than Ego. Address: *tata;* also *ŋalai,* "big," for male siblings (m.s.).

tɛŋgu
Junior siblings, parallel and cross-cousins. Address: *tɛŋgu;* also *mota,* "small," for male siblings (m.s.).

manɛŋgu
Siblings, parallel and cross-cousins of the opposite sex. *manɛŋgu taine* (m.s.); *manɛŋgu tamoni* (w.s.).

natuŋgu
Son or daughter; child of a sibling of the same sex as Ego.

nuŋgumbela	Sister's son; child of sibling of the opposite sex (m.s.).
nuŋgumoa	Brother's son; child of sibling of the opposite sex (w.s.).
nɛŋgusoko	Great-grandparent.
nɛŋgukinakina	Ancestor of the fourth ascending generation.
nɛŋgumeme	Ancestor of the fifth ascending generation.

AFFINAL

kiwɔŋgu	Spouse. Reciprocal.
anɔŋgu	Spouse's parent.
iwɔŋgu	Spouse's sibling. Reciprocal.
lawɔŋgu	Child's spouse.

Appendix II

GLOSSARY

ABBREVIATIONS: S = Sio; Si = Siassi; Se = Selepet; Ko = Kovai; K = Komba; N-M = Neo-Melanesian.

ai munogon   Twenty, load of one hundred taro (Ko).

amaŋ topŋe   Source of pots (Se), refers to Sio.

atam   Exchange partner (Si).

baliŋ waro   Exchange relationship (Si).

barata   Sibling of the same sex as Ego (N-M).

barɔwe   Ancestral spirit (S).

be   Taro (K, Se).

bik Siassi   Umboi Island (N-M).

bilum   Woven net bag (N-M).

bisnis   Relative, kin, kindred (N-M).

bosboi   Native foreman on plantation (N-M).

bukawa   Belt of dogs' teeth (K).

buku   Friend, clansman, trade-friend (K).

bush bilong Sio   Sio's hinterland, the Kwawa River drainage; people of the hinterland, principally Komba and Selepet tribesmen (N-M).

255

bushkanaka	Bushman, mountain dweller; pejoratively, an unsophisticated native (N-M).
dasɛn	*Tambu*-shell ornaments (K).
deŋa	Taro (S).
dewa	Large yam (S).
dinau	Debt (N-M).
dir	Unit of five taro (Si).
dir tamot	Load of one hundred taro (Si).
dɔŋgu	Low mounds formed of the rubble removed from garden plots; a boundary (S).
dumui	Spokesman and chief assistant of the club-house leader; nowadays, any person in charge of allocating shares of pork and food at a feast (S).
goka	A kind of small yam. Staple crop at Sio (S).
gud taim	Time of peace, usually refers to period prior to World War II (N-M).
haus boi	Men's clubhouse, serves as a social and recreational center, and as a dormitory for unmarried men and boys in modern New Guinea villages (N-M).
haus tamberan	Ancestral spirit house (N-M).
hipau	Tree producing a resin used in hafting arrow tips (Se).
hiri	A trade system linking the Motuan people of the Port Moresby area and communities of the Papuan Gulf (Motu).
jana	*Tambu*-shell ornaments (S).
jili	Debt (S).
jombe	Magic (S).
kaboi	Island dwellers of Arop, Tolokiwa, and Siassi (S).
kandiri	Mother's brother, maternal relative (N-M).
kano	Nothing, perishable manufactured goods, goods of little value (S).
katonɔŋa	Trustee, guard (S).

kazalabu	Dugout canoe without wash strakes (S).
kɛta	Women's large net bag (S).
kiniŋa	Dancing festival (S).
kınsa	Two-piece ornament of *tambu* shell embroidered on coconut bast (K).
koipu	Big-man, leader of men's ceremonial house (S).
korokoro	Platform for display of food associated with men's houses (S).
kula	Interisland trade system in the Massim area of eastern New Guinea, which involves the circular movement of shell bracelets and necklaces.
kulo	Sio pot (S).
kulo katuŋa	Standard cooking pot (S).
kulo ŋgaŋga	Small pot (S).
kulo tabageri	Oversize pot (S).
kumboi	Bushman (S).
kumboi kalawe	Remote bushmen, upper Komba and Selepet villagers (S).
kumbwai	Bushman (Si).
kunai	Wild grasses of the genus *Imperata* (N-M).
labuna	People of the Rai Coast (S).
lain	Group of native laborers headed by a foreman; also generation, group of age-mates (N-M).
laplap	One and a half yards of cotton cloth which is worn like a skirt by men and women (N-M).
lapoto	Coastal people east of Sio (S).
luamin	Wife's mother, wife's elder sister (Ko).
luluai	Government appointed village headman (N-M).
mai	Shame (S).
mami	A kind of small yam. Staple crop at Sio (N-M).

maro	Great, great one (S).
maron	Big-man, leader of men's ceremonial house (Si).
masawa	A small and swift ocean going canoe employed by the Dobuans, Trobriand Islanders, and other peoples in the western half of the *kula* ring.
matin	Headband of dogs' teeth (K).
mbaliŋa	Wealth, durable manufactured goods (S).
mbaliŋa ŋalai	Important wealth (S).
mbawnza	Men's clubhouse (S).
mbole	Banana (S).
mbuer̃a	Southeast Trade winds (S).
mbute	Winged bean (S).
mete	Friend, trade-friend (S).
mundo	Tobacco (S).
mutu	Siassi Islanders (Ko).
namatawuk	Yellowish disc-shell beads made in northwestern New Britain (Si).
naw	Market, meeting place for trade (S).
nia tamɔta	Stranger, unknown being (S).
ŋalai	Large; elder brother (S).
ŋasin	Mother's brother, sister's son (Ko).
ŋge	House site, patrilineally inherited (S).
ŋgoa melamela	Breastplate of dogs' teeth (S).
ŋgosa	Sugar cane (S).
ŋgu	Group; residential section, village or moiety organized for the preparation and distribution of food on ceremonial occasions (S).
panair	Dogs' teeth, ornaments of dogs' teeth (S).
patawuku	(S). See *namatawuk.*
pitpit, edible	*Saccharum robustum,* the flowering tassels of the plant are eaten.
plet bilong Siassi	Carved wooden bowls manufactured by the Siassi and Tami Islanders, which are

	distributed throughout the Vitiaz Strait region in trade (N-M).
pren nating	An acquaintance (N-M).
pren tru	A good friend (N-M).
pus	Five pounds' worth of shillings (N-M).
rota	Work, labor, task (S).
rumi	Men's ceremonial house (Si).
sæŋgo	Maize (S).
saŋgiŋgi	Type of canoe built on the New Guinea mainland, consists of railing erected on a crudely shaped solid hull (S).
saŋiri	Boars'-tusk pendant (S).
sapu	(S). See *kɪnsa* and *senam*.
se	Blood, relative (S).
se laiti	Close kin.
se maliwai	Distant kin.
senam	*Tambu* shell embroidered on a rectangular piece of coconut bast (K).
se tetu	Kindred, descendants of a common pair of great-grandparents.
se toŋge	Other kindred, nonkin.
sia	Island (S).
siasia	Archipelago (S).
Sigaba (*Sigawa*)	Old name of Sio Island village.
singsing	Dancing festival (N-M).
sisi	Island (Si, Tuam).
s'kamau	Bad, evil (S).
skoŋa	A transverse brace; figuratively, a member of a clubhouse leader's faction (S).
tambu	*Nassa* or small cowrie shells; affinal relative (N-M).
tamot	Man, twenty (Si).
tamɔta	Man (S).
taro kongkong	*Xanthosoma*, Singapore taro (N-M).
taumbwa	Edible *pitpit* (S).

tok Siassi haphap	Broken Siassi; a pidgin based on a Siassi vocabulary that reputedly served as a trading language in coastal and island areas of the Vitiaz Strait prior to the spread of Neo-Melanesian (N-M).
tono	Land, garden (S).
tono dɔŋgu	Garden land divided into small rectilinear blocs and bounded by low mounds of rubble.
tono gale	First yam garden of the annual gardening cycle beginning in March or April.
tono luwatu	Second yam garden.
tono ŋalai	Third and final yam garden.
tono pweoŋa	Land in which individual rights are established by cultivation.
tono tama	"Father of the land," senior male of land owning group.
toŋa	Men's small net bag (S).
toŋa panair	Net bag decorated with dogs' teeth (S).
ulum	Patrilineage, men's clubhouse (Ko).
us	Big-man, leader of men's ceremonial house (Ko).
waru	Pumpkin (S).
weŋa	Feast, ceremonial distribution of food (S).
wokboi	Native plantation laborer (N-M).
wořa	Northwest Monsoon (S).
wɔŋga	Canoe (S).
wɔŋga ŋalai	Twin-masted, ocean going canoe; also *wɔŋga pinora rua* (S).
wɔŋga pinora tetu	Single-masted canoe.
yabi	Sweet potato (S).

Appendix III

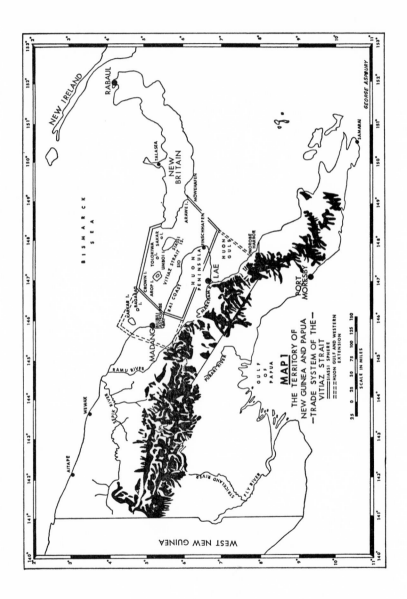

MAP 1

THE TERRITORY OF
NEW GUINEA AND PAPUA
—TRADE SYSTEM OF THE—
VITIAZ STRAIT

····· SIASSI SPHERE
- - - - HUON GULF AND WESTERN
======= EXTENSION

SCALE IN MILES
25 0 25 50 75 100 125 150

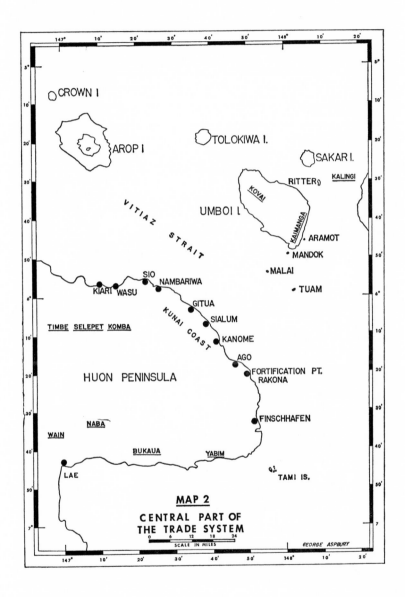

CROWN I

AROP I

TOLOKIWA I.

SAKAR I.

RITTER◊   KALINGI

KOVAI

UMBOI I.

KAIMANGA

• ARAMOT

• MANDOK

• MALAI

VITIAZ STRAIT

⌐ TUAM

SIO

NAMBARIWA

KIARI WASU

GITUA

SIALUM

TIMBE SELEPET KOMBA

KUNAI COAST

KANOME

AGO

HUON PENINSULA

FORTIFICATION PT.

RAKONA

FINSCHHAFEN

NABA

WAIN

BUKAUA   YABIM

TAMI IS.

LAE

MAP 2

CENTRAL PART OF
THE TRADE SYSTEM

0   6   12   18   24
SCALE IN MILES

GEORGE ASPBURY

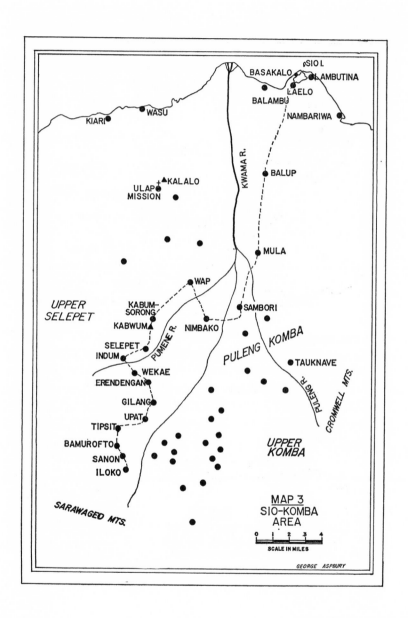

SIO I.

BASAKALO

LAMBUTINA

LAELO

BALAMBU

NAMBARIWA

WASU

KIARI

KWAMA R.

BALUP

+ KALALO

ULAP
MISSION

MULA

WAP

UPPER
SELEPET

KABUM-
SORONG

SAMBORI

KABWUM

NIMBAKO

PULENG KOMBA

SELEPET

INDUM

PUMENE R.

TAUKNAVE

WEKAE

ERENDENGAN

GILANG

UPAT

TIPSIT

BAMUROFTO

SANON

ILOKO

UPPER
KOMBA

PULENG R.

CROMWELL MTS.

SARAWAGED MTS.

MAP 3
SIO-KOMBA
AREA

0   1   2   3   4
SCALE IN MILES

GEORGE ASPBURY

N

MANTAGEN

AUPWEL

KABIP

KAMBALAP

MARARAMU
AIYAU
OROPOT
GASAM
GOM
OMON
BARANG
AWELKON MISSION
OBANGAI
TARAWE
OPAI
GOMLONGON

AROT

KOVAI

MARLI

GIZARUM
PLANTATION

BARIM
(PARAMOT)

UMBOI
ISLAND

KAIMANGA

LABLAB ✝
BIRIK

SAMPANAN

YANGLA
GAURU

ARONAIMUTU

ARAMOT I.

PORE I.
MANDOK I.

MUTUMALA I.

MAP 4

THE SIASSI-UMBOI
AREA

MALAI I.

SIASSI ISLANDS

0 1 2 3 4 5 6
MILES

6 S

148 E

TUAM I.

GEORGE ASPBURY

265

Bibliography

Allied Geographical Section, Southwest Pacific Area [AGS]
1943   "Area Study of Western New Britain," *Terrain Study,*
        No. 57.
Barrau, J.
1958   *Subsistence Agriculture in Melanesia.* Honolulu, Hawaii: Bernice P. Bishop Museum, Bulletin 219.
Barton, F. R.
1910   "The Annual Trading Expedition to the Papuan Gulf,"
        in Seligman, *The Melanesians of British New Guinea,*
        Chap. VIII, pp. 92–119.
Belshaw, Cyril S.
1950   "Changes in Heirloom Jewellry in the Central Solomons," *Oceania,* XX, 169–84.
1954   *Changing Melanesia.* Melbourne and Wellington:
        Oxford University Press.
1955   *In Search of Wealth.* American Anthropological Association, Memoir No. 80.
Bodrogi, Tibor
1959   "New-Guinean Style Provinces, The Style Province
        'Astrolabe Bay,'" in Bodrogi (ed.), *Opuscula Ethnologica Memoriae Ludovici Biro Sacra,* pp. 39–99.
        Budapest: Akadémiai Kiadó.
1961   *Art in North-East New Guinea.* Budapest: Akadémiai
        Kiadó.

Bücher, Carl
1907   *Industrial Evolution.* New York: Henry Holt.
Burling, Robbins
1962   "Maximization Theories in the Study of Economic An-
        thropology," *American Anthropologist*, LXIV, 802–21.
Chinnery, E. W. Pearson
n.d.   *Certain Natives in South New Britain and Dampier
        Straits.* Anthropological Report No. 3, Territory of
        New Guinea; Melbourne: Government Printer.
Codrington, R. H.
1897   *The Melanesians: Studies in Their Anthropology and
        Folklore.* Oxford: The Clarendon Press.
Dalton, George
1961   "Economic Theory and Primitive Society," *American
        Anthropologist*, LXIII, 1–25.
Dampier, Captain William
1906   "A Continuation of a Voyage to New-Holland, etc.,
        In the Year 1699 (1709)," in John Masefield (ed.),
        Dampier's Voyages, II, 453–573. London: E. Grant
        Richards.
Davenport, William
1961   "When a Primitive and a Civilized Money Meet," in
        *Proceedings of the 1961 Annual Spring Meeting of
        the American Ethnological Society*, pp. 64–68. Seat-
        tle: University of Washington Press.
Durkheim, Emile
1960   *The Division of Labor in Society*, tr. by George Simp-
        son. Glencoe, Ill.: The Free Press.
Epstein, T. S.
1961   "A Study of Rabaul Market," *Australian Journal of
        Agricultural Economics*, V, 1–18.
Finsch, Otto
1887   "Abnorme Eberhauer, Pretiosen im Schmuck der
        Südsee-Volker," *Mittheilungen der Anthropologischen
        Gesellschaft in Wien*, VII (N.F.), 151–59.
1888a   *Samoafahrten: Reisen im Kaiser Wilhelms-Land und
        Englisch-Neu-Guinea in den Jahren 1884 u. 1885 an
        Bord des Deutschen Dampfers "Samoa."* Leipzig:
        Ferdinand Hirt.
1888b   *Samoafahrten, Atlas.* Leipzig: Ferdinand Hirt.

1914   *Südseearbeiten.* Abhandlungen des Hamburgischen
          Kolonial-Instituts, 14; Hamburg: L. Friederichsen.
Firth, Raymond
1954   "Money, Work and Social Change in Indo-Pacific Eco-
          nomic Systems," *International Social Science Bulletin*,
          IV, 400–410.
1963   *We, the Tikopia.* Boston: Beacon Press.
Flierl, John
1927   *Forty Years in New Guinea: Memoirs of the Senior
          Missionary John Flierl*, tr. by M. Wiederaenders.
          Chicago: Wartburg Publishing House.
Forde, C. Daryll
1937   "Land and Labour in a Cross River Village, Southern
          Nigeria," *Geographical Journal*, XC, 24–51.
Fortune, R. F.
1932   *Sorcerers of Dobu.* London: Routledge and Kegan
          Paul.
Frerichs, A. C.
1957   *Anutu Conquers in New Guinea: A Story of Seventy
          Years of Mission Work in New Guinea.* Columbus,
          Ohio: Wartburg Press.
Friederici, Georg
1912   "Wissenschaftliche Ergebnisse einer amtlichen For-
          schungsreise nach dem Bismarck-Archipel im Jahre
          1908." II. Beitrage zur Volker- und Sprachenkunde von
          Deutsch Neuguinea. *Mitteilungen aus dem Deutschen
          Schutzgebieten* (Berlin), Erganzungsheft 5.
Goldschmidt, Walter
1959   *Man's Way: A Preface to the Understanding of Hu-
          man Society.* New York: Henry Holt.
Grace, George W.
1964   "Movement of the Malayo-Polynesians: 1,500 B.C. to
          A.D. 500, The Linguistic Evidence," *Current Anthro-
          pology*, V, 361–68.
Greenop, F. S.
1944   *Who Travels Alone.* Sydney: K. G. Murray.
Groves, W. C.
1934   "The Natives of Sio Island, South-Eastern New
          Guinea," *Oceania*, V, 43–63.

Haddon, A. C.
1891   "The Tugeri Head-Hunters of New Guinea," *Internationales Archiv Für Ethnographie*, IV, 177–81.
Haddon, A. C., and James Hornell
1937   *The Canoes of Melanesia, Queensland, and New Guinea.* Vol. II. Honolulu, Hawaii: Bernice P. Bishop Museum, Special Publication 28.
Hagen, B.
1899   *Unter den Papuas.* Wiesbaden: C. W. Kreidel.
Hogbin, H. Ian
1938–39 "Tillage and Collection, A New Guinea Economy," *Oceania*, IX, 127–51, 286–325.
1939   *Experiments in Civilization.* London: George Routledge.
1947   "Native Trade round the Huon Gulf, North-Eastern New Guinea," *Journal of the Polynesian Society*, LVI, 242–55.
Hoyt, Elizabeth E.
1926   *Primitive Trade, Its Psychology and Economics.* London: Kegan Paul, Trench Trubner and Co., Ltd.
Johnston, Bruce F.
1958   *The Staple Food Economies of Western Tropical Africa.* Stanford, Calif.: Stanford University Press.
Knight, Frank H.
1952   "Anthropology and Economics," in Melville J. Herskovits, *Economic Anthropology*, pp. 508–23. New York: Knopf.
Krieger, Maximilian
1899   *Neu Guinea.* Berlin: Alfred Schall.
Kunze, Georg
1896   "Krakar oder Dampier-Insel," *Petermann's Mitteilungen*, XLII, 193–95.
Lawrence, Peter
1964a *Road Belong Cargo: A Study of the Cargo Movement in the Southern Madang District, New Guinea.* Manchester: Manchester University Press.
1964b "Work, Employment, and Trade-Unionism in Papua and New Guinea," *Journal of Industrial Relations*, pp. 23–40.

LeClair, Edward E., Jr.
1962   "Economic Theory and Economic Anthropology,"
        American Anthropologist, LXIV, 1179–1203.
Lesser, Alexander
1961   "Social Fields and the Evolution of Society," *South-
        western Journal of Anthropology*, XVII, 40–48.
McSherry, C. J.
1962   "The Largest Society in the Territory," *The Kibi* (Co-
        operative Journal, Papua and New Guinea), II, 33–36.
Malinowski, Bronislaw
1915   "The Natives of Mailu," *Transactions and Proceed-
        ings of the Royal Society of South Australia*, XXXIV,
        494–706.
1922   *Argonauts of the Western Pacific*. London: Routledge
        and Kegan Paul.
Mead, Margaret
1930   "Melanesian Middlemen," *Natural History*, XXX,
        115–30.
1956   *New Lives for Old*. New York: William Morrow.
1961   "The Manus of the Admiralty Islands," in Mead (ed.),
        *Cooperation and Competition among Primitive Peo-
        ples*, Chap. VII, pp. 210–39. Rev. ed.; Boston: Beacon
        Press.
Miklukha-Maclai, N. N. (Baron Maclay)
1875   "Ethnologische Bermerkungen ueber die Papuas der
        Maclay-Kuste in New-Guinea," *Natuurkundig Tijd-
        schrift voor Nederlandsch Indie*, XXXV, 66–93.
1951–54 *Collected Works* (in Russian). Moscow: Soviet Acad-
        emy of Science. 5 vols.
Miracle, Marvin P.
1961   " 'Seasonal Hunger': A Vague Concept and an Un-
        explored Problem," *Bulletin de l'I.F.A.N.*, XXXII,
        273–83.
Mulvaney, D. J.
1964   "The Pleistocene Colonization of Australia," *Anti-
        quity*, XXXVIII, 263–67
Murdock, George Peter
1949   *Social Structure*. New York: Macmillan.
1964   "Genetic Classification of the Austronesian Lan-

guages: A Key to Oceanic Culture History," *Ethnology*, III, 117–26.

Murray, J. H. P.
1912   *Papua or British New Guinea*. New York: Charles
         Scribner's Sons; London: T. Fisher Unwin.

Neuhauss, Richard
1911   *Deutsch Neu-Guinea*. Berlin: Reimer. 3 vols.

Odum, Eugene P.
1959   *Fundamentals of Ecology*. 2nd ed.; Philadelphia and
         London: W. B. Saunders.

Parkinson, R.
1907   *Dreissig Jahre in der Südsee*. Stuttgart: Strecker and
         Schroder.

Polanyi, K., C. Arensberg, and H. Pearson (eds.)
1957   *Trade and Market in the Early Empires*. Glencoe, Ill.:
         The Free Press.

Pospisil, Leopold
1963   *Kapauku Papuan Economy*. Yale University Publica-
         tions in Anthropology; New Haven, Conn.: Yale Uni-
         versity Department of Anthropology.

Reay, Marie
1959   *The Kuma, Freedom and Conformity in the New
         Guinea Highlands*. Melbourne: Melbourne University
         Press.

Reche, Otto
1954   *Nova Britannia. Ergebnisse der Südsee-Expedition,
         1908–10*. Bd. 4, Hamburg.

Reina, Paul
1858   "Ueber die Bewohner der Insel Rook, ostlich von Neu-
         Guinea, nebst einigen Notizen uber Neu-Guinea und
         Benachbarte Inseln," *Zeitschrift für Allgemeine Erd-
         kunde*, IV (N.F.), 353–65.

Rowley, C. D.
1958   *The Australians in German New Guinea, 1914–1921*.
         Melbourne: Melbourne University Press.

Sahlins, Marshall D.
1960   "Political Power and the Economy in Primitive So-
         ciety," in Gertrude E. Dole and Robert L. Carneiro
         (eds.), *Essays in the Science of Culture in Honor of*

Leslie A. White, pp. 390–415. New York: Thomas Y. Crowell.
1965 "On the Sociology of Primitive Exchange," in Michael Banton (ed.), *The Relevance of Models for Social Anthropology*, pp. 139–236. ASA Monographs, I; London: Tavistock.

Saville, W. J. V.
1926 *In Unknown New Guinea*. London: Seeley Service.

Scheffler, Harold W.
1964 "The Social Consequences of Peace on Choiseul Island," *Ethnology*, III, 398–403.

Schmitz, Carl A.
1955 "Zur Ethnographie der Huon-Halbinsel, Nordost-Neuguinea," *Zeitschrift für Ethnologie*, LXXX, 298–312.
1960 *Historische Probleme in Nordost-Neuguinea*. Wiesbaden: Franz Steiner.
1963 *Wantoat, Art and Religion of the Northeast New Guinea Papuans*. The Hague and Paris: Mouton.

Schurig, Margarete
1930 *Die Südseetopferei*. Leipzig.

Seligman, C. G.
1910 *The Melanesians of British New Guinea*. Cambridge: Cambridge University Press.

Service, Elman R.
1962 *Primitive Social Organization*. New York: Random House.

Souter, Gavin
1963 *New Guinea: The Last Unknown*. Sydney, London, Melbourne, and Wellington: Angus and Roberston.

Stolz, M.
1911 "Die Umgebung von Kap König Wilhelm," in Neuhauss, *Deutsch Neu-Guinea*, pp. 244–86.

Todd, J. A.
1934 "Report on Research Work in South-West New Britain, Territory of New Guinea," *Oceania*, V, 80–101, 193–213.

Tueting [Thompson], Laura
1935 *Native Trade in Southeast New Guinea*. Honolulu, Hawaii: Bernice P. Bishop Museum, Occasional Papers, XI, No. 15.

Uberoi, J. P. Singh
   1962   *Politics of the Kula Ring.* Manchester: Manchester
          University Press.
Vogel-Hamburg, Hans
   1911   *Eine Forschungsreise im Bismarck-Archipel.* Ham-
          burg: L. Friederichsen.
Watson, Virginia
   1955   "Pottery in the Eastern Highlands of New Guinea,"
          Southwestern Journal of Anthropology, XI, 121–28.
Werner, Eugen
   1911   *Kaiser-Wilhelms-Land.* Freiburg im Breisgau.
White, T.
   1952   Patrol Report, Siassi. Typescript, Subdistrict Office,
          Finschhafen.
Wirz, Paul
   1933   "Head-Hunting Expeditions of the Tugeri into the
          Western Division of British New Guinea," *Tijd-
          schrift voor Indische Taal-Land-en Volkenkunde,*
          LXXIII, 105–22.
Worsley, Peter
   1964   Personal communication.

Index